Escape from

Someday Isle

The Best of *Living Aboard*

Escape from

Someday Isle

The Best of *Living Aboard*

Edited by Linda Ridihalgh

Living Aboard
Austin, Texas

Escape from Someday Isle

Living Aboard
P.O. Box 91299
Austin, Texas 78709 U.S.A.
(512) 892-4446 • fax (512) 892-4448
info@livingaboard.com • www.livingaboard.com

Printed in the United States of America

Publisher's Cataloging-in-Publication

Ridihalgh, Linda, 1942- editor
    Escape from someday isle : the best of Living aboard / edited by Linda Ridihalgh
    Austin, Tx, Living Aboard, 2003
    xii, 228 p., 25 cm.

    Articles previously published in *Living Aboard* magazine.
    Includes index.
    ISBN 0-9741991-0-9

    1. Boating living.   2. Houseboats.   3. Boats and boating.
I. Ridihalgh, Linda, 1942-   II. Title.   III. Living aboard.

GV777.7   797.1'2

for John,
my first and always mate

CONTENTS

INTRODUCTION

"When I was planning my transition, your magazine was a great source of comfort to me that even though I might be insane, I wasn't the only one in the asylum."

– Jillian Simensky

This is a book about making dreams come true. It's about leaving the confines of daily life and looking at the world from a new perspective — and it's about living aboard a boat. If that's a crazy idea, then this is also a book about crazy people. Here you will meet folks who rearranged their daily lives to live and travel on their boats. You will read, in their own words, how they fulfilled a dream many share. For anyone who hopes to someday do Something Else, their stories are interesting, informative and inspiring. They are the best stories from the last ten years of *Living Aboard* magazine.

For nearly 30 years, *Living Aboard* magazine has been a community forum for liveaboards — a place where people who are living their dream on the water can exchange information, share experiences and work together to preserve the right to live aboard.

The newsletter that grew into *Living Aboard* was founded in 1973 by Roland and Janice Smith. In 1982, Janice and Roland turned the publication over to George and Maureen Breen followed by Linda Grover and Tom Daughtery in 1985. Michael and Raf Frankel guided development of *Living Aboard* from 1987 to 1990 when Craig and Lynn Wanous took over. Tim Murray was at the helm from 1993 to 1997 before handing it to Fred Walters, our current publisher. It is a tribute to each of these people that *Living Aboard* has grown from a newsletter — inspired by the desire of a small group of cruisers to keep in touch with one another — to a magazine that serves liveaboards on four continents and in all 50 states of the U.S. It is still the only magazine dedicated to the liveaboard way of life.

When I was reviewing back issues of the magazine for this anthology, I was struck by the quality and timelessness of so many of the articles, letters and columns. *Living Aboard* is a reader-written magazine, and the information is truly the voice of experience. Sadly, it is a fact of magazine journalism that much of this hard-won wisdom is lost in a few months when a particular issue is removed from the newsstand or cleared from the coffee table. Gathering it again for this, the second *Living Aboard* collection, has been immensely satisfying.

In 1990, Michael Frankel, former editor of the journal, took on the job of surveying liveaboards and compiling articles from the first 18 years of *Living Aboard*. His book, *Gently with the Tides,* has become a classic and is still must-reading for anyone who shares the liveaboard dream.

However, it has been more than ten years since Michael published the first *Living Aboard* anthology, and that was a decade in which technology transformed society. Nowhere is that more evident than for people living aboard. Advances in telecommunications made the liveaboard lifestyle more accessible to greater numbers of people — it is now possible for many to work "at home" wherever that may be. With the growth of the Internet homeschooling became an attractive option for parents who may otherwise have waited until the kids were out of school to move aboard. And cruisers have new ways to communicate with the folks back home or, happily, with us here at the magazine. More information, new ways to share it, and more people participating in this unique lifestyle have helped the magazine grow in scope and content.

When the Smiths started *Living Aboard* magazine in 1973 (then the newsletter of the Homaflote Association) they stated that it was for "mutual benefit through shared experience." Now, a generation later, that statement still goes to the heart of *Living Aboard* magazine and is central to its vision and purpose. We are grateful to all who have, over the years, so generously supported the liveaboard community by contributing their knowledge and their experience to the pages of the magazine and to this book.

I hope that the stories we've collected here will inspire you to escape from "Someday Isle" — and maybe even help convince your relatives that you aren't so crazy after all.

- Preface -

SOMEDAY ISLE

We met him on the Isle of Margarita, a small island off the coast of Venezuela in the Caribbean, whose name means "guardian of the sea." Venezuela used its oil profits to build an aqueduct under the bay from the mainland to supply water to high-rise hotels and make Margarita a free port. We took advantage of the frugal vacations offered and had not much to do except watch the small, open fishing boats go out in the evening and come back in the morning. Eyes painted in the bows helped the boats find their way home.

We watched "quick-and-dirty" boat repair on the beach as carpenters would replace one bad plank and send the boat out until another plank needed replacement, minimizing downtime.

A liveaboard 39' sailboat anchored in the bay, and when the owner came ashore in his inflatable we were at the dock to meet him. Tanned and grimy, he held an encrusted piece of PVC pipe. He had been working on his boat and was trying to replace some plumbing. He had spent several months sailing from Mississippi down the islands with wife and child and west from Grenada to Margarita, because Margarita is much cheaper. He was contemplating whether to go through the canal or sail down the coast of South America. When I asked if he liked this kind of life, he said emphatically, waving the PVC pipe for emphasis, "I love it!" When I asked how his wife liked it, he said, just as emphatically, "She hates it!"

He went on to tell us that his older brother who was immersed in business would always say, "Someday, I'll sail away," until a fatal heart attack put an end to his dreams of "Someday Isle." He knew then he made the right decision to go sailing while he was still able and not wait for a future that might never arrive.

We waited while he went back to his boat to get a few envelopes for us to mail when we got back to New York. One was addressed to a bank, another to the IRS. Apparently he had more trust in two fellow sailors he would never see again than in the Venezuelan postal system.

We wrote to let him know that we had mailed his letters and eventually received a reply in which we learned that he was dismasted off the coast of

South America. His wife, tired of the cruising life, left him to go home. Another letter, some months later, told us of signing on another crew more amenable to the rigors of the sea. Undaunted, and still loving it, he continued through the canal and sailed eventually to Australia.

We had our own dreams of "Someday Isle," but put them to rest some years ago and content ourselves with living aboard during the summer while sailing the local New England waters. We recall with admiration, and not a little envy, our brief encounter with this true liveaboard who did what most of us only dream about.

— Art Krieger

As Good As It Gets
Why We Live Aboard

Who hasn't dreamed of chucking it all, moving onto a boat, and sailing to far-away places with strange-sounding names? Sailing off into the sunset may be just a distant dream, but living on a boat is still an appealing lifestyle. It combines the serenity of nature with the promise of adventure — and always offers a waterfront view. As one Connecticut liveaboard who commutes from his New York City job to his home afloat put it: "I am the view they pay hundreds of thousands of dollars for . . . And if people think life aboard is roughing it, they haven't seen my boat — my life is good!"

Living aboard is a dream many share and more and more are achieving. As jobs become more flexible, home offices become more powerful, and people demand more from their lives, the trend is on the rise. Many thousands of people from all walks of life live on all kinds of boats, forming a diverse community with a wide range of personal interests and experience. It is a lifestyle that transcends economic and social boundaries. A sailor in Seattle described the liveaboard community in his marina as comprised of engineers, nurses, mechanics, naval architects, entrepreneurs and salespeople. There are families with young children who live aboard, there are retired couples, single men and women, college students, and nine-to-five professionals. They live wherever there is water on all kinds of boats — of all sizes and makes. They live on lakes and rivers and oceans, north and south, east and west, in all kinds of climates. Some live in marinas, some live on the hook, some cruise, some stay put, leading different lives in different places. What they hold in common is a fierce independence, love of the water and a spirit of adventure. They are a community, albeit a diverse one, bound by their unique lifestyle.

So why do people live on their boats? The best way to learn who lives aboard and why is to hear first-hand from those who have dared to realize their dream. There are as many stories out there as there are liveaboards, and here we tell you a few of the best.

It's Better on the Boat

Nancy L. Mills aboard Summer School

We've lived in a house and we've lived on a boat and we're convinced that, for us at least, it's better on the boat. Among the advantages: it's simpler, it's cozier, and it's closer to nature.

Before and After — Then and Now

We were college professors of engineering, with six degrees between us. Our professional positions enabled us to lead a very comfortable life: a nice house with a fireplace and hot tub, dinners out at fine restaurants, vacations in the tropics, and most important to us, a boat on which to spend our summers.

Now we're retired liveaboard cruisers. Our home is our boat: a 34' trawler, aptly named *Summer School*. Although Dave has a small pension, the rest of our "retirement" income comes from savings and the proceeds from the sale of our house (after Uncle Sam got his share). And against all the recommendations in the books on living aboard and cruising, our boat is not paid off.

So for me, retirement may be temporary. But we've worked out what we think is a reasonable budget — not requiring us to watch every penny or compromise our standard of living excessively. We expect to be living this life for at least two years. Any additional income earned along the way will extend the time we have for this adventure.

Because of Dave's myriad of health problems, including leukemia, we decided not to postpone "our escape" any longer. After spending two summers and a semester-long sabbatical on the boat, we knew it was the life we wanted to lead.

> Dave Perkins and Nancy Mills live and cruise on their 34-foot Marine Trader trawler. They found that cutting the ties to land gave them a simpler life, one that brought them closer to nature and closer to each other.

It's Simpler

Because of the limits on space, we have fewer of everything on the boat. For example, on land we had china service for eight; on the boat, we have service for four (which is two more than we usually need). Since we have fewer dishes, no dishwasher, and no place to hide dirty dishes, we wash them up as we use them, which means it's not ever a very big job. Keys have also been simplified. From a keyring holding four keys to various offices, supplies and laboratories at work, four car keys for two cars, a house key, a key for the padlock on the door of the boat, and one unidentified key (there's always one, isn't there?), or eleven keys total, we're now down to four keys, one for the boat, two for the one car we kept, and one for our bicycle padlock. (We disposed of the "mystery" key.)

We have fewer clothes and personal possessions, although we did rent a storage locker on land for books, a few pieces of furniture, winter coats and certain personal mementos that we couldn't quite give up. We hired an auctioneer to dispose of everything else we didn't want. After being subjected to considerable comment from movers on my "tons" of clothes, I thoroughly enjoy the freedom of a reduced wardrobe. I've gone from 16 pairs of shoes (I'm no Imelda Marcos,

really) to three, from five purses to one all-purpose tote bag. Having to maintain a large wardrobe and dress to present a proper professional "role model" image at work is a burden that I don't miss. Instead of trying to remember what I wore to class two days ago so as not to repeat the same dress, it doesn't matter if I wear the same clothes every day until they need to be washed. Since laundry requires a trek to the laundromat at the marina, we both try to reduce frequent changes of clothes. Jeans and sweats, shorts and T-shirts are our usual attire with dress-up clothes stowed carefully away for special occasions.

But we're not roughing it either; we've just reduced the possessions that often own us instead of the other way around. We have air conditioning, a CD player, TV and VCR, a cellular telephone, a full-sized bed in our aft cabin, two heads with showers, a four-burner propane stove with oven, refrigerator with freezer (but it is small!) and all the comforts of home, except the fireplace and hot tub, which we occasionally still miss. We actually have a great deal of storage space on our boat, but it's not all easily accessible. For example, there are huge storage areas under the V-berth and aft cabin bed, as well as spacious areas under the seating in the main saloon, but access to all these areas requires lifting of mattresses or cushions — and everything that is on them. These areas are best for items we don't need frequently.

Our personal business affairs have become simpler as well. Once we cut the ties to a land home, we no longer had all the utility bills: electricity, gas, fuel oil, telephone (two lines: one for voice, the other for computer) plus the cellular phone, cable TV, water, sewer and trash, lawn service and firewood deliveries. Now we pay our slip fees and our cellular phone bill. Slip fees generally include electricity, water and cable TV, although we've stayed at marinas that metered power and water and charged separately for these as well as cable. But it's still

"We love to watch the birds. . . . We've seen egrets, herons, ibis, roseate spoonbills, osprey, gulls, ducks, loons, coots, cormorants, Canada geese, pelicans. . . . We've been awed by the soaring ability of osprey. . . . We've awakened to the honking of the Canada geese on the Chesapeake in the fall. . . ."

only one check to be written to the marina. As needed, we fill the diesel fuel tanks and propane tanks. Neither of these require frequent attention as our trawler has a range of approximately 1,000 miles and in eight months of cruising, we used about half of one of our two propane tanks. We operate primarily with cash (ATMs are great for getting cash as you need it wherever you go) which means that our only other regular monthly bills are the boat payment and AT&T long distance charges.

We're also attempting to reduce other complications and commitments. We've reduced our subscriptions to magazines and catalogs. We've dropped our professional memberships with their attendant communications, publications, conferences and meetings. We don't accept invitations if we don't want to go and we don't do things we don't enjoy. We try to avoid schedules, especially when cruising. It is almost impossible to meet set deadlines given the vagaries of weather. We're striving to reduce our stress levels — with less to do, there's less to worry about. However, we should add that although in many ways, our life is simpler, the boat is full of complex systems, including a generator, that do require attention. But the feeling of independence that comes from having a self-contained living environment is definitely worth it.

It's Cozier

Now, if you spend a lot of your time trying not to be in the same room with your spouse, you won't understand the appeal of closeness. But we're sure that we will never have enough time together so we cherish every minute. The compactness of the boat keeps us in constant touch and we like that.

We moved onto the boat from a three-story, ten-room, 100-year-old house on a hill with 18 steps from the sidewalk to the front door. Our trawler has three good-sized cabins. The forward cabin is a V-berth which we have converted into an office (you wouldn't really expect two engineering professors to be without a computer and printer). The main saloon contains the galley, built-in settee, L-shaped banquette with table for dining, and the lower helm station. It is raised three steps from the forward and aft cabins. We never complain about these few steps! The aft cabin is our bedroom, with full-sized bed and excellent built-in storage. The forward and aft cabins each have an adjacent head with shower. We also have walk-around decks, a cockpit and a huge bridge for our outdoor living areas.

In the house, we were always looking for the other person. As much as possible, we tended to stay in the same room at the same time, leading us to wonder why we needed so many rooms. On the boat, we don't have to go searching for the other person to tell them something. Even though we might be in separate cabins, doing different things, we can see and talk to each other easily. We even have an intercom between the galley and the bridge, just in case the helmsman wants to change his or her lunch order. What some might consider cramped and crowded, we consider cozy, a source of great joy in our relationship.

It's Closer to Nature

One of our favorite things about living aboard is the closeness to nature, although when we're at anchor and the wind is howling, it's pouring rain and the sky is filled with lightning, nature may seem a little too close. While it's true that boaters are more at the mercy of weather than land dwellers, we don't have to go anywhere if the weather is bad. Most of the time, it's hard to beat the peace and serenity that come from living on the water. The gentle swaying of the boat reminds us that we are in the middle of a fascinating environment. With windows all around our cabin, we have a 360 view of all nature has to offer.

We love to watch the birds and have added two bird books to our library to help us identify them. We've seen egrets, herons, ibis, roseate spoonbills, osprey, gulls, ducks, loons, coots, cormorants, Canada geese, pelicans, and turkey buzzards, among others. We've been entertained over and over by pelicans crash diving into the water all around us as they fish. We've been awed by the soaring ability of osprey and watched them close up in their nests on the ICW markers. We've awakened to the honking of the Canada geese on the Chesapeake in the fall. We've been surprised by cormorants suddenly popping up from the water like corks. We've seen egrets: great white, snowy and cattle. We've seen green herons, night herons, little blue herons, and the magnificent great blue herons from the Chesapeake to the Florida Keys, where we've seen their white phase.

Birds aren't our only contact with nature's creatures. We've had dolphins leaping around our boat as they ride the stern and bow waves. What incredible animals they are! So sleek and yet so strong. Without appearing to move a muscle, they swim alongside the boat, turning over in the water to take a good look at us, leap into the air and dive under our bow. We've also been lucky enough to snatch quick looks at huge sea turtles in the Keys and watch alligators on the ICW. We've seen tarpon and manatees, river turtles and muskrats. Snorkeling in the Keys and the Bahamas has revealed an amazing array of tropical fish life: triggerfish, angelfish, sergeant majors, barracudas and many more. (We bought another book to help us identify the fish.) We've also seen rays, sharks, dolphin fish, shrimp and conch.

Having a boat has enabled us to visit some of the most beautiful and secluded beaches in the Bahamas. With sand as fine and soft and white as talcum powder, warm, clear, turquoise water and few other boats, the Exumas are a premiere cruising area. I guess we could say that "it's better on the boat in the Bahamas" but that's another story. We enjoyed our trip there and hope to return. The unspoiled and uninhabited cays are most relaxing and restful. It's a perfect place to do nothing!

And at the end of a day on the boat, whether cruising, at anchor or tied up in a slip at a marina, we look forward to relaxing with a drink as we watch the sunset. The unobstructed view from our bridge can be breathtaking. The colors of the sunset reflected in the water bring a perfect end to another day in touch with nature and each other. We consider ourselves to be very fortunate to have the opportunity to experience this liveaboard life for which we seem so suited and from which we derive such pleasure and satisfaction. For us, it's best on the boat!

A Dozen Things I Have Learned About Myself, My Boat & Living Aboard

I was lying in bed, listening to the water lapping at the hull, reminiscing about stepping aboard my "new" 30' sailboat four years ago, when I got up, scratched the ears of my puppy and scribbled down a few things I've learned since moving aboard:

- It's difficult to explain to friends, co-workers and grandma the true depth and meaning of what it is to live aboard.
- The boat was the cheap part.
- It's important to listen to all of the advice offered to you and then politely dismiss the majority of it.
- It's hard not to throttle the next person who says "Gee, you don't actually do very much sailing."
- If there is water on the floor, resist the temptation to ignore and pretend it came from the dog's dish.
- I will fall hard on my butt once a year. This is good, however, because that's where I keep my brains and it reminds me why I should not walk on wet sails, step between life lines and descend the companionway holding groceries, laundry and a briefcase.
- Never let the facts get in the way of a good story.
- If on a gorgeous sunny Sunday afternoon, your fenders look absurdly large – they are just the right size.
- It's difficult not to yell obscenities every time my dinner rolls off the stern-mounted grill – scares the neighbor's kids.
- No matter what you say now, eventually you will sell or give away all that stuff in storage.
- It's not the speed that kills, it's the humidity.
- Island time is a state of mind, not a place you have to visit.

Living aboard has become my life's grandest adventure – and to think I would have missed the last four years if I had listened to the advice of others, waited for the perfect time, or until I had enough money. Do it now!

– Kevin Hinsdell

Why Do We Live Aboard?

Peg Travis & Dave Hirchert

"*Live aboard? You live on a boat?!*" This is our favorite — when someone asks, "Where do you live?" Our reply is a simple answer, "On *Gypsy*, our boat," and that is when we see this astounded look while they picture in their minds a boat they have seen or had experiences with. "On a boat? You live on a boat?" "Yes" we reply.

"Where?" they ask.

"Today here, tomorrow there, and who knows the next day," we answer.

But what can we expect, our own family and friends consider us eccentric. My very own sister says she can't keep up with us and only knows where we are when she "sees the whites of our eyes."

"Walkabout" is an Australian aborigine expression for people who throw up everything and take to the bush for awhile. People say a person has "gone walka-bout" when they seek to get away from it all, to cleanse the soul, or possibly to just satisfy a yearning for adventure.

We call ourselves "sailabouts."

We abandoned the security of four solid walls and a shingle roof over our heads; a yard to mow and a cantankerous vehicle to maintain; neighbors to contend with and a regular 8-to-5 job. We gave up the "rat race," moved aboard *Gypsy* and became "sailabouts." Gypsies of the sea, wanderers, nomads, drifters, vagabonds. But, we didn't give up life — real living just began.

Gypsy was built by us, with spare time and spare money, which translates into — we didn't do or go much of anyplace for many years. We moved aboard October 8, 1992. Dave, the captain, had been a self-employed metal boat designer/builder for 28 years and I, the first mate, had worked clerical for, *hmm-mmm*, many years. We had no idea of the opportunities that would be open to us living aboard a boat. Many of the experiences and adventures we have had are indeed awesome.

Revisiting the question, "Why do we choose to live aboard?" The answer varies with who you ask and when you ask.

I spent one of my birthdays — all day — cleaning and melting 2,000 pounds of lead into 12 pound ingots for ballast. We ended up moving them no less than 14 times to get them in place in the keel. Many times during this day-long process, I asked myself "Why, dear God, am I doing this?" My answer came later when we crossed the Gulf of Alaska and *Gypsy* tossed, heaved and rolled while contending with winds, waves and rain. I now know lead on a deeply personal level.

Peg Travis and Dave Hirchert live aboard a boat they built themselves. *Alaskan Gypsy* is an 83' motor-sailing schooner launched in 1992. For Peg and Dave, *Gypsy* is a perfect boat and a perfect home.

Alaskan Gypsy,
*looking picturesque in
her natural habitat.*

Many times when we drop anchor in a remote cove or bay the silence is unreal. We often sit quietly, watching and listening to the wildlife and the weather. Our eyes dance as a bald eagle glides across the bay, repeatedly dipping to the water and finally surfacing with a writhing salmon in his grip. The congregations of ravens or seagulls drifting in the cove unceasingly chatter and cry to each other. We silently watch as a chubby little black bear waddles to the beach looking for spawned out salmon for dinner; we see a doe and her fawn as they exit the woods to find tender beach grass.

We watch the fog drift in to cover us at night as we sip our tea, snug and warm in the wheelhouse. In the morning we watch the mist rise from the water and the bay come awake. Sometimes we watch a storm cloud come our way and soon hear the rain on the roof or witness slow, feathery snowflakes fall. We hear the wind as it blows and makes the water dance and the trees whisper.

Why do we live aboard? I don't know exactly. There are too many reasons why.

Quality of Life

Rob & Barbara Davis as told to Gary Graham

At the time of the accident, Rob and Barbara Davis were building a 45' Sampson-design ferro-cement sailboat in their backyard.

"I opened my eyes and there were a bunch of people dressed in white and green all around me. My arms and legs feel really heavy, and yet they don't feel anything. I think maybe I'm strapped down because I can't move anything, any part of my body. People start asking me things like, 'Mr. Davis, do you know what day this is? Mr. Davis can you feel this?,' things like that. And then there is this pain, like fire and ice and needles, all over my body . . . ."

This is how 46-year-old Rob Davis describes regaining consciousness in a hospital emergency room, unable to move or control any part of his body. He was paralyzed from the neck down. A quadriplegic. That was 22 years ago. He was only 24 years old.

When bad things happen to good people dreams are too often destroyed. But for Rob and Barb Davis, it was their dream of owning a boat that kept them going through a terrible ordeal — and it is the boat that has enabled them to once again appreciate and enjoy life.

We had been talking for over an hour in the big aft cabin of the *Barbara Lynn* and Rob said "Hey let's take a break and go up on deck." It was a warm Florida spring morning, the coffee pot was empty, so it sounded good to me. Rob scooted himself off the settee, plopped down on the floor, dragged himself over to the ¹/₂-ton chain winch and struggled into his bosun's chair. After a couple of minutes of getting straps and chains organized, Rob began winching himself straight up through the open hatch.

"I have an electric winch, but I'm better off doing it this way." Rob hoists himself another few feet. "The more exercise I get, the better off I am."

Rob wiggles out of the bosun's chair and squirms into a resting position against the cockpit seat. He flashes me a confident grin and says, "This is a lot better. A perfect morning." We watch a few pelicans shopping for breakfast in the Indian River as we soak up the warm sun.

I first saw Rob, Barbara and their son, Zack, the same day I came into Melbourne Harbor, Florida. They're a hard group to miss. I had just anchored my Catalina 27 when I saw a man in a wheelchair, a woman, and a small boy make their way out onto the dinghy dock, and load up a catamaran dinghy. The empty wheel chair was taken back to the van, then they putt-putted out to a large sailboat at anchor, and scrambled aboard, transferring all the bags and water jugs. They obviously had lots of practice at the routine, but it was still fascinating to watch. In fact, it was a little hard to believe. The next morning I saw the woman and the boy headed for shore. I couldn't resist checking out their dinghy.

Rob and Barbara Davis enjoying their life on the water.

It is two identical canoes, each about 12 feet long, lashed together with two 2 x 6s, with about 3 feet between the two canoes. The three-horsepower outboard motor is mounted between the two hulls. Very ingenious indeed. The craft can carry a lot of weight, would be extremely stable, and can be assembled or taken apart in a couple of minutes. Obviously, someone is pretty creative.

Later that day, I saw the woman carrying some shopping bags and about a half dozen, 8-foot 2x4s out to the dinghy, load them, and putt-putt back out to the sailboat. She pitched all the stuff up on the deck, then scrambled onto the boat and disappeared below. What a gal.

Still later, she putt-putted to shore to retrieve the boy, apparently home from school. The boy, once on the boat, spent the next hour or so having imaginary sword fights on the mast which hung many feet beyond the bow. He'd thrust and parry, but ultimately get run through and plunge in a dramatic death dive to the warm waters below. A few minutes later he'd be back on deck for a rematch with his imaginary foe.

A man in a wheelchair living on a boat at anchor. A woman who brings home a loaf of bread, a quart of milk, and pile of lumber — in a catamaran dinghy. A young boy who isn't glued to video games or terrorizing the mall. I knew I had to meet this family and find out more about them.

They met my dinghy with a cheerful hello and very graciously invited me aboard, complete with my notebook, camera and obvious curiosity.

"Rob and I met on a blind date when I was 17 and I knew from the moment I saw him I was going to marry him." Barbara is fixing lunch aboard the boat and she grins affectionately at Rob. "Rob knew he wanted to build a boat and sail the world. I'd never even been on a sailboat in my life, but it sounded like a good idea to me," Barbara says laughing.

Rob said he saw a ferro-cement sailboat and decided to build one. "I spent $300 with a Sampson representative in Grand Rapids, Michigan, for the plans and another $7,000 for some training sessions and the 800 sacks of ferro cement. As far as I know, this is the only boat just like this, and we built most of it after my accident.

"Without this boat I probably would be dead. This boat gave me a focus when I really needed it. It gave me a goal, a determination. It gave me and Barb something to do besides just deal with me. It gave us something to dream about and work on together. And, as we got the boat together, it gave us freedom. When I sit at the tiller of my boat, it doesn't matter that I'm a cripple. I'm the captain and I can still sail my boat. And that idea, that knowledge, that dream, helped me and us more than anything else to deal with me being paralyzed."

Seeing Rob and Barbara and Zack, together, and watching Rob get around the boat, I forgot he was a quadriplegic. But Rob has absolutely no use of his legs — zero. He has about 10% use of his left hand and arm, and about 2% use of his right hand and arm. He can't make a tight fist with either hand, and he can't close the fingers of his right hand at all. When he shakes hands in greeting, his right hand has no grasp to it. Watching him at work, I realized that most of the time he has to use one arm to steady himself, otherwise he collapses like a rag doll. This means that whatever he is doing, he must back himself into a wedge or support of some kind to get the use of both hands. But even at that, he has no strength and no grip. He tires very quickly, and has to take several Tylenol every day for pain management.

"I can have all the painkillers I want, but I don't want to spend my life in the twilight zone. I've done that, and I don't want to do it any more. I've got too much to do to be whacked out on drugs all the time."

Barbara is equally as amazing as Rob. The word "can't" simply isn't in her vocabulary. And she's not one to just sit around and talk. If I wanted to talk with Barbara, we'd have to do it while working. So I spent several hours with Barbara, sanding the main mast on the *Barbara Lynn*, while Rob sorted "stuff" down below.

"I guess the doctors didn't like me very well, because they'd spend a lot of time getting Rob used to the idea that he was going to be a total cripple all his life, then I'd come into the hospital and tell him to hurry up and get better because we had a house to finish, a business to run, and a boat to launch.

"You know, most people with broken necks stay for at least a year in the hospital, sometimes two or three, but Rob was out of there in five months. And that rehab program was a joke, everything was a negative. You can't do this, you'll never be able to do that — we just didn't have time for that stuff. So one freezing day, I just went and got him and took him home.

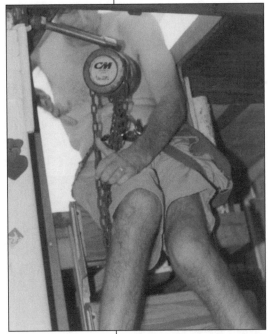

Rob is able to winch himself up through the hatch, preferring the exercise of doing it himself to using the electric winch.

"You see, Rob is an extremely active and creative person and he has to be able to create and do things or he'll just wither away. That's what makes the boat such a great place for Rob. There's always something to do, and he'll always figure some way to get it done. Maybe he can't do it all himself, but it will get done."

I asked Rob about that later and he agreed. "Sure, it takes me longer to do some things, but I get them done. And what difference does it make if you're crippled or not if you can watch your kids grow up on the water, living on the boat. In fact, living on a boat is the best life I can imagine for a cripple.

"I'm the president of my own boat company. I know how to weld, I know how to fiberglass, I know how to fix engines, I know how to rig, I know how to do anything on this boat. Maybe I can't do it myself, but I can tell someone else how to do it. That's how we built the boat."

Barbara stood up from sanding the mast. The Florida sun was getting hot. Sweat was beading and running on her face and body. The white paint dust from the mast was smudged all over her arms, legs and face. I asked her if she would like to move back on land. Just at that moment a dolphin surfaced a few feet from us.

"Nope, you don't get this kind of view on land. And we have a freedom here that you just don't get on land. No, I don't want to move back on land. Besides, it's a lot better for Zack out here."

I asked Barbara how they had modified the boat to accommodate Rob. She thought about that for a few moments of sanding while I worked on my side of the mast. "Well, do you see any wheel chairs around?" she finally asked. I had to admit I didn't.

"That's because the wheel chair stays on land. No, we haven't done much of anything to the boat. I mean, what is there to do? What we have done is to modify Rob's head. And I guess that's another big difference of a boat over a house. Everybody tries to modify a house to fit the cripple. Here, we modified the cripple to fit the boat. We just have to be creative."

While Barbara was fixing lunch, I checked on Rob and he was in his "shop." By sitting and leaning against a door jam and against some steps, Rob began dragging out tools. It was an impressive array. Several electric tools, and an assortment of hand tools. "I have a gas welding outfit, a wire feed electric welder, several pumps, and a scuba outfit. I can do all kinds of repairs to anybody's boat,

Rob and Barbara have the systems worked out for transferring Rob – their "catamaran" dinghy is very stable.

and I've made a lot of money doing just that." And it was the same principle, if he could see it or be told about it, he could see that it got fixed. Rob then ticked off several rescue repair jobs he had done: water pumps, head gaskets, generators, water heaters, things like that.

Rob took a drink of water but dropped the glass. Barbara tossed him a towel, refilled the glass, and Rob went on with the discussion. "Look, when Hugo hit, every boat in the Charleston area went down. There were hundreds of boats sitting on the bottom. And you couldn't get a pump of any kind for any amount of money. But a guy had a pump that was frozen up, powered by an old Wisconsin engine with no carburetor. He gave it to me for free. So I got the pump working. Then I got the engine working by feeding it gas through a Coke bottle with cotton over the end. I turned the intake manifold over so it became a downdraft, and shook the gas into it from the coke bottle. It took me four days with that outfit to pump out my boat enough to get it light enough so I could start winching it to shore with my ½-ton winch. I'd sit there all day feeding that Molotov cocktail carburetor and Barb would move the hose around. After we got our boat to shore, we raised three more boats. We pumped them out with me feeding the little engine and dragging them ashore with that little winch." He pointed with his eyes to the winch he uses to lift himself onto the deck.

I had to comment, "You know, being physically disadvantaged hasn't slowed you down a whole lot."

He smiled a little and said "I'm not physically disadvantaged or physically impaired. I'm a cripple, a gimp. I have to figure out a whole new system to survive every day. But the worst thing I could do is to fit into society's little box of being physically disadvantaged and want everybody to help me. I'm grateful for the doctors and the hospitals for saving my life when I first broke my neck, but after that, they just were in my way."

As the day drew to a close, we watched the sun begin to set and agreed that there is a magic to life on the water. Living aboard redefines priorities, refocuses the trade-offs. Barbara at one point said, "You know, it's funny, but the easiest thing to do is live in a house, the next easiest thing to do is live in a marina, and the hardest thing to do is live at anchor. I guess that's true for anyone, but especially for us. I mean I'll admit it, it's just a lot of hard work to always have to bring every drop of fresh water and food out to the boat, and drag all the garbage and laundry back to shore. And getting Rob back and forth to shore can be a real pain. He's gotten dumped more than once. Getting Zack to shore every morning for school is an effort, especially if it's raining. The work on the boat never ends. But on the other hand, we just love the feeling of being out here, just a few minutes away from pulling up the anchors and setting out."

What's ahead for them? As they both agree, "We want to live around the world. Not just travel around the world, but live around the world. We want to go to new places and get involved in the communities and be productive. We like to help people, that's what life is all about." ✍

"When I sit at the tiller of my boat, it doesn't matter that I'm a cripple. I'm the captain and I can still sail my boat. And that idea, that knowledge, that dream, helped me and us more than anything else to deal with me being paralyzed."

Weren't You Cold in There?

Robyn Coulter

Whack! Bang! The noise jolted me from my sleep. I pried open my eyes and stared at the clock. It was 3 a.m. Maybe I had just dreamed I'd heard something. Whack! Bang! There it was again, and it sounded like something was going to drive a hole right through our hull. I slid out of the V-berth and threw on pants, sweater, socks and coat. I struggled into my boots. As I tossed the hatchboards aside, and jumped into the cockpit, the icy cold of the December night hit me. Zipping my down jacket, I stepped over to the tent door and opened it.

Whack! Bang! Gingerly, I stepped off the boat and edged my way along the icy T dock to the main dock, examining the boat's hull as I went. The night was cold and clear. Next to our hull the marina's bubblers were humming away nicely. As far as I could see there were no chunks of ice or logs near our hull. Nothing was floating in the water but a few geese. So what was causing that noise?

Less hardy souls might wonder what makes people stay on their boats enduring the ice and cold of northern winters. For those who would always rather live on a boat than on land, it's just part of the adventure. Winter brings its own kind of beauty as well as the promise of spring.

Gently one goose picked up our slack spring line in her beak and pulled back. Whack! went the spring line as she released it. Bang! went the spring line as it hit the hull of our boat. The slingshot effect was absolutely professional. I shook my sleepy head and laughter overtook me. My deep belly laugh rang out in the night air. As I turned to go back to my warm berth, I think — no, I'm sure — those geese were laughing too.

My partner, Manny, and I were spending our first winter living aboard a Catalina 27. We'd bought this sailboat the previous summer and after refitting, repairing, and completing a new interior, we named her *Free Spirit*, and moved aboard. Small as she was, she was what our pocketbooks could afford. As we joined a small community of liveaboards in Ontario, Canada, we never imagined the adventures that this winter would bring.

On Lake Ontario, around the city of Toronto, there are four main marinas that service winter liveaboards. Among those marinas, there are perhaps 100 boats with liveaboard owners, at any given year. Too short summers and long freezing winters characterize the Toronto climate. Winter temperatures frequently dip to minus 20° C (-4° F); snow storms and dreaded ice storms complete the picture. The liveaboards in our marina were a tough bunch and would while away those cold February nights with dreams of "next summer . . . ."

Our winter liveaboard experience began in late October, when mysterious piles of lumber appeared next to many boats. Not lovely mahogany, or teak, but plain construction pine, in bundles of one-by-twos and two-by-twos. Frames started to rise off many decks and talk turned to winter covers, or "tents" as liveaboards called them. Neighbors discussed windproof designs and the pros and cons of different types of plastic coverings and tarps.

Around this time, marina staff began to prepare the winter bubbling system. Long hoses were strung in the water around the docks and boats and weighted. These submerged hoses would bubble air up to the water's surface and prevent ice forming next to our boat hulls. As Manny and I mourned the end of the sailing season, the marina activity and chilly weather reminded us that preparing for the oncoming winter was important.

One day in mid-November, we had our winter "tent" frame completed and estimated a couple of hours work to put on the plastic covering. Five hours later we were caught in the first snow and the finger-numbing cold was making it impossible to continue. Only half the boat was done. We climbed inside the cabin to sip mugs of Irish coffee. Manny and I looked at each other feeling foolishly like the squirrel who'd forgotten to prepare for the cold. Obviously there was more to this northern liveaboard experience than we'd bargained for!

Later that evening, I trekked back from the marina showers — down the path, across the parking lot, and along the dock. It was snowing hard and the moon shone through a fog of flakes. The bitter cold was accompanied by a cutting wind. As I hunched into the warmth of my winter coat, I wondered what else Mother Nature would have in store for us.

A few days later the temperature rose a little, and things began to thaw. We took the opportunity to quickly finish the plastic. With our "tent" completed, our home became a winter cocoon and my gloomy outlook lifted. Heaters blasted away indoors, keeping us comfortable and able to cope with ever colder temperatures.

In December the flagpole at the entrance to our bay was strung with colored lights. Many of our neighboring boats strung up some of their own, adding cheer to our dismal winter skies. On December 26, I woke to find we were frozen in solid. The temperature had fallen to minus 20° C. Overnight, big chunks of ice had floated in from across the bay and shut down our bubbling system. By morning we were sitting in the middle of a skating rink.

January brought with it the realities and pleasures of a deep Canadian winter. At the first of the month, we awoke to find our sweaters frozen to the cabin walls backing their shelf. Little ice crystals lined the V-berth and sparkled in the dark. We lay there, warm under our down comforter, with t-shirt weather blasting from our cabin heaters, and condensation causing frost to form on our cabin walls.

Often that month, I'd get up to the sound of soft pitting against the tent and lots of snow. As I'd step out to shovel our dock, everything would look soft and white. In the evening the lights coming on across the bay would appear pink through the picture postcard mist of snow. Then I'd forget the cold realities of winter for a while, as I marveled at the beauty around me.

Mornings we'd find Canada geese asleep on ice islands, off our stern. Little ledges of snow piled on their backs as, oblivious to the weather, they continued in their normal routines.

Manny put two vents under our V-berth. He hoped they would circulate warm air and help prevent condensation. The bubblers worked fast and furiously now, gurgling next to our hull. Inside it sounded like we were living in a pot of soup. A noise far better than the awful crunching and grating sounds that came through our hull, when we were iced in.

One night in late January we "sailed" to the sounds of slatting plastic, banging wooden trap doors, and wind screaming through the rigging. Halfway through the night, Manny moved to the pilot berth, and slept in a sleeping bag. The heeling motion was making it impossible for the two of us to sleep in our little V-berth. Heavy winds put a strain on our neighbor's tight lines. By morning they'd pulled out a dock board and one of the cleats as well.

Early in February, the temperature skyrocketed to plus 10° C (50° F). The sun shone and everyone was eager to get outside and ease their cabin fever. I walked past *Sea Dove*, a large ketch at the end of our dock. They were hanging out laundry. A sharp, sweet wave of nostalgia washed over me, and I could almost taste summer.

Throughout the winter, filling our water tanks, was a nasty job. The marina had turned off all dockside water supplies in the fall. Some liveaboards had installed an ingenious system. A long hose, which reached from the beginning of our dock to the end, where we lived, was sunk with the bubbling system. The farthest end, near land, had an extra hose with a cap on its end. This hose was filled with water and the capped end was attached to the dock by a chain. The hose was then sunk, to prevent freezing.

To retrieve this end, we had to pull up the chain, unhook the hose, and uncap the end. We would pull the hose to the nearest working water outlet, hook it up and turn the water on. At our end of the dock, a similar uncapped end was held by a chain. Once this end was retrieved and uncapped, our hose could be attached and fed through a trap door in our tent and the water tanks filled. Dealing with water in the cold is a finger-numbing job. Each week we'd put off the inevitable, hoping the weather would turn milder, before we'd have to refill our tanks.

I remember the last winter that I lived on the *Northstar*. It was December and I hadn't gotten around to putting up the old winter bimini top on the flybridge.

One weeknight we got a good foot of snow. I got up at sunrise, which in Massachusetts at that time is around 6 or 6:30, threw on clothes and boots, and went out to shovel off the boat.

I vividly remember that morning. The snow had just stopped falling. The sky was a slate gray. The kind of gray that won't let you figure out if the snow is going to stop for good or not. There was a dead quiet all around. No wind, just cold. Only the occasional sound of a shovel scraping ground somewhere.

I was shoveling off the flybridge, pushing the snow into the water, and it hit me kind of sudden: Other people are breaking their backs shoveling driveways, and I'm up on the top of my boat, with a commanding, un-obstructed view of the harbor, the water as calm and slick as glass.

This was my home. I remember feeling very good at that moment. My writing can't do that moment justice, but believe me, it was great.

– Kevin Neenan

March came in and the temperature dropped quickly. By night we had freezing rain. We arrived home and everything was like glass. The steps to the washroom sparkled in the night and when a hand reached for the rail, to balance, it too was slippery. Trees, bushes and grassy reeds were all an eerie, glassy white. Boats dripped icicles from their stanchions, lines and rigging. *Sea Dove* had unfortunately hung out laundry and it was bent over the lifelines, cardboard stiff. "Tents" were windblown and frozen into strange shapes.

Our walk down the dock was perilous. We managed the first 50 feet quite well, with the security of boats along side us. However, the next 100 feet was an open stretch of unattended dock. There were no rails, no boats alongside, just one endless, icy pier. Aware of the risk of hypothermia in those icy waters, Manny and I edged our way to our boat always within arms reach.

The next morning, neighbors strung safety lines, and stories abounded of slippery walks home. One couple had taken off their boots, hoping the warmth from their feet would melt the ice and provide traction.

One morning in late March, the rumble of thunder and our first downpour of rain greeted me. I almost jumped out of my berth to close the hatches, when I remembered the "tent." We had our own umbrella and did not have to worry about incoming rain.

Here and there, around the marina, signs of spring began to show. Boats on land were being aired out and cleaned up. I packed away one heater and used the other two only occasionally. The sun shone and the marina was busy. Dinghies were out, lineups had started at the broker's offices and weekenders were talking antifouling over mugs of coffee. Along the dock, our neighbors were celebrating winter's end with a barbecue.

With the onset of spring, we liveaboards took down our tents and put winter far behind us. Summer friends were launched and joined us dockside. Inevitably the questions arose: "How was your winter? Weren't you cold in there?" Smugly we smiled and shook our heads.

Living aboard in the middle of a Canadian winter is a unique experience. For us, it was a choice made because we'd always rather live on a boat than on land. These days we are beginning to realize our dream, and moving on to cruise in warmer climates. Often we look back on those northern winters with pride. Our adventures there will always embellish the wonderful kaleidoscope of our life afloat.

"In the evening the lights coming on across the bay would appear pink through the picture postcard mist of snow. Then I'd forget the cold realities of winter for a while, as I marveled at the beauty around me."

Doctor's Orders

Shirley McGoldrick

When I was told that I had a heart blockage and I needed cardiac catheterization and possible angioplasty, I figured, "OK, no problem — overnight in the hospital and then home with a couple days rest and good as new," home in this case being our 41-foot Formosa ketch, *Ariel* where I have lived for five years with my husband, Fran, and Sinbad, our African grey parrot.

Thinking it over, however, I have to admit I was scared, especially when I was told I would be awake for the procedure. I don't think a person should be awake for *any* hospital procedure. But off I went for what I thought would be a simple procedure. It was, but then the drugs wore off and I learned that I needed bypass surgery. I was sent home to make the arrangements and told not to wait too long. That was a problem, because at the time my mother was dying from congestive heart failure. So I decided to wait, worried that my mom didn't have much time left and she would need me. I waited a week and then one day Mom sent me to the mall on an errand and I discovered I couldn't even walk halfway through the mall without being totally exhausted and out of breath. Needless to say, she didn't get what I went for, and I went home to our boat and made the arrangements for surgery.

When well-meaning relatives urged her to move ashore after major surgery, Shirley McGoldrick was forced to re-examine her commitment to living on her boat. She decided she wanted to be in her own home, aboard her boat. It turned out to be a good place to recuperate. The small space on a boat put things conveniently at hand, and she was surrounded by a caring marina community.

Immediately upon learning of my problem my brother the landlubber decided that after the surgery I had to come and stay with him because there was no way I would be able to get back on the boat after surgery. Now, I don't know about you, but when a doctor tells me that I'm walking around with a time-bomb in my chest I really don't need the added stress of knowing that I won't be able to return to my home — my boat — after major surgery.

So there I was crying hysterically, not because I could die, but because I couldn't come home to my boat! I finally decided that after the surgery I would spend the recovery period aboard our boat and if I died, so be it. My husband, being of sounder mind at the time suggested that I let the doctor decide what was best. Whoa, why didn't I think of that? Thank God for understanding doctors! His decision was, "If that's where you live and that's where you will be most comfortable, then that's where you should be — on your boat" — but try to explain that to well-meaning relatives who think I'm crazy to live on a boat even when I'm healthy.

So, the date was set and just to make things really difficult, my mother died five days before scheduled surgery. I didn't reschedule, I figured she would understand. Meanwhile, my brother kept insisting that I stay with him to recuperate after surgery. *Not!*

After five days in the hospital, I was sent home. The marina guard met me at the car and drove me down to the boat in the golf cart. I hobbled out as everybody watched to see if I really could get on the boat. We have a 41' ketch, so I had to hobble up three steps, drag my gimpy leg across to the boat and back down four steps into the boat. Piece of cake. Still convinced that I needed to stay in a house, my brother called to argue his case. He lost.

The hardest part of being on a sailboat when your chest has been opened up is sliding the hatch open and closed. After my husband oiled it really well, I can now move

Sinbad, aboard Ariel.

it without a problem. Luckily we have doors and not slats. Actually I have found that a boat is a great place to be when you are incapacitated. Everything is very close at hand, the shower is easy to use and the people in the marina are at least as helpful — maybe more so — than any neighbors you would ever find on land.

Sure there are a lot of things I can't do, but then I realized that I couldn't do them no matter where I was. I did spend one weekend with my brother in his house. I couldn't get out of the bed by myself. I had to walk entirely too far to get to anything. The toilet was too low and I absolutely refused to use the shower for fear I would slip in the tub.

Major surgery and being a liveaboard do mix. It's just what you're used to. Don't let those landlubbers talk you into coming home to a house just because you're temporarily incapacitated. Hey, they think you should live in a house when you're healthy. ⬢

Cruising Alone

Jim Akers

I have traveled by myself, with my little Yorkie puppy, Kristi, acting as my first mate, for nearly 8,000 miles on our river system. I have cruised the Black Warrior, Cumberland, and Ohio rivers, the Tenn-Tom Waterway, the Mississippi to St. Louis and out the Missouri River and I have enjoyed every scenic minute of it.

It all started when I was in high school. I spent two summers on a towboat, the *Tommy Herbert*, working the Cumberland, Tennessee, Ohio, and Mississippi rivers. I learned to love the river system — the peaceful serenity at morning's light, the ever changing scenery and sights around every bend and the many beautiful sunsets as the day turned into night.

Jim Akers has cruised our nation's rivers for nearly 50 years, so when he found himself alone after many years of marriage, he sold his house and moved aboard his Chris Craft Fly Bridge Express. It turned out to be the right thing for him to do. As Jim says, "it just doesn't get any better than this."

As time went on, I finished college, went to work and married a wonderful lady, Sybil. We had one child, a daughter we named Lynda. With hard work, it was not long before I bought a boat — much to my wife's dismay! She could not swim and was totally afraid of the water. I tried to get her to take swimming lessons, but she refused, so I carefully explained to her the safety features of the boat. She reluctantly agreed to give it a try and we planned a trip on the Cumberland River in Tennessee. The first night out we anchored behind a small island on the Cumberland. When she got ready for bed that first night, she put on her life jacket and continued to sleep that way for the next week and a half. Every night aboard she wore that blasted life jacket. I tried to explain to her that the life jacket kinda gets in the way when. . . . Needless to say, it was not long before I bought a much larger boat — safer, more sea worthy and with a steel hull — a Chris Craft Roamer.

Sybil seemed pleased and on our first trip aboard our new boat we really enjoyed the beautiful weather, the great scenery and our new Roamer. After anchoring, we had dinner on the aft deck enjoying the peacefulness of the surroundings, then we prepared to retire for the evening. When she came to bed she was not wearing a life jacket — she was wearing a ski belt! Well, that was somewhat of an improvement and I felt we were making progress. As time went on, she finally felt secure and the belt went as well. She was a wonderful wife, a super mother and a great first mate.

That was many years ago. In 1975, the Lord decided he needed my wife and since then I have cruised alone. I have sold or given away all my land-bound stuff and now live aboard full time.

I am often asked by my land-locked friends (who think I have lost my ever-loving mind for wanting to live on a boat) how I managed leaving a big house and moving onto a small boat. I tell them that, when I was in the house, I used one side of the bed in the bedroom, used one bathroom, used the kitchen to cook popcorn, make coffee and not much else, used one chair in the living room and watched one TV. On the boat, I have the same conveniences, I just don't have to walk as far between the queen-sized bunk, the head, the galley and the living area — I still sit in one place and watch one TV.

I have met so many great people on my travels and they are always interested in how I manage to dock the boat, go through the locks, how I anchor out by myself, and how I have maintained my sanity cruising and living aboard alone. I have a boat that I can handle myself and have developed systems that work well for me.

Traveling alone, you need to know how your boat handles in most situations and water conditions. That took practice, patience, and more practice. Experience helps, of course, but it is important to have the right boat, one that is not too big or too small. I needed a boat that has a low aft deck — so I can easily and hurriedly get off the boat; one that has fairly wide gunnels and walk-around decks to aid in locking through and anchoring; has a fly bridge so I can easily see the many floating props and shaft villains; has a lower station to make it nicer and safe in severe thunderstorms and cold weather cruising; one that has the convenience of home in the cabin; and, most important, one that has two engines. I now own a Chris Craft Fly Bridge Express that I purchased when I retired. Our daughter, Lynda, loved the boat, the water and all the many trips we made — so I named the boat *Missa Lynda.*

I usually captain the boat from the flybridge. I don't have bimini curtains — I am from the old school. I love the wind in my face and a little rain never hurt anyone. (I don't think my first mate, Kristi, agrees with that though — she hides under the fly bridge console when it rains.) The only time we come down to the lower station is when there is a lot of lightning nearby or when the temperature gets below 40 degrees.

Keeping my sanity and enjoying life while traveling on my boat by myself with Kristi, my little Yorkie first mate, is a breeze. First of all, I am up and down my flybridge ladder many times a day so I keep my girlish figure. I eat when I get hungry, sleep when I get sleepy and when I wake up — I've got to get up. I fix coffee, enjoy two cups, take Kristi out when I am at a marina and then I am ready to go.

I love the water, I love my boat, and I love our nation's rivers. How fortunate we are to be able to travel this great country — from the magnificent Great Lakes to the beautiful Gulf of Mexico, from the industrial east to the wilderness west — entirely by river.

I would not trade my way of living and traveling with anyone. Those who are land-locked cannot know the beauty and tranquillity that can be found on the river nor know all the wonderful people I meet along the way. It just doesn't get any better than this.

"I think we live a little closer to the world this way."

– Louise,
aboard m/v Caper

People Who Live on Their Boats

Gary Graham

- Why do you live aboard a boat?
- What was the biggest adjustment you faced in moving from a house to a boat?
- What's the best part about living aboard a boat?
- What's the worst part about living aboard a boat?

With these four question in mind, and a notebook in hand, I did my survey of 11 liveaboards. I was after feelings, not facts. There are dozens of books, hundreds of articles, and thousands of opinions about how to store pancake mix, fix leaking windows, kill cockroaches, take care of dogs, and install holding tanks.

Gary Graham interviewed residents of Bear Point Marina in Orange Beach, Alabama, to learn why they choose to live on the water. Here eleven liveaboards describe what living aboard means to them and discuss why they do it and what it's like.

But how do we really *feel* about living aboard? What is there that compels some of us to compulsively flee land and seek the water for our home? After we do it, how do we feel about living aboard? Is it what we thought it would be? Are we glad we did it? What do we like most about it? What do we fear? What did it do to our relationships?

You'll be amazed at the variety of answers I got to my four questions. Our experts (four married couples and three bachelors) are as diverse as the boats we live on. Jim and I each live on boats in the mid 20-foot range, valued at around $8,000. From there we move up the scale to Bill and Sandy, who are at home on a 50-foot trawler worth about 80 times more. But we all live quite contentedly in a little marina on the Alabama/Florida line.

Sonny & Anne

First meet Sonny and Anne. They've been married 40 years and recently retired from their own business. They still own a home and one acre in Parsons, Tennessee, where they have "lots of stuff." They have lived full time on their 38' Cheoy Lee sloop, *Different Drum*, since October of '94. They plan to circumnavigate. They have a car at the marina.

Why do you live aboard a boat?
Anne: "I love the water. We've had lots of boats and we always had such fun with them. We've had several sailboats and even a big old houseboat. When you're on the water, you just don't have all the problems and things to do when

you're on land. Life is simpler on the water. So we decided to retire and get a boat and live on the water. And I like to travel and see new places, but I just hate traffic. Getting a boat just seemed like the sensible thing to do."

What was your biggest adjustment?

(At this point, I'm conveying what I think Anne feels is the big adjustment.) She says she *wants* to live aboard a boat and thoroughly *enjoys* it. But there is that part of her that wants the security of the cement foundation, the two-by-four studs and the stone fireplace. She wants unlimited fresh water and the big tree in the front yard. She misses the availability of all the conveniences of a land-based lifestyle, whether or not she actually uses them. But "I want to be *able* to use them if I want to." Balanced against these thoughts are the questions that face her as she looks forward to an uncertain length of time living on a boat. If a single thought had to be used to describe Anne's biggest adjustment, it might be "facing uncertainty."

What's the best part?

"Oh, everything is so easy, so relaxed. We have lots of time to do what we want to do. On land, we seem to always have to go places and do things, people to see, meetings and stuff to go to. And it's a lot easier to keep the boat clean than to keep a big house clean. I don't spend nearly as much time just cleaning. I have more time to enjoy myself and my husband. Besides, Sonny helps with the cleaning and laundry, so it doesn't take any time at all. And I love sailing with the engine off, listening to the wind in the sails and the sound of the boat gliding through the water."

What's the worst part?

"There isn't any worst part. I think it's great. I really enjoy it — except for the fresh water. When we're cruising, I'm always afraid we're going to run out of fresh water. I even have about 150 two-liter jugs filled with water and stashed all over the boat."

You mean in addition to the storage tanks on the boat?"

"Yes. Oh I know I may be silly, but I just don't want to run out of fresh water. Besides, the water in the jugs is good Tennessee water."

Why do you live aboard a boat?

Sonny: "Well, like Anne, I love the water. We had our flying service and air-field for almost 20 years, and I just wanted to retire from it. I want to travel but I want to do it on the water. *And,* I'm going to circumnavigate the world before I die. I've always *wanted* to do that, and I'm *going* to do that. I'm going to sail around the world."

What was your biggest adjustment?

"*Space!*" (It took me over a half hour to realize exactly what Sonny was talking about. He doesn't mean space on the boat to put his shoes, hang up his pants, store the corn flakes, or a place to put the dinghy motor. That's boat stuff requiring boat space. That's no problem. But Sonny doesn't have space for his welder, drill press, table saw, extra sheets of plywood, impact wrench, 17 boxes of nuts and bolts, four kegs of nails and his rototiller.) "I get so frustrated having to

"That's what I like about living aboard a boat — it makes you re-examine what's important to you!"

– Anonymous

run to the hardware store every time I need some little tool or part when I must have six of them back home."

What's the best part about living on a boat?

"Oh, that's easy, *no* telephone. I *love* not having a telephone. I've waited all my life to not have a telephone. In fact, let me tell you a story. Last Christmas our daughter gave me a brand new cellular phone and it was all paid for, for the whole year. I mean this thing was the newest and the best. I thanked her for it, and told how much I appreciated the thought, but I told her to take it back, I didn't want it. I've spent my whole life talking on telephones, talking on radios, carrying pagers, carrying telephones around. But I'm retired now — I live on my boat, and I don't want to hear telephones ringing *any more*. At first my daughter was mad, then she was hurt, but she finally understood that I *just* don't want a telephone. If anybody really has to get hold of us, they can call the marina. Or if we're out cruising, then we'll surface sometime, somewhere."

What's the worst part?

"Like I said, space."

Veijo

Next meet Veijo (pronounced Vay-oh). Veijo is in his early 60s, a recently retired tool and die maker originally from Finland. He lives alone on *Vagabond*, a 32-foot sailboat. He doesn't have a car, but he's an enthusiastic bicycle rider. Veijo has a few things stored with his daughter, "about a 6-by-6-foot space." When Veijo left, we all missed him very much.

Why do you live aboard your boat?

"I bought the boat to live aboard and cruise. I enjoy going to different towns and visiting the museums and interesting places. I like to see the cities. To live on a boat is a very cheap way to live and travel. Besides, it's fun. I like boats and I like the water."

What was your biggest adjustment?

"Well, for me it's a big adjustment to be retired and have a lot of time to do nothing. So, in a way, the boat has been good because there is always something to do on a boat. It's also an adjustment to not have a car. It means I have to use the marina car (if they have one), go with someone else, or ride my bike. If I ride my bike, it means I have to make lots of little trips to the grocery, and I can't buy anything really big. But it's good because when I move, I don't have to worry about moving my car."

What's the best part about living aboard?

"Well the best part is why I bought the boat; I'm able to cruise to new places and see new things."

What's the worst part?

"For me the worst part was finding the right boat. I looked for a year to find the right boat. I spent about $16,000 in phone and gas and motel bills looking at boats. I wanted a full keel and keel-hung rudder boat, but it had to be something I wanted and could afford. I finally found out about *Mauch's Sailboat Guide*, and

"There is something very soothing about being surrounded by water. I don't feel nearly as much stress as I used to."

– Nancy Cowell,
aboard m/v *Tartan*,
Brisbane, California

that really helped me. I wish I had found that book earlier. The boat I finally bought cost only $32,700, but I spent so much money to find it." (*Mauch's Sailboat Guide*, 2 volumes, by Jan Mauch; specifications, interiors and illustrations on over 1,200 new and used boats.)

"After that, the worst part is the trashy marinas, with dirty showers and loud parties."

Bill & Sandy

Bill and Sandy live on a very lovely 50' trawler, *River Walker*. They're both retired from successful businesses, he from contracting, she from interior design. They live full time on their boat, summering in eastern Alabama, wintering in southwestern Florida, with other cruises interspersed. They have a car at the marina.

Why do you live aboard a boat?

Bill: "Well, I've always liked boating, always had boats, and I have many fond memories of boats. Also, I don't like being tied down. I move a lot. I *like* to move a lot. The move onto the boat was my 51st move, so I guess I'm sort of a Gypsy. But boats are unique for me in a special way. You see, I don't like rented beds, or rented bedrooms. I like to travel, but I want to sleep in my own bed at night. I like familiarity in my personal surroundings, but it doesn't matter where my personal surroundings are. So the boat allows me to travel wherever and whenever I want, but I always have my own bed and personal surroundings. That's very important to me."

What was your biggest adjustment in moving aboard?

"One big adjustment was certainly closet space. Along with the quantitative adjustment, I also changed my wardrobe to be more in line with the boating lifestyle. I no longer own a suit or a tie. I had to downsize and adjust everything I wear.

"It was a big adjustment to get rid of everything we own that wouldn't fit comfortably on the boat. We didn't put anything in storage someplace, we got rid of it. Now, absolutely everything we own is on the boat. We live on the boat, period. This also means, the boat is as full as we want it right now, so if something comes on the boat, something else has to leave. For instance, if I see a shirt I'd like to buy, I have to think about what shirt I'm going to get rid of, because only so many shirts will fit in my closet on the boat. If we see a picture we want, we have to decide which picture is going to have to go. If Sandy wants a new dish or set of glasses for the galley, that means a dish or set of glasses will have to go. That's the rule we live by, and that's a big, big adjustment.

"Another big adjustment was the learning of all the mechanical and technical skills involved in owning a boat. As a contractor, I'm used to *coordinating* things, but not really *doing* them. Now, I have to know how to actually *do* things. After we purchased the boat, but before we retired and moved aboard, I'd just make a phone call and everything got done. My involvement was to write the check. For instance, maintaining the teak used to cost about $4,500 a year. Now Sandy and I

"The beautiful souls are they that are universal, open, and ready for all things."

– Michel de Montaigne

do it for under $50. The waxing used to run about $3,000 a year, now we do it for about $100. But you know, when people stop and admire the woodwork, I feel really good about it, knowing we did it ourselves. Nobody ever told me how nice my garage door looked after I had that painted."

What's the best part of living aboard?

"The best part is the people. We often will get to talking with people on the dock and invite total strangers aboard for a visit. You can do that in a marina, and we enjoy that. In a marina you can enjoy good camaraderie without clinging involvement. However, some of those meetings have evolved into friendships which continue over space and time.

"Another good part is the fun of learning about boating, learning about navigating, anchoring out — the fulfillment of cruising in your own boat. We've enjoyed wonderful experiences while cruising. And my wife and I have become much closer because of the boat."

What's the worst part?

"I think it's the fear that this lifestyle might end, eventually will end. One of us might become physically unable to live aboard. Or perhaps we might not be able to come back to the marinas we enjoy, like this one. Or I just may get too old to operate the boat. I think about that. I don't want to move back on land."

Why do you live aboard a boat?

Sandy: "Because of the adventure and enjoyment. Both of us get bored easily, and with the boat we get all the adventure of traveling and all the comforts of home. Actually, we're both miserable without a boat. But both people have to be 'boat people' for it to work. I don't think living aboard a boat will work unless both partners really want to and are committed to making the necessary changes."

What was your biggest adjustment?

"Space. We downsized for several years, moving to smaller and smaller houses and apartments. That was easy for us to do, because Bill was constantly building and selling houses and apartment buildings. We just moved into his latest project until the next one was done. With every move, we kept getting rid of things.

"I was also faced with re-projecting my energy. I was accustomed to running my own business, and now I have a lot of time on my hands. Bill was busy learning about the boat, and we shared some of that, but I still had time on my hands.

"Then there was the adjustment of having two 'captains' on the same vessel. We were both accustomed to being the boss of our own separate business, and now we are together on the boat. So we worked out a schedule and we stick to it. When we're cruising, we take turns operating the boat. When I'm on duty, Bill does something else somewhere else. When I'm at the wheel, I have total responsibility for the boat. Bill usually goes below to rest, because in a while it will be his turn again. We honor that schedule and responsibility very faithfully. But that was a big adjustment for us, to figure out how to share the command responsibilities while cruising."

What's the best part of living aboard?

"The best part has been the growth of our relationship, the sharing, the companionship. Also, being on the open ocean or anchored out somewhere; I enjoy the wonders of God's creation. I see so much of God in nature. I feel we are a part His creation. I love cruising on the ocean."

What's the worst part?

"Selecting the time for the Gulf crossing, traveling across the open ocean from Florida. I love to make the Gulf crossing, it's a wonderful trip, but I don't like rough water. The worst part is trying to pick the right time so the weather will be good. Also, cleaning is more difficult on a boat."

Jim

Jim lives on *Last Resort*, a 1948, 28-foot homemade wooden cruiser. It could use a little work. He's going to start fixing it up "soon." Jim has lived on his boat for four years. He's of working age, a philosopher and an entrepreneur.

Why do you live aboard a boat?

Jim: "I love being on the water, and I hate being tied down. I hate being tied to an *it*. A house is an *it*. I have to work close to *it*. I have to make lots of money to support *it*. I have to insure *it*. I have to pay taxes on *it*. I can't be gone too long from *it*. With a house, my life revolves around *it*, my whole life style is based on *it*. Have you heard the expression 'I have to get home'? You'll never hear me say that, 'cause I don't.

"With a boat, I can live in a marina and my lifestyle is what I want it to be, not based on *it*. Nobody cares what I live on. I'm friends with everybody here and they're friends with me. The friendships are based on people, nothing else, certainly not on an inanimate *it*.

"And with a boat, you're always ready financially, mentally and *emotionally* to go. With a house, even if you sell it, you always have that emotional dock line, which is a lot harder to cast off than the physical dock line. With a boat, I'm always home, no matter where the boat is. I cast off the physical dock line and leave, but the emotional dock line stays on the boat. I take my emotional home with me.

"Have you ever heard anyone say, 'Boy, if I won the lottery I'd sure sell my boat and buy a big house and just stay there'? Of course not, but you always hear it the other way. They'd sell their house and buy a big boat."

What was your biggest adjustment?

"Space, going from several thousand square feet to 61 square feet."

" . . . despite the fact our homes float, we really are quite normal."

– Millie & Jack Rose

What's the best part?

"It's just the *knowing I can untie four lines and leave anytime I want,* that makes life tolerable."

What's the worst part?

"Trying to live in a 61-square foot-floating shoebox."

Dave & Sissy

Sissy is a bookkeeper by trade. She now works part time for a selected group of clients — but as a housekeeper. She regularly turns down work. "I don't want to work any more hours than I already do, and I won't work weekends. I want to spend my weekends with my husband."

Dave does something technical in the printing business, but not all day, every day. He, too, could work more hours if he wanted. They have two cars. They have lived three years on their 38-foot sloop, *Creola*. They don't have anything in storage anyplace else. Everything is on the boat.

Why do you live aboard a boat?

Dave: "Mainly to get away from the insanity of suburbia. We got tired of the big mortgage payments and the stress of trying to keep up with the neighbors, who are trying to keep up with their neighbors, who are trying to keep up with us. Also, we lost our house in a fire several years ago, and that was a real revelation about life, about how temporary everything really is. I guess moving on the boat was a move *away* from suburbia as much as a move to the boat.

"Also, my brother-in-law lives on a boat. I saw his lifestyle and the more I thought about it, the better it looked. So I decided to try it."

What has been your biggest adjustment?

"Actually, it's been a positive adjustment. I wasn't ready for how much I'd enjoy this. It's very rewarding. I really like living aboard a lot more than I thought I would."

What's the best part of living aboard?

"The freedom I feel. This little patch of water under the boat is like a sidewalk that leads all the way around the world. I can go anywhere I want. All I have to do is untie the boat and go. That's why I spend so much time just working on the boat and making sure that everything works the way it's supposed to. I like the feeling that I can leave anytime I want to. Maybe it's just to another marina, but I like the feeling of knowing I'm not tied down. I'd say another good part is how living on the boat has strengthened my marriage relationship."

What's the worst part of living aboard?

"Well, at first it was the lack of knowledge about the boat. Now, it's the lack of privacy. My wife and I are quite content with each other's company, we like to spend time together. A marina is a very social place. People, strangers, are always strolling down the walk and looking in the boats, stopping and asking questions. Sometimes we have to stay below deck just to get some privacy. That gets old."

"One of the best parts is that I'm going through the back alleys of America. The waters haven't been totally homogenized yet like the rest of the country. You know, a suburb in Phoenix is going to look the same as a suburb in Saint Paul, but on the waterway, you still get a sense of uniqueness. For me, that reinforces the sense and pleasure of living aboard and being on an alternative life journey."

– Dick, aboard s/v Murmur

Why do you live aboard a boat?

Sissy: "Well, it's nothing I would have done by myself, but when Dave wanted to do it, I thought, 'why not?' I mean, we'd already lost all our stuff in the fire and I was tired of all the money it takes to live on land. So we decided to try it. I figured if we didn't like it we could move back on land. So, why not?"

What has been your biggest adjustment?

"The laundry. It's just a big pain to have to lug the laundry up to the car, drive to the laundromat, wait around, come back, drag it back to the boat. It takes half a day. I was used to just doing a load while I was doing other things."

What's the best part?

"I love the simple life we lead now. I look back on all the money I wasted on cars and fancy clothes; stuff that doesn't really mean anything. But you get caught up in it, because everybody you know and work with are all caught up in it too. The boat life is just so much simpler."

What's the worst part?

"The laundry, the mildew and the cleaning. It's really hard to keep the boat clean. I thought it would be easier, but it's not. It's a lot harder to keep a boat clean than a house. And it's a constant battle with the mildew."

Alan & Kathy

Alan is, quite honestly, a genius. His academic and professional résumé brings you to no other logical conclusion. At 36 he has accomplished what most people can't do in a lifetime. He has owned *Precipio*, his Morgan 41, for six months, and recently moved aboard. He plans to cruise extensively for two years, then re-evaluate his future. Kathy is his companion, a very perceptive and intelligent woman with remarkable business and organizational skills, but little sailing experience. They have two cars at the marina.

Why do you live aboard a boat?

Alan: "The thought excited me. I've just sold my business and I want to take some time off. It's the old story that if you have the time, you usually don't have the money, and if you have the money, you usually don't have the time. Well, right now I have the time *and* the money, so I'm going to take two years off and go cruising. I mean, how often do you hear older people say, 'Gosh, I sure wish I would have worked longer hours when I had the chance'? Not often! So I'm going to take some time off while I'm still young enough to enjoy it."

What's the biggest adjustment you faced?

"Organizing my stuff. I'm really not a neat person, but you can't be a slob on a boat. When you need something, you usually need it right now, not in an hour and a half, after you've torn the boat apart looking for it. I probably have a dozen screwdrivers on this boat, and I'll be lucky if I can find one in a hurry. I have to get organized."

What's the best part?

"The adventure of all this; feeling the freedom to go; getting the boat ready to live on it for a long time — it's all a lot of fun. I'm having a ball."

What's the worst part?

"Getting organized. That and finding the right boat to buy. I could have gotten a larger boat, but I had to think about selling it. I got a good deal on this boat, and it's a lot easier to sell a $90,000 boat than a two-million-dollar boat. The more expensive the boat, the fewer the people who can afford to buy it when you want to sell it. And like the old saying, you always make the money when you buy something, not when you sell it. If you put out too much money when you buy something, you'll never get it back when you sell it."

Why do you live aboard a boat?

Kathy: "Well, we wanted to travel and not live out of a suitcase or a hotel or a tent, so that meant a boat."

What's your biggest adjustment?

"My biggest adjustment is dealing with Alan's disorganization. When Alan can't find something, he will usually start asking me where it is. Most of the time I can find it before he can, but then when he's through with whatever he's doing, he doesn't put stuff away again, or when he does, it's in a different place and then he can't remember where the new place is. It's really frustrating trying to get the boat organized with Alan around.

"After that, I'm having a hard time feeling productive. I just sold a business, too, and now I have a lot of time on my hands. I used to manufacture jewelry, plus I had my own retail outlets. I'm used to doing things, lots of things."

What's the best part of living aboard?

"The boat is causing us to evaluate our relationship. Living in a boat does that. Also, I'm looking forward to traveling and meeting new people. I think marinas bring out the best in people. I think the boat is going to set the rest of our lives in action."

What's the worst part?

"I think boats are primarily 'guy things.' Alan gets to talking with all the guys in the marina about boats, and he spends *hours* doing that. He's always off on some other boat looking at chains and motors and boat stuff. I think it's harder for women to make friends in a marina. The women tend to stay on their boats more than the men. I miss having close women friends. Like, I enjoy going to the movies, but Alan doesn't. He'd rather rent a video. So where does that leave me? I like to go shopping and maybe just look, but Alan hates that, so where does that leave me? Of course I could go alone, and sometimes I do, but it would be nicer if I had some women friends to mess around with the way Alan goes messing around with you guys in the marina. I don't mean to rain on his parade, but I wish I had a parade too."

Me (Gary Graham)

I live on a 25' O'Day sloop, *Simplicity*. I have two boxes of stuff shoved way in the back of a friend's closet a continent away. I have a truck and a motorcycle at the marina. I'm living on minimum-wage jobs, freelance writing (like this), and I teach writing workshops. I have lived aboard since I made the big move back in '95.

Why do I live on a boat?

Like everyone else, I love the water. I don't like lots of possessions, and I love the feeling of freedom. I'm also a fairly solitary person; I enjoy reading, writing, sailing, motorcycling, and hiking. These are all mainly solitary pursuits.

What was my biggest adjustment?

In my head. Making the decision to become a full-time Gypsy. Giving up high-paying pressure cooker jobs for a low-income nomadic existence. Making the decision to re-adjust my life style. Overcoming the fear of economic hardship. Committing myself to living off my writing abilities and minimum-wage, transient jobs. The biggest adjustment was between my ears, not space or transportation or laundry.

Space is a problem, but I work around it. I set up the computer, modem, printer and files in the morning, then take them down at night. It takes about five minutes to convert from boat to office, but that isn't much time compared to driving 25 miles to work.

What's the best part?

The satisfaction of realizing I can *do* it. I am *doing* it. I have *done* it. I never have to live on land again. I never have to dread going to work at a job I hate again. I never have to deal with a boss I don't respect again. I'm learning I can live on less than minimum wage. This means I can just be a permanent drifter, which is what I want. I've spent a lifetime doing *things*, being a human *doing*. Now I'm slowing down and being somebody, a human being. I like the new me.

Another best part is the continual motion of the boat. My spot in the marina gets a lot of wake action, plus being on a small sailboat, I rock a lot. I absolutely love the continual motion.

A totally unexpected benefit for me is my vastly improved health. I can't afford any junk food; no colas, no spicy, processed meat, no candy, no smokes, no snack treats, no fast food. I just can't afford it. As a result, I eat a lot of whatever produce is the cheapest. Lots of potatoes, yams, carrots and apples. My morning beverage is warm water and lemon juice. (Then I drink two cups of the marina free coffee.) I drink lots of plain old water. I have never felt this healthy.

What's the worst part?

The fear that I will be forced to live out my last days on land, incapacitated in some tiny, sterile room at the end of a long hall, in a publicly run warehouse for the indigent, feeble, aged. I fear being moored to impartial machines and tended by uncaring medocrats. I much prefer to die alone, at home on the water.

" . . . you better not dream too hard or long; your dreams just might come true."

– Jimmy Buffett

My prayer is that as my earthly voyage comes to an end, I'll have the strength to pull up the anchor and set the sails one last time, heading *Simplicity* out to sea for the start of my eternal journey.

I want my last sight to be her sails full before a freshening breeze, my last sounds to be ocean water tapping her hull in time to a Jimmy Buffet tune on my little boom box. I want my last smell to be the clean ocean air, and my last taste to be good straight slug of hearty sailor's rum.

God, what a way to go!

- 2 -

WHAT'S LOVE
GOT TO DO WITH IT?
Finding the Liveaboard Boat

In this section, liveaboards tell us about their boats and discuss why their boat is the right boat for them. Buying a boat is a huge undertaking. The search alone eats time and money and can chew you up emotionally. One Living Aboard reader estimated he spent over $16,000 on research materials, telephone and travel costs before he found a suitable boat. While it is true that the process of finding the right boat for living aboard can be lengthy and frustrating, it can also be loads of fun. As you look at boats — and visit as many as you can — you'll begin to see your dream take shape.

It is likely that your idea of the perfect boat will change as your search progresses. Keep in mind that a boat that is fine for weekends or short trips may not be a good boat on which to live full time. Give a lot of thought to not only what you intend to do with the boat but how you live on a daily basis.

So where do you start? You can find a lot of help in books, magazines and on the Internet. Best of all, walk the docks, visit boats, talk to other liveaboards. Most boat owners like to talk about their boats and show them off. You will find, by the way, that the boats you tour will start to blend together in your mind. The more boats you see, the harder it will be to remember the particulars of each. If you can, take a video camera to record your visits. You'll not only have a record of what the boat looked like, but also of your comments and the comments of the broker or owner as he or she shows you around.

Once you start looking at boats, you'll know what you want even if you can't articulate it. You'll be able to walk into a marina and tell by looking which boats you would like and which are not for you. You'll develop a feeling for a certain boat and when you find that boat she'll be beautiful and just the boat for you. You'll fall in love.

Choosing the Right Boat for Living Aboard

One Woman's Perspective

Pamela Wendell

For anyone who has ever thought about living aboard a boat, the decision is difficult and often frustrating. Of course, the biggest part of the decision is what kind of boat will make you both physically and economically comfortable.

My husband and I spent four years in the process of selecting the boat and equipment which would suit our needs, and this article hopes to help those who are at the beginning of this process.

Although my husband and I had sailed for years on a 37-foot sailboat, we both knew, and discussed many times, the shortfalls of this boat for full-time living. Even though we thought it was a great boat for weekend sailing, it lacked sufficient space and storage capacity and overall comfort, which we felt we could achieve by having a larger, roomier boat.

When selecting a boat for living aboard, it is important that partners are both involved in the decision-making process. Mars and Venus often have different ideas about what will make a comfortable home.

I had never imagined living on a boat full time. This was my husband's dream. However, as time went on, my goals changed and I warmed to the idea. Not having children or much family left helped, too, as most women want to be near their loved ones. Also, most women want to feel secure and have their treasured possessions around them. Boats have limited space, so giving up your material things, which you have worked so long and hard to get, is not only difficult, it is incomprehensible to many women.

Hygiene is another huge obstacle. It is a well known fact that you just cannot stay as clean on a boat a you can in a house. So if you are thinking of living aboard and this is as important to you, as it was for me, then a proper head, shower and potentially a washer/dryer are important items to include on your list of priorities.

When selecting a new boat, one of the most important issues for couples is to make sure that both are involved in the decision making. My husband went out of his way to make sure that I was included in almost every decision. However, ultimately, because of his years of racing experience and extensive research into new boat materials and equipment, I deferred to him on many issues. Nonetheless, he always asked. This kept the arguments to a minimum. As time progressed and we saw each other's strengths and interests, we split the work; I handled aesthetics and he handled mechanics. Before the final buy, however, we would present to each other our findings and choices to get concurrence that this was a good decision. I should mention here that aesthetics does not mean picking colors and fabrics only. I worked heavily on both the interior and exterior layout, including where dorade boxes and ports should be positioned, how high and large built-in items should be, and designing custom cabinetry. All this had to be done to optimize space while accommodating the equipment on board and providing maximum comfort.

Fortunately for us, at the beginning of our search, we had decided to move to Europe for a few years. My job took me there, and we thought this would give us a golden opportunity to see what Europe had to offer in the form of sailing and boats, not to mention culture. We sold our 37-foot boat and ended up living in Germany for over four years. During that time we traveled extensively, seeking out harbors and boats whenever possible.

Because we had had a boat we enjoyed for nine years, we started there and worked from lists of what we liked and disliked about it. Then we added ideas we liked from other boats we saw. We determined that our choice would be based on the following criteria:

Size

It had to be big enough to give an open feeling and allow us to have separate space. It needed to feel as though we weren't bumping into or tripping over things all the time; it needed adequate storage space; and it needed to do all this in a size which two people could handle easily — one person under unusual circumstances. Based on discussions with other liveaboards, as well as our own findings, we decided that 40- to 50-foot was the range that seemed right.

Quality

It had to be well constructed. Of course, this is a relative concept, and how one ultimately uses the boat, as well as how much one can spend, will bear greatly on this decision. If you are planning on living at the dock only, then it is not as important to have offshore construction. We are planning on extensive cruising, potentially to remote locations, so a solid, well-built boat was a must.

Sailability

It had to perform well while sailing. Although our old boat was a cruiser with a performance keel, we felt a full keel would give us more stability. Also, we wanted a full cutter rig using furling systems for all primary sails, and a sliding spinnaker pole for handling the spinnaker more easily. All lines had to lead to the cockpit and all winches had to be oversized. This would make a larger boat more manageable.

Comfort

Based on discussions with dozens of women, this was an extremely important issue for non-liveaboards and liveaboards alike. We wanted every part of the boat to feel comfortable, from the cockpit to climbing the mast, to pumping the head. Initially, I was adamant that I had to have a queen-sized master berth, aft. If I was going to live on a boat, I wanted a decent bed and bedroom. However, after looking at hundreds of boats in our size and price range, we simply couldn't find one with this amenity, as well as with all our other layout requirements.

Price

It had to be within our price range. We knew that for a new boat in the 44-foot range what we would end up paying depended on construction and options. Many used boats cost less, (depending on age, make and options, and how eager the owner is to sell), but we never found a used boat that didn't need a lot of renovation work to get it the way we wanted. We decided that we would set our price and look for a new boat.

Gear

The equipping of a boat can be a tedious and never-ending process. However, we felt if this was going to be our final boat, as well as a home we could travel in, it must have well made, reliable equipment to include: engine; feathering prop; sufficient electronic and navigation equipment (autopilot, depth/speed/wind instruments, radar, GPS, VHF radio, single side-band radio, weather FAX cellular phone, laptop computer); air conditioning, which was a must for living anywhere between Washington D.C. and Florida; a diesel-fueled heater to complement the central beating system; oversized batteries; a power inverter; a water purification system; TV/VCR; stereo; washer/dryer; fans; oven/stove; refrigerator/freezer; sufficient electric bilge pumps and oversized manual bilge pump; electric windlass, and rigid rowing dinghy with outboard.

A generator was outweighed initially by the air conditioning because of price, but room was built for one to be added later.

Homeyness

We wanted it to feel like a home rather than a camp or a weekend retreat.

Looks

This was more important to me than my husband, as he was more concerned with construction and sailability. However, I felt I wanted a boat that was nice to look at after spending all this money, and that potentially had good resale value if we ever elected to sell it.

After having sent away for information on numerous boats and flying around the world to look at a dozen or so, we decided to build a 44-foot cutter-rigged sailboat in Canada. Although it was the right decision for us, building tends to be more expensive and very time-consuming. Our anxiety was compounded by the fact that we were still living in Europe and couldn't just pop in to see how the boat's construction was going. From the first visit to the builder's site, to completion, it took roughly one and a half years. During that time my husband and I each went to Canada two times to survey the construction, approve changes, and make necessary decisions and adjustments. The builder was amazed at this, but otherwise we kept in constant contact through telephone, faxes and mail.

The ultimate product, to us, was worth the wait. Although the boat was to have come mostly equipped, my husband and I were able to change and incorporate all the items we felt were so important, such as makes or models of almost everything on the boat. This included such things as a four-stage bottom application which retards blistering and inhibits barnacles, type of sails and furling systems, hatches and ports, electronics, winches, batteries, ground tackle and propeller. All tanks are accessible and can be removed for repair or replacement, and extra capacity was added for long hauls.

To me, it was a delight decorating the interior. The boat came with a semi-standard interior, but because we wanted to add storage and separate the refrigeration from the freezer, we were able to customize the cabinetry to better utilize space. The two heads on board were reduced to one large one, and one for a washer/dryer. This allowed the head and shower to be enlarged. The quarter berth in the nav station was eliminated and made into what we call the "garage," which is a large storage compartment for miscellaneous items. From our travels throughout Europe, we had purchased tiles and wood carvings which we incorporated in the head and galley of the boat, giving it a homey feeling. We chose a cherry wood interior for a warmer feeling, but picked light fabric colors to give the interior a tropical feeling. The galley is large with two sinks in a center island, and a workbench can be attached to the back. A permanent dinette allows meals to be served without having to set up a table at every meal, although a hide-away dining table is available to drop in on top of the cocktail table in the forward saloon, should we have company. Five-inch foam was used everywhere for added comfort while sitting and sleeping, and extra bookshelves and cabinets were built to hold CDs, movies and reading material.

The layout gave us both the openness and separate space we desired. My husband designed the nav station to suit himself, because I knew he would be spending much of his time there. Additionally, the entire cabin gained a large airy feeling by placing the main saloon forward of the mast in the bow. The V-shaped couch converts quickly and easily to a queen-sized berth for visitors. For such occasions, a door was added from the main cabin to the shower for access to the head, without disturbing the aft master cabin.

My desire for an aft master queen-sized berth was met with a seven-by-seven-foot berth, which I decorated with tropical sheers and comforters, giving it an inviting feeling.

One of the biggest features to me was the large cockpit and real staircase companionway. Many sailors prefer small cockpits because of the danger of swamping at sea. As a result, we had the builder incorporate a flap into the drop-down transom which purges water quickly. We felt that in the tropics, the cockpit would become our second living room, and most of our time would be spent there. Having this additional room for entertainment and relaxation is a

"To furnish a ship requireth much trouble."

– John Manningham: Diary (1602)

feature I would find hard to do without. The bimini overhead protects the cockpit from the sun most of the day.

The boat came with a rigid dinghy on davits which easily lowers to the water. This has been a blessing, along with the drop-down transom, as we have two dogs that need to be taken ashore frequently when we're at anchor.

The boat does have bright work on it which doesn't make it as low maintenance as some would like, but this was a trade-off for what I considered to be a prettier boat.

Teri and I own a Krogen Manatee 36' x 13'8", with a single queen stateroom, complete galley, very large (full beam) saloon, plus large aft deck, nearly flat floor front to back – a true pleasure to be on and live aboard. This model is very well suited to life aboard.

– Randy & Teri Horn
aboard Sirenia, *Lake St. Claire, Michigan*

As mentioned, building a boat is not for everyone. Fortunately, there are many good used boats on the market at quite reasonable prices, which can make the dream more affordable. Also, used boats usually have worked out the new "bugs," and are normally equipped with at least the essentials for sailing. This makes it a little easier to add things later, as much of the added cost to new boats comes from electronics, navigational and safety equipment.

All boats are a compromise. However, we felt this boat came closest to our ideal at the price we were willing to pay. The information above is not all-inclusive, however it is intended to give the reader a good idea of what we felt was important and why. The final price of the boat ended up being more than our original cap, although we believed the cost was justified relative to what we felt we had to have. As in building a house, people should allow for added costs, even with the best of planning.

Naturally, there were hundreds of discussions around should we or shouldn't we, what should we include, what did we have to have, and what could we live without. As time went, on our goals and targets changed a bit. In the end, we determined that to get everything we wanted on a boat, we would have needed around 60 feet, which for two people (in our opinion) is too large to handle, and for us, too expensive both from a purchase and maintenance point of view.

For us, the ultimate choice between used and new was extremely difficult, and filled with anxiety. Couples should look at it as if they are buying a home, because for many women, this can be a much more difficult and emotional decision than it is for a man, especially if you are dipping into life savings.

Our boat was built to be a pleasure to live on as well as to sail. Every time I go aboard, I feel good about our decision and our efforts. Of course, part of this includes learning seamanship and having a positive attitude. If this is attained, the experience will be more pleasurable.

Finding a Boat on the Web

Nina Pratt

"You're nuts!" my family and friends said. "You're right!" I said, and began the process of moving from land to water. When I decided to sell my co-op apartment in New York City and move aboard a boat, I didn't have a particular boat in mind. Most wannabe liveaboards either already own a boat or have a larger boat in mind to buy and perhaps fix up. Not me. My first task, then, was to find a boat to move aboard.

I was not a complete neophyte, however. As a kid, I'd sailed with my family, mostly on Buzzard's Bay. I learned how to navigate coastal waters and steer a straight course, how to judge the sky for good and bad weather, how to tie a bowline behind your back while treading water (a useful skill if you have happened to irritate the skipper) and how to provision a boat for a week's cruise. For a variety of reasons, I had been beached since my late teens. Now at age 50, I was about to launch myself into a new life afloat.

> Searching for the right boat for living aboard can be an expensive and frustrating process. Nina Pratt discovered that the Internet was a great place to start her search. She saved time and travel costs; she also found lots of friendly advice and encouragement from other boaters on the Internet.

Being a New Yorker without a car — we pride ourselves on taking the train (known to out-of-towners as the subway) or walking everywhere — I found it difficult to get around to see many boats. So I decided to explore the resources of the Internet in search of the perfect liveaboard boat. Up until then, I'd used my computer as a writing tool and had explored only sites of interest to writers. When I began to search for my home on the water, I found a whole new world on the net that I'd never suspected existed.

In some ways, being out of touch with reality is an excellent way to start when you enter the liveaboard and yachting worlds. I not only was vague about what sort of boat I wanted, but the boats I remembered from my childhood were, if not obsolete, then at least hopelessly old fashioned. That description fits me too, so I didn't let that stop me. I knew that my dream boat had to be large enough for me to turn around in without knocking myself out with an elbow. I needed full standing headroom below which for me was 5 feet 4 inches. My crew, two cats, also needed sufficient room. They don't share anything, so I had to have room for his and her cat boxes, his and her food dishes, his and her water dishes, his and her . . . you get the picture. Finally, since I have no human companion, my dream boat had to be easily handled by me alone.

Raised on sailboats and being ecologically minded, I ruled out powerboats. Since I wasn't interested in sailing far or fast, that eliminated bluewater or racing boats. Although I had a prejudice for classic hulls, I also have a strong distaste

"She starts — she moves — she seems to feel the thrill of life along her keel!"

– Longfellow; "The Building of the Ship"

for hard work, so I scratched wooden hulls from my list. Not much to go on, but it was enough to get me started and I began cruising the cyberseas.

One excellent site led to another and I happily rose two hours early every morning so I'd have time to paddle about on the Internet. I looked at a lot of pictures which, with my antiquated equipment, took forever to download. I e-mailed individual sellers (very fruitful), brokers (less helpful), and manufacturers (got a snail-mailbox stuffed with information of varying quality). I also joined several Internet mailing lists. These I found packed with good, not-so-good and downright stupid advice. I liked them better than the newsgroups or bulletin boards, because I found them easier to cope with as they came directly to my computer in digest form rather than my having to search them out each time. And I began to appreciate some of the "locals" who populate each list.

Once I fixed on a boat that I thought might suit me, I'd sign up for the mailing list specific to that boat. For a time, I was on the catboat list, the Rhodes list, the trawler list. You'll find a list for virtually every boat somewhere on the 'net. These were especially useful in getting detailed information about the pluses and minuses of each type of boat. They are also good sources for finding a used boat of a specific class. And you meet some nice (as well as some charmingly peculiar) people.

After several months of sifting through all this information I began getting serious about looking at the boats in the flesh, or fiberglass, I should say. The first boat that took my fancy was a 26-foot catboat. Small and with only one sail to worry about, but roomy down below, she seemed the perfect solution to my problem. I located several on the Internet and then chose one to travel to see.

Boat visiting should be fun as well as instructive. I picked a boat located in Ft. Lauderdale so that I could leave cold and wintry New York for a weekend and, incidentally, get in a visit to my father who lives on Key Largo. Another reason I chose this particular boat was that she was in the water and ready to sail. Further, air fares are competitive from New York City to Florida so even if I hated the boat, I wouldn't be out a packet of money. Several fellow members of the various mailing lists I was on at the time gave me tips on good places to stay, interesting activities and sights to see, and also invited me to stop by to visit with them when I was in the area.

However, one look at the catboat and I knew she wasn't right for me. She looked great on paper, but seemed ungainly on the water and poorly designed below. Undaunted, I canceled the survey I'd arranged (yup, I also found the surveyor on the Internet, then checked references with the folks on my mailing lists) and had a lovely few days seeing the sights, visiting my father, hanging out at the marinas and meeting a few of the folks I'd been corresponding with over the Internet.

At this point, a thread got started on one of the lists about having cats aboard. I began to worry that my older cat, a neurotic feline named Buddy, might not take too kindly to the sea, especially heeling in a stiff wind. He doesn't take kindly to any break in his routine, to tell the truth. A friend offered to take Buddy and me off for a day sail. We arrived, Buddy hissing and screaming in his carrier, and we sailed off up the Hudson River. It was freezing cold, but wonderful to again feel a boat moving under my feet. However, Buddy, was less than thrilled. He threw up on every cushion he could reach, shredded a small carpet and pooped on the owner's berth. I don't think we'll be invited back. I hasten to add that I replaced all that the little furry monster destroyed.

So I added new criteria to my list: the boat should be power, not sail, and be very easy to clean. Several Internet friends suggested that I jettison the cats, but this was unacceptable to me, so I went back to the Web to look at more pictures, study more plans, daydream about how I and my cats might live together on a boat. I was drawn to those modeled on work boats. I almost bought a tug/yacht, but she turned out to have some serious structural flaws so I kept looking. I flirted with a lobster boat, dallied with a trawler, and then I found her, my dream boat.

I had seen pictures of the Scout 30 made by Express Yachting and designed by Ben Ostlund. She looked like an old Elco commuter yacht from the 1920s — plumb bow, raised foredeck, big square wheel house with a long canopy extending over the cockpit. She looked exactly like what I was searching for: roomy below, stately on the water, full of teak and brass, but made of fiberglass and so not too hard to keep up. Since there were only a few of these made during the late '80s, I logged onto the Internet to search for one that might be available.

I found *Puffin* in Nova Scotia. I e-mailed the seller and we corresponded for a while. Friends on the Internet offered lots of advice about the mechanics of buying a boat in Canada, who a good surveyor was, and how to assess for myself whether or not *Puffin* would suit me. The surveyor agreed to do a "walk through," a cursory inspection of the boat. It turned out that he knew the builder and designer, so he was familiar with her. We talked at length over the phone about what kind of cruising I planned so that he and I were both sure this kind of boat would suit me. Based on this information, I made an offer, and, after the requisite amount of dickering, the seller and I came to an agreement, subject to a personal inspection and a full survey. Soon I was on a plane bound to see *Puffin*. I knew the moment I saw her sitting at the dock in picturesque Chester that she was my boat. Fortunately, she passed her survey with flying colors!

Throughout the purchasing process, my Internet friends offered help. They sent me their buy/sell agreements on which to model my own, counseled me on potential pitfalls of negotiating a sale without a lawyer, steered me to a good shipper, recommended a customs broker to make sure she got across the border alright, and held my cyber-hand when I got nervous about the magnitude of the step I was taking. I never would have found *Puffin* without the Internet. I never would have had the courage to buy her without the support of my online friends. I never would have had the pleasure of looking out over the marshes at sunset from *Puffin*'s cockpit, my cats purring by my side, Vivaldi on the stereo, a cold drink in my hand. The Internet is a miraculous tool for liveaboard boat buyers.

There is only one trawler on the market that truly meets both the captain's and the first mate's requirements. That is a Krogen '42. Besides coming equipped with a washer and dryer, microwave and some with an ice maker, it is a very beamy boat with lots of storage and plenty of living space. It is truly a long-range trawler and a liveaboard's delight.

– Ann Gordon,
Westport, Connecticut

My husband and I have lived aboard full-time on our sailboat, a Hans Christian 33, since buying it in October, 1991. We would buy another sailboat for now, but would consider a trawler-type powerboat (or a Nordhaven if we win the lottery!) when we are no longer physically able to handle a sailboat. I would like to charter a catamaran someday, just to try something different. We plan to cruise full-time.

– Linda Hill & John Gratton,
aboard s/v Nakia, *Redwood City, California*

Buying a New Boat

Some Things Work and Some Things Don't

Ted & Ann Gordon

The Tayana 37 is a wonderful boat for cruising; it's a stable double-ender with full keel and 20,000 pounds displacement. This was the boat we wanted; we were taken with her pleasing lines and exquisite teak joinery work and finish. It was roomy — more room than we had ever had before. How could we ever fill it? And it was new; we could order just what we wanted — from cabin layout to winch placement on deck. After suffering the requisite months of anguish and indecision, we ordered hull #522, our first brand new boat.

The Tayana is built in Taiwan by the Ta Yang yards and is ordered in the United States through a local importer, who has the job of helping buyers select the exact boat design that will be built and delivered. This

> One sure way to get exactly what you want in a liveaboard boat is to buy a new boat. The trick, of course, lies in knowing exactly what you want.

is one of the joys of buying a new boat; within limits, and money permitting, you can get what you want. Some boats come in alternate configurations — select model A or B — but the Tayana comes like a blank slate. The alternatives are almost infinite. As soon as you've paid your deposit, you specify your boat in great detail, but the gods and fate still play a big role in determining what's finally produced. There's always a slip or two between down payment and delivery. And we found out that what seemed so logical and right in design concept may not work out as planned. Therein lies this tale: how our boat evolved and how what we wanted changed when we saw it in the flesh, or at least in real fiberglass and teak.

Here's what we chose: a cutter as opposed to a ketch, on the basis of simpler sail handling. The cabin consisted of a double berth up forward rather than a V-berth because we thought it would be simple to make the bed; and enclosed quarter berth aft to provide our guests with a modicum of privacy; galley at the companionway, and an aft-facing nav station opposite the galley. The saloon table was fixed with a drop leaf surrounded by an L-shaped settee, and another settee opposite. We opted for propane to fuel a three-burner gimbaled stove and cabin heater. The mast was to be deck stepped to minimize any deck leakage and a 30-horsepower Yanmar diesel was selected for auxiliary power. One thing that we really wanted was placement of engine controls near the helm. The standard design had the controls on the cockpit bulkhead near the companionway and out of reach. We wanted to be able to call for engine power quickly in tight situations.

We wanted a mass — more than that, a crowd — of drawers behind the settee cushions for everything that had to be stored, from tools to silverware. Most of the electronic equipment was scheduled for installation in the United States during commissioning, but we planned where everything would go so that we were sure there would be enough room in the nav station panels. On deck, we thought through the winch sizing and placement, the layout of the running rigging, the deck material (fiberglass, if you please) and the companionway cover (teak would be fine). There was more — much more — in this process of selection and design. And it was fun.

Through luck, Ted had a trip in the Far East two weeks before hull #522 was scheduled to be shipped and he stopped over at the yard in Kow Chung. It was a scene of great industry. People swarming all over the boat in an obvious frenzy to complete it before the shipment date. It sure looked like our design, but there were a few small differences. Like the mast — it was keel stepped; like the engine controls — they were in the standard place, far from the helm. And while he didn't have the dimensions with him, the spot for the cabin heater looked much too small and the cutout for the stove seemed too narrow. Much discussion, in English and gesture, followed with their engineers. Nothing could be done about the mast — keel stepped was stronger, anyway. The engine controls might be moved, but it was a big job and involved extending all of the engine wiring and mechanical connections. We settled for a parallel engine start switch near the helmsman's knee.

Because he was sure the heater space was too small, we redesigned the cabinet on which it was to mount. As for the stove cutout, we'd wait and see. (It turned out to be too small for the stove we had selected, so we switched later to a two burner model.)

Don't get us wrong, the boat was magnificent. The helmsman's seat was a work of art. The stanchions were gleaming and braced against the bulwark like a brick fort and the winches were placed and sized as planned. The layout looked terrific and the boat had happy owners.

After 18 months, some of it in extended cruising (the ICW, the Florida keys, and the Bahamas), we really liked some of our choices. Other decisions were simply wrong. First of all, the next time we'll have the yard install most of the major equipment, like the stove, heater and propane system, rather than installing these systems during commissioning. The factory can build in what has to be built in and sizing mistakes won't survive this process. Sometimes they can get better prices, too.

We had our salesman perform the commissioning, and this, in retrospect, was a bad decision. We think that this was his first, or close to his first, post-delivery assembly. Simple things took too long. Tubing kinked where it shouldn't have and quality was suffering.

The assembly job is inevitably complicated by the fact that the factory is halfway around the world. Things that the factory supplied fit together very well, but the trouble came in the installation of the new equipment. We became so dismayed by the process that we took the boat before it was finally commissioned, gave it a sea trial, had a surveyor look it over, and finished it ourselves. It became *Candide,* after Voltaire's character who was always searching for the best of all possible worlds.

That crowd of drawers didn't work out so well either. We found that drawers are neat all right, but nothing taller than the drawer itself can fit. So one unforgettable Saturday, I attacked the drawers, made large cutouts and plywood covers, and converted the space behind the port settee into a major storage hold — the cave — which can now take a pot for boiling lobsters. The double bed in the forward compartment is probably just as hard to make as a V-berth would have been, and when heeling there is sometimes a lee edge which can dump the resting person. On deck we would have chosen to have even less teak, if possible.

In the class of "I wish we had done it at the start, rather than later" are the electric windlass (we started with a manual one), the all-chain rope (we started with a chain-rope combination), and the air conditioner which we found a near necessity in the southern summer, fuel and water tank gauges to replace the original unreadable dip sticks, and a 100-amp generator to replace the inadequate factory-standard 30-amp device.

We bought and installed an integrated set of instruments; knotmeter, depthmeter and wind speed and direction. The main instrument is mounted at the nav station and is repeated via digital cable at the helm. The setup is ideal except for one fault. When one instrument goes out, they can all go out. Sending the main unit back to the factory (twice) blinded us completely.

The wiring to the nav station instruments turned out to be too puny, so it was replaced. The compressor unit for the 12-volt refrigerator was badly placed behind one of the settees, but moving it to the deep lazarette has apparently solved the matter. Access to the lazarette is constrained, we wish there was more room to climb down. In making the modifications to the boat, we learned another

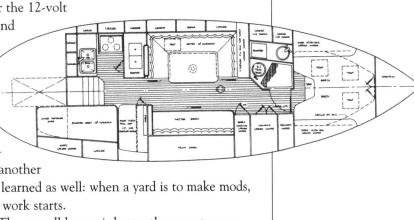

lesson that others before us have learned as well: when a yard is to make mods, always get a firm price before the work starts.

Many things worked out well. The overall layout is better than most, even though the next time privacy for our quarterberth guests won't be a high priority. The prism we mounted in the deck over the shower lights up the whole head area. The opening ports and hatches are a delight, although we've given up on cleaning the bronze. The enclosed shower is what we had hoped it would be. The no-leak stuffing box doesn't leak. The Yanmar just runs and runs (where's

"There's a lot of us in the boat — thought, love and money."

some wood to knock on?). The stainless steel water and fuel tanks are adequately sized and well placed amidship. The arched helmsman's seat gives visibility that otherwise would be absent. The quarter-wave ham radio antennas work like a charm. The roller furling jib has never let us down and it turns out that, as we thought, the staysail is small enough not to require furling gear of its own. For the main though, we added lazy jacks. The dinghy davits are working out well; it's a lot better to hoist the inflatable than to tow it. The list is longer, but you have the idea.

We're off *Candide*, now, but will be back on board in a month or so. When we go on board it will be like going to our second home. There's a lot of us in the boat — thought, love and money. And, all things considered, it's been worth the effort.

After six boats, both sail and power, I've found the one which will also be the next one I buy. Presently, I have a Carver aft-cabin 36 cruiser which I enjoy as a liveaboard here in Key West, Florida. It's just big enough for living, and great for cruising. It's well laid out space-wise, and has many advantages over my previous boats. Many after a tour, comment that "they could live aboard something like this as it's bigger inside than it looks on the outside." I've lived aboard for eight years now and surely enjoy every minute along with my cat. I think the cat has found places that I haven't as it disappears and reappears often. I'm a retired Navy chaplain (Roman Catholic priest) who is always glad to show off and answer questions about boating and living aboard. I will someday buy another boat just like this one and hope to have as much fun and enjoyment as this one affords. The Latin name says it all: *Quam Bonum II* – "How good it is!"

– *Rev. Jerome R. Turner,*
aboard Quam Bonum II, *Key West, Florida*

It's a Wonderful Life

Kevin LaGraff

Back in 1986 my wife, Susan, and I were living in Monterey, California, as two perfectly happy, middle-class homeowners. Our pursuits were the typical golf, tennis, and bridge variety with a hefty load of travel both here and abroad. Life was good, we were happy. Then one weekend things got even better.

We drove to Santa Cruz one Saturday for an event that was billed as a "Sea-Fest." The harbor was alive with all kinds of boats covering sail, power and personal craft. As we were leaving we came across a 16-foot Alden rowing shell that the owner was selling for $1,000. We tried our best to bargain, but the young man said the boat should be selling for twice that amount, so we wrote him a check with the condition that he would deliver the shell to our home in Monterey. "It's a deal!"

That little shell, known as an "Appledore Pod," was to open a door to a whole new life for us — a water-based life. Every morning we'd set out for a morning row before heading to work. Since the shell had only one seat, Susan and I would take turns. The non-rowing person could enjoy the marine life while sipping hot tea. The morning rows expanded into weekends, and we met some other ocean rowers who invited us along on half day excursions along the pristine Monterey-Carmel coast. Our world was opening up to sea otters, harbor seals, pelicans and a too-close encounter with a spouting whale that left us both wet and terrified. And eventually laughing ourselves silly.

The rowboat convinced us that we needed more water in our lives, so we started looking for a boat that we could berth in the Monterey Marina and use as a home base for our rowing excursions.

Our search ended in the California Delta when we found a pretty decent looking Bayliner Victoria about ten years old. Since the Monterey Marina was full and had an eight-year waiting list, we had to buy a 25-foot Folkboat in order to get the slip, and then sell the Folkboat at a loss. This is a fairly common procedure in California municipal marinas and I'm still not sure I like it, but, when in Rome . . . .

Once our Bayliner was ensconced in the slip, we gradually started moving in some creature comforts: stereo, toaster oven, some bedding for the V-berth, and a few pots and pans. She became our *Pied-a-Mer* — a nice place to drop in and sip some Chardonnay while watching the sun set over the Pacific.

Kevin LaGraff and Susan Atkins made the transition from land-locked suburbanites to full-time liveaboards one step at a time. They started with a 16-foot rowing shell, moved up to a 28' cabin cruiser and now live full time on *Mana*, a Krogen Manatee. Thanks to lower overhead since moving aboard, they both retired at 50 and are enjoying their life on the water. In fact, they love it!

One thing led to another, and before we knew it we were spending considerably more time on the Bayliner than in our house. And, we were both loving it. But alas, all good things must come to an end, and so we thought the worst when the Monterey city council asked the harbormaster for a report on "persons living illegally on boats berthed in the marina." The harbormaster began preparing his report and was surprised to find that many of the non-liveaboards, especially fishermen, were in favor of having people on their boats full-time as a crime deterrent. Electronics and gear thefts were down on the docks where there was some activity on a regular basis. The harbormaster included this in his report, as well as dismissing many of the other misconceptions about "boat people."

Kevin and Susan often take weekend cruises to San Francisco from their home port of Sausalito, enjoying big-city benefits without big-city hassles.

The report led to a proposed ordinance allowing 10% of the boats in the marina to be designated liveaboards. The hearings on the ordinance were lively, but the opposition wasn't nearly what the council members had expected. The ordinance was adopted and the call went out for applicants to serve as the liveaboard guinea pigs.

Susan and I had never thought the liveaboard life was for us, but we both agreed that since we started hanging out in the marina we didn't miss golf or tennis that much. One Saturday afternoon we sat on *Pied-a-Mer*, after a glorious day of rowing in the kelp beds off the Monterey Bay Aquarium, contemplating our future.

Out of the clear blue Susan said, "I like being on this boat more than in our house."

I thought, "Then what-in-hell are we doing paying out $1,500 a month on a mortgage?"

So I asked her, "If you had to choose right now, would you live ashore or on a boat?" She looked up at the clear blue Monterey sky and murmured, "B-O-A-T!"

The harbormaster was somewhat surprised to hear that we were interested in living aboard, since we didn't exactly fit the mold. He was also concerned that since we owned our home, we would be taking the place of an applicant that had no other residence.

Then I'll sell my house," I told him.

As it turned out, the boat inspection process set up by the ordinance ruled out some of the applicants, so the 10% allowable allotment was never met. We moved aboard as soon as we got the green light. And for good measure, we sold the house and just about everything in it. I guess you could call that a change in lifestyle!

Life Aboard

Living on a 28-foot cabin cruiser can be an adventure. Fortunately, my wife owned her own business several blocks from the marina where we set aside a room for storage of clothes and whatever. At the time, we were both dressing up in business suits everyday, so we needed the extra space. The boat leaked some, so I became a pretty good caulker until we got a dry boat. The other stuff, like installing an Electrosan sanitation system, rewiring the electrical, and replacing some of the canvas was interesting because it gave me a better "feel" for the boat. Susan and I did as much of the work as we were technically able to, and then hired professionals for the in-depth jobs.

We lived very happily this way for two years. At that point we both felt confident that this would be our new way of life for some time to come. I recall having a conversation with a boat broker around that time.

"You see all these big fancy boats I've got for sale," he said to me. "Well, I'd say at least half of them were owned by people who just up and decided to move onto a boat. After several months, one of them, usually the wife, says, 'That's enough . . . I've had it . . . I'm moving back home.' You and your wife did the smart thing by starting off with a small investment boat and seeing if this is really the life for you before plopping down a ton of money on something you never use."

Looking back, I'd call that pretty good advice. Because we realized we had the bug, now we were ready for "the bigger boat."

The Bigger Boat

We did things somewhat "bass ackwards." Instead of finding a boat and then getting the financing, we went to the bank and obtained a $50,000 loan. After we were approved, we went on a boat search that took us all over northern California. But it was fun seeing what was out there.

Instead of "kickin' the tires" we were "kickin' the fenders." Looking back, I'd say that several times we almost went way out on a limb and bought too much boat for our needs. Our goal in finding a suitable boat to live aboard also encompassed a change in lifestyle that would lower our cost of living so we could enjoy the fruits of our labors. A dream that we both shared was to retire at 50. The right boat could be our ticket.

At first we thought we wanted a houseboat. We looked at several and even made a low offer on one that was refused. In future years we would look back on that as a blessing, as we evolved from river cruising to bay and coastal cruising. I was pretty convinced that my ideal boat would be a trawler-style diesel with a single screw. After several weeks of looking, we got a call from a broker in Stockton who said, "There's a funny looking boat over here you might like. You could get her pretty cheap."

We drove to Stockton and ended up on a dusty levee road that took us to the "funny looking boat." She was a 1985 Krogen Manatee, 36 feet long and covered with cobwebs, but, nonetheless, a great floor plan and full of goodies like washer/dryer, full-size refrigerator, compact 100-horsepower Volvo diesel, and

"In less than a week we were starting to move aboard and felt like we were on our second honeymoon."

lots of dark, interior teak. Susan was put off at first by the exterior looks, but once aboard she fell in love.

The sales transaction took several days, but having the $50,000 as a partial payment helped move the sale along. In less than a week we were starting to move aboard and felt like we were on our second honeymoon. The work was a labor of love. I started on the outside while Susan worked on the inside. The boat cleaned up real good. We were very proud of *Mana* and our efforts.

At about this time I had accepted a job in Sacramento, so our timing couldn't have been better in terms of having a new home in Freeport, just south of Sacramento on the river. After a day's work at a desk job in the state capitol, it was sheer heaven to drive down to the marina and escape to our boat. Many warm, sultry evenings were spent fishing off the fantail while barbecuing and listening to baseball on the radio.

We have a 1977 42' Hatteras Sportfisher. We made some significant changes to the interior. We replaced the 3-burner electric stove and oven with a house-size Jenn-Air range top, put in a full size refrigerator with ice maker, replaced the microwave with a microwave/convection combination, replaced the "boat furniture" with a three-piece sofa, two wicker rockers, wicker footstool, and wicker end table, all from the three-story house we sold and emptied!

We have a large TV, VCR, and CD player, also from the house. We installed lots of teak bookracks to house our many cookbooks. You can see we wanted many of our favorite things with us. Living aboard has been great!

– Sharon Barrett,
aboard Almost Midnight, *Ft. Pierce, Florida*

Perhaps the only thing we missed while berthed on the Sacramento River was blue water. After developing a work proposal that relied heavily on "telecommuting," we were able to relocate our boat to the San Francisco Bay area in a charming little town called Sausalito. Thanks to cellular phones, faxes, and an understanding boss, our trawler became my office 90 miles away from Sacramento. Whenever I needed to be in the capitol for extended periods, we'd cruise back through the Delta and up the Sacramento River to a downtown marina. We had become fully portable in both our living and working environments.

The Sausalito living aboard experience is now going on ten years and we feel this has been the most enjoyable period of our lives together. The little rowing shell that we acquired in Santa Cruz still sits alongside *Mana*, and we row her every morning in Richardson Bay when we take our fruit and tea for breakfast. On weekends we usually cruise to San Francisco and spend time messing around in the "big city." We have become quite proficient with getting around using the buses, trains, and bicycles. And besides, San Francisco is a great town for just walking. We feel fortunate to be able to enjoy the city's attractions without the hassles of living in a metropolis.

Every morning we awake and say a prayer of thanksgiving that we are fortunate enough to be living aboard. It's a wonderful life!

A Boat for the Present

Tim Murray

"What is the perfect boat for living aboard?"
Well, there is no perfect boat," but the more you know about boats, the better chance you have of selecting one that will do what you want done at any particular state of your life. Perhaps the things that I like about my present boat will help you in your choice.

I have been thoroughly and most enjoyably involved with boats all my life. My childhood summers were spent on the shores of the South River, just outside of Annapolis, Maryland. We swam, canoed, rowed, sailed, water skied and just messed around in boats of all types and descriptions. As a newlywed I was unsuccessful in convincing my wife to trade her silver service for a boat, but being on the water at every opportunity continued as a way of life. I'm still amazed at the amount of cruising we did on a 23' sailboat with three little boys. Over the years I have thought of boats as an important intergenerational communication device, and have been fortunate enough to enjoy a wide variety, both power and sail, ranging in size from 8' to 50'. From my viewpoint, the choice of a particular boat at any given time depended on a number of factors. The amount of money that you have to apply to both the purchase and the care and feeding of a boat is a factor, but only as an upper limit. How you want to use the boat and the amount of time available to enjoy it, is more defining.

There may be no "perfect boat", but, for the Murray family, this Pearson motor yacht comes close. A former publisher of *Living Aboard* calls his *Interlude* an "intergenerational communication device."

A few years ago I tried a 42' cruising sailboat. She was a ketch-rigged Pearson 424. For various reasons we never became attached. The timing was just wrong. I didn't have time to cruise. Our sons were grown and not easily available, and our daughters, while they enjoyed being aboard, had no interest in the workings of the boat.

I then bought a 27' racing sailboat, a J27, which I still have and race frequently. She is a simple boat, easy to sail in and out of the slip, very competitive on the race course, but definitely not the cruising type. Once quite by accident, my wife and two of our daughters ended up having to spend a night aboard. They abandoned ship at 7 a.m. and have never been below since. As they left, there were mutterings about a portable head out in the open.

While enjoying the J27, I started looking for an all-out cruising boat. The original image of the boat was very fuzzy. The prime motivating factor was that I wanted something that would be fun to wake up on while anchored in the lee of a barrier island. I had more time to spend aboard, but was not planning on extensive cruising in the immediate future. I could envision keeping the boat in other harbors and using her as a getaway.

In some ways, knowing too much about boats made the process more difficult. I was fond of so many — from old wooden boats to flashy new ones. After 20 years of selling boats, I was now acting like the typical, confused, pain-in-the-butt buyer.

Then I saw an ad for 43' Pearson Motor Yacht. It was a boat that I was familiar with, from my days as a Pearson sailboat dealer, but there weren't many made. Pearson built very good boats, but they had no idea how to market powerboats.

The particular boat in the ad was not nearby, but I remembered one in the area. When I contacted the owner to take a refresher look, I found out that the local boat was very much for sale.

Then I made a serious mistake. I took my wife to see the boat. She fell in love with it, particularly the bathtub in the bathroom. We all have our priorities.

Pearson called her a motor yacht, which is not very descriptive. I would describe her as part trawler, part houseboat and part typical motorboat. The combination works very well. We call her the *Interlude*.

The hull is modified V, starting with a sharp entry and flattening out to five degrees aft. There is a skeg on the center line, with its deepest point by the props and rudders. I consider the skeg a very important feature for protection for the underwater equipment, directional stability at slow speeds, resistance to windage when docking, and rolling at displacement speeds.

According to the manufacturer, the displacement is 22,000 pounds, which is moderately light. A Grand Banks 42 has a stated displacement of 33,000 pounds.

The moderate displacement, combined with twin 200-hp diesels, Perkins 6-354 turbo located aft with v-drives, gives a top speed of 15 knots and a comfortable cruising speed of 12 knots. Yes, I know that cruising at 12 knots burns more fuel than 8 knots, but I have never understood the penitent fixation on fuel economy. It sometimes appears that one can justify any outlay for a boat as long as it doesn't burn much fuel per hour.

Aside from getting you there more quickly, 12 knots also produce the benefit of a much less rolly ride. The flow of water under the hull is the source of this added stability. I play with the idea of repowering her with 300-hp engines and cruising at 18 knots. When appropriate, she is still comfortable at displacement speeds. The 300-gallon fuel tanks provide ample range, but her large windows don't really make her suitable for long, open crossings. If my plans change, and I want to cruise oceans, I will go back to a sailboat. When the winds are over 15 knots, I would rather be in a sailboat.

A short aside concerning the difference between planing hull and displacement hull power boats: At about eight knots a 40-foot boat will start to try to climb over its bow wave. For this to happen, there has to be a combination of sufficient horsepower and hull shape (wide flat stern and hard chine — where the side and bottom meet — enhance this). At about 12 knots the boat settles down and gets in the groove. If I wanted a displacement speed boat — one that goes through the water instead of riding on top of it — I would prefer one that has more of a whale-shaped underbody

Having the engines under hatches on the aft deck doesn't create a walk-in engine room, but it does con-tribute to an overall lower pro-file. Six-foot headroom in an engine room is nice, but it raises everything else, which raises the center of gravity, which adds to the rolly-roll, both at anchor and when cruising at displace-ment speeds.

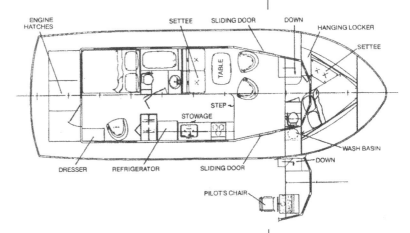

I particularly enjoy the sedan type layout — main and aft master cabin on the same level — as opposed to the more com-mon tri-level. When I sit up in our queen-size bed, I can look out the large win-dows and see the world around me. This layout also puts the upper deck on one level, which provides ample space for an 11-foot Whaler and a very sociable area under bimini. A disadvantage is the ladder climb to get there.

The sedan layout also helps create very workable side and aft decks, which makes it easier to dock and transfer on and off of small boats, and makes me feel more a part of the water instead of being removed from it. The almost 15-foot-wide hull accommodates the side decks and still leaves an interior beam of almost 12 feet. It's a compromise that I like.

Did I get what I want in a boat? Absolutely! Some of the reasons for choosing her were logical, some whimsical; but the first morning that she was mine to feed and care for, I woke up, sat up and looked out at the beauty of a fantastic barrier island.

If you want to upset my wife, mention that you heard the *Interlude* is for sale. That will get me into trouble.

Editor's note: Pearson is no longer in business. The company manufactured mostly gasoline-powered boats in the 1970s; about 20 Pearson 43s were built in the mid-1980s, most with diesel engines. As far as availability, any BUC-system boat broker should be able to locate a vessel for you.

In Praise of the Nordic Tug

Karen L. Fisher

Engine warming . . . shore power cords disconnected . . . ropes untied . . . everyone on board . . .

"Alright, Captain, ready to go!"

"Everything unhooked?"

"You bet." *Whistling Gopher*, a 32' Nordic Tug, eases away from the dock. The first mate gives the all-clear as she enters the pilothouse.

The captain nods and smiles as he says, "Off to another great adventure!"

Sounds like a perfect dream, doesn't it? For my husband, Andrew, and me, it is our dream come true. We've been avid boaters for 10 years, traveling many miles in the New York Finger Lakes and Canals, Canada's Trent-Severn and Rideau canals, St. Lawrence Seaway, and Lake Ontario. Our 268 SeaRay, *The Phantom*, was a wonderfully competent vessel, but we began to want a little more living space for our cruising. Just out of curiosity, we attended boat shows in Annapolis and the Trawler Fest in Solomons, Maryland (where I picked up my first *Living Aboard* magazine). These places are full of information, people, and unbelievable boats!

For ten years, Andy and Karen Fisher spent vacations cruising aboard their SeaRay and they knew that before they moved aboard fulltime they needed a bigger boat. But what kind? And how big? Confusion set in – so many boats, so little time – until they saw the Nordic Tug and fell in love.

Confusion set in . . . what kind of boat did we really want? How much space did we want? How much did we really need? What did we want to invest financially? Could we afford this adventure?

We needed a plan. (We had a goal — we wanted a larger boat.) We were sure of two things: 1. We needed to organize ourselves financially; and 2. We needed to gather lots of information about different styles of larger boats. This was not going to be an overnight process; we figured it would take five years. There would be no immediate gratification. Andy and I were committed to the long haul, so we began reading all the boat magazines we could find, visited boat shows, and talked with owners, dealers, boaters. Andy researched engines, chines, hulls, interior layouts, electronic equipment, etc. This technical information was lost on me and I trusted his judgement. Slowly, we were defining items we would like on a boat and items that were not realistic to our needs.

Life has a way of letting reality intrude into dreams. Andrew had a scare about possible heart problems. Fortunately, after having a heart catherization, we found that not to be the case. Then, while teaching my 6th grade inner-city students, I was assaulted by a female stranger who made it to our 3rd floor classroom. This incident was traumatic for me and I took early retirement. Both our situations brought home the fact that we may not be here in five years, so we looked for ways to reach our goal sooner. We scrutinized our finances, advertised our SeaRay for sale, and continued our research through magazines, books, and the Internet. We figured out that we wanted a trawler-type vessel, but still didn't know which one. If you've ever looked at trawlers, you'll know there are so many types: Albin, Monk, Grand Banks, Krogen, Island Gypsy, Chris Craft, Mainship, etc.

Then Andy came across the photograph of a great looking boat, a 42' Nordic Tug, in a magazine. In another publication, he found an article about a 32' Nordic Tug liveaboard. These boats had looks, personality, and character. We concentrated our research on Nordic Tugs, new and second-hand. Neither one seemed to remain on the market very long. We subscribed to the Nordic Tug newsletter (Andy even purchased all the back issues), surfed the 'net, and conversed with various Nordic Tug dealers.

In March 1998, we flew to Seattle, Washington, to look at a used 1994 32' Nordic Tug, and discovered that the manufacturing plant was nearby. We called, asked for a tour, and were escorted through the place.

We saw everything from filling the mold with fiberglass, to the finishing work on teak and paint. What a personal, hands-on process! Everything was hand fit for each boat. Watching these people work verified that Nordic Tugs were quality-built boats. They have been in business since the 1980s. We noticed they were only on hull #121 with the 32' boats. To us, this meant they took their time building each boat for quality, not quantity. Along with the 32' boats, Nordic Tugs manufactures 37' and 42' tugs also. Before leaving for home, we made an offer on a new Nordic Tug, hoping to set it up with a charter business in Washington. We were told that the money we'd make from projected charters would cover 75% of the boat's costs. The evening we made the offer, Andy and I contracted a major case of buyer's remorse. We were presented with an additional $2,000 counter-offer the next day. Being a real estate investor/broker, Andy has always said, "Don't be afraid to walk away from a transaction if you can't get the terms you want." Therefore, we rejected the counter-offer and flew home a little relieved and disappointed. Actually, it would have been very costly to fly back and forth to see the boat, not to mention the cost of having it shipped to the East Coast eventually. Still, we were very impressed with the boat and the Nordic Tug "family."

Whistling Gopher, a 32' Nordic Tug, is Karen and Andrew Fisher's dream come true.

We were becoming attached to the Nordic Tugs, but we had only been on one while underway for about 30 minutes. In order to see what they were like while cruising, sleeping, and living aboard, we decided to find one to charter. A Nordic

Andrew Fisher on board Whistling Gopher. *Karen calls this photo "Happy Camper."*

Tug owner referred us to Southwest Yacht Club at the Marinatown Marina in Ft. Myers, Florida. They chartered the *Carol Ann,* a 32' Nordic Tug, built in the late 1980s. We were eager to try her out, so we booked her for 10 days in July 1998. We cruised Pine Island Sound where dolphins surfed our wake. The scenery was great, *Carol Ann* was great (a lot slower than our SeaRay, but that was no surprise), but Florida's July weather was hot and sticky. Never having visited Florida during the summer months, we were surprised by the intense heat and humidity. But we found the boat to be a sturdy and steady cruiser.

We encountered a wide range of reactions to the Nordic Tug while cruising. Since we were considering purchasing one, we took note of these reactions. One afternoon easing through Pine Island Sound in the rain, we approached a boat that was stopped. It appeared everyone was on deck and one man seemed to be flagging us. I thought they were having trouble and might need to be towed, so I put on my life preserver and started gathering my ropes. Andy pulled along side when one man asked if we were the towboat from BOAT/U.S. where he had radioed for help.

We encountered another reaction late one afternoon while we sat on deck enjoying the mild breeze drifting through South Seas Plantation, Captiva Island. A little girl walked along the dock holding her father's hand, curiously looking over our boat. As she approached *Carol Ann,* tugging at her father's arm, she pointed to us and asked, "Daddy, can I go in the playhouse?" Andy and I laughed. These Nordic Tugs seemed to attract a lot of attention and appeal to all ages.

Andy and I were convinced we wanted a 32' Nordic Tug, but my unexpected retirement changed our financial structure. After much thought, talk, and frustration, we consulted a financial advisor to assist us. We put together an investment portfolio, sold our SeaRay and one land parcel, and began restructuring and refinancing our rental properties. During our refinancing process, we visited the Annapolis powerboat show again and talked with Gene McCray and Ed Shelton, Nordic Tug Dealers. It was great seeing the new Nordic Tugs. Ed and

Gene informed us that they had a 32' green hull in Florida for sale, which was outfitted exactly like the one we offered to purchase in Washington.

We all talked and talked. When Andy and I went to lunch, we talked more. Being in real estate, before he makes large purchases, Andy has to get the figures to work. So, he got out his calculator and started punching keys. Within a few minutes, a smile crept onto his face and I laughed, "You made the figures work, didn't you?" He nodded and we talked some more. Instead of refinancing our investment properties for 10 years as planned, we would refinance for 15 years. The difference between the mortgage payments would cover the majority of the boat payment. Sounded good to us, so we went back to see Ed Shelton and Gene McCray of Nordic Tugs. They were patient and supportive with all our questions. They understood all the hard work we had done to achieve our goal and they were pleased with our interest in the Nordic Tugs. By the time Andy and I left the boat show, we made a deposit on the new boat in Florida, which Ed had named *Whistling Gopher*. (Ed loves to tell the story of how he came up with that name!)

As soon as Andy reached home, he logged onto the Internet booking us flights to Florida for the following weekend. Therefore, within the week we met *Whistling Gopher*. Needless to say, we took to her in a big way. Andy grinned from ear to ear! We spent four days with Ed, Gene, and *Whistling Gopher*, coming home with lots of pictures after finalizing the transaction.

We left Pennsylvania and drove back to Florida and *Whistling Gopher* with a truck full of old and new boating "stuff" and a 10' Zodiac with motor. Andy and I spent three weeks on the boat over the Christmas and New Year holidays exploring the St. John's River in Florida. We made a turkey dinner for Christmas, three pecan pies (from scratch), and the traditional pork and sauerkraut for New Year's Day, all prepared aboard our 32' Nordic Tug. We enjoyed the Florida sunshine and acquainting ourselves with *Whistling Gopher*'s every nook and cranny. We love her. She's beautiful, comfortable, capable, dependable, and ours! It feels good to enjoy the benefits of all our planning and hard work. ✍

We have a 1967 vintage Cal Cruising motorsailer, 46 feet. Our boat was designed for a purpose. Bill Lapworth designed the Cal 46 so two people could live aboard comfortably and travel anywhere in the world. We have an active Cal 46 Association, even though no boats have been built in more than 20 years.

We have been active sailors, racers, cruisers, anglers for almost 40 years. We have sailed across the Atlantic, left southern California in 1988, spent two years in Mexico, Central America, and through the Panama Canal. We have sailed the Caribbean and Bahamas extensively, plus the north coast of South America.

– Tom & Bobbie Vandiver,
Pensacola, Florida

I have a 1984 42' Nova semi-displacement, aft-cabin, motor-yacht type trawler. I feel it has the following attributes for living aboard (including single-handed cruising while living aboard): two staterooms separated by the main cabin, two heads with showers, bathtub (small), 300 gallons water (20 gallons hot), diesel heat with setback thermostat, inverter, generator, 500 gallons fuel, twin diesel engines, dual control stations, autopilot with twin remotes, CO detector, three 8 D batteries for house (plus engine battery), battery monitor (tracks amp hours used), propane stove, double galley sinks, enclosed bridge, GPS, remote control windlass with all chain rode & Bruce anchor, minimal exterior teak, TV antenna, radar, double bed in each stateroom, Borg-Warner straight drive transmissions (can be freewheeled, allowing running on one engine), mid-engines (can be worked on in bad weather), cored cabin (insulation), Davis weather monitor, indicator lights for pumps, lights, etc.

I feel it has the following drawbacks: twin engines (more maintenance and fuel), lack of covered aft deck, high aft deck (difficult to board or fish from), any exterior teak at all, no dinette, non-electronic autopilot (will not interface with GPS), mid-engines (noisy), lack of outside storage area (no lazarette), lack of compartmented bilges for safety (previous boats were Cruise-A-Homes), single pane windows (no insulation).

I have lived aboard full time for seven years. I still work full time; however, when (if) I retire (10 years?), I plan to live on the boat in Desolation Sound, Canada, six months a year and motorhome around the states the remaining six months.

If money were no object (I buy lottery tickets), I would probably buy a single-engine, full-displacement trawler of about 50' overall (I own a 50' slip).

> – Earl Munday,
> Seattle, Washington

In Defense of the Catamaran

Michael Beattie

In all of sailing literature there's never much written about multihulls, so I shouldn't be surprised catamarans aren't often mentioned in *Living Aboard*. Heck, I lived aboard a monohull for eight years and cruised it as well, without giving a thought to trimarans or catamarans.

Condos Afloat

Until, that was, I came across a Prout 37 tied up to the town dock in Labelle, Florida. The owner used the *Snowgoose* as his home on the Waterway, while continuing to run his publishing business back in New England. I couldn't believe the space I saw below deck.

I mentioned the catamaran to my then girlfriend as a possible replacement for our salty looking but desperately cramped monohull. She dismissed the idea out of hand: "They look like condos afloat," she sneered contemptuously.

Michael Beattie and his wife, Layne, have found that their 34-foot Gemini catamaran is not only a good home but a comfortable, reliable cruiser. She has taken them and their dogs, Emma and Debs, on many wonderful adventures down the coast of California, to Mexico, Central America and on to Florida.

Seven years later she's living in a house on a canal in Southwest Florida, I'm married in California, and my wife and I are aboard our new Gemini 105 catamaran. The faithful monohull went to a good home in Miami, and its sale constituted the down payment on our 34-foot catamaran.

My wife Layne and I own a bright and comfortable three-bedroom home a couple of blocks from the beach in the northern California university town of Santa Cruz. The harbor has a liberal liveaboard policy and welcomes one and all, provided you can pay over $300 a month and have neither cats nor dogs. Unfortunately, the sailing on Monterey Bay is boring, lacking destinations, and is excessively challenging with a rugged coastline battered by daily breezes in the 25-knot range and massive Pacific swells. We keep the catamaran in Alameda, 70 miles away, in the heart of San Francisco Bay where the climate is milder, the sailing is still challenging, but there are many, varied destinations for a boat. Thus, we lived aboard on weekends, meeting on the boat Friday nights and departing for our respective jobs Monday morning until we left on an extended cruise.

The Search

When we were looking for our future home afloat, Layne had few, but very firm, criteria. She wanted a bright and airy cabin, an unobtrusive saloon table without any masts or supporting pillars in the middle of her entertainment area, and a sleeping cabin with lots of light and room, a "nice place to lounge," as she put it. So we looked at many used boats in the $100,000 range. It was a parade of beautiful cruising boats, Cabo Ricos, Crealocks, Pearsons, Nauticats, Fishers and Cals. We inspected custom designs and strange floating condos crammed into a single hull. We even looked at an early French cruising catamaran, but we found it to be an uncomfortable "bleach bottle" interior with cramped sleeping accommodations buried in the hulls. Even that was at a price we could not afford.

After two years of fruitless looking and with me in despair, we checked out the new catamaran dealership in Alameda, and there we found our future home. Of course the $95,000 Gemini cost considerably more when we added in a "few" options, sales tax and delivery, but at $133,000 it is still, in our opinion, a heck of a lot of boat for the money.

Catamarans have suffered a lot of criticism in the boating press over the years. Early home-built boats had a tendency to break up in heavy seas and overly enthusiastic racers have managed to tip their machines over to the accompaniment of much publicity, but for a very few of us catamarans are superb homes afloat, all too often overlooked by people scared off by the negative stories. We never gave serious consideration to a trimaran, as there were only homebuilt boats, Searunners mostly, on the used market, and brand-new trailerable tri's simply don't offer sufficient room for our liveaboard lifestyle, even though they can easily outperform our Gemini on any point of sail.

Miki G is the home of Michael Beattie, his wife Layne Goldman, and two large dogs.

The Pros

Layne and I love many features of our Gemini and I hardly know where to begin . . .

We live on a stable platform 14 feet wide and 34 feet long. Essentially it gives us the living space of a 45-foot monohull, with three double berths in separate cabins, in an astonishingly stable platform — so stable that we've sailed across the bay in 30-knot winds with 4-foot seas with a teapot sitting in the middle of the saloon table. Our seasick-prone guests return regularly to sail on the only boat that doesn't have them feeding the fishes, and with a 14-foot beam we can easily get a slip anywhere around the bay for an overnight stop. At anchor, of course, we have a huge space in which to lounge, including a wide foredeck for sunbathing, a cockpit that can seat eight or nine comfortably, and a saloon on the same level without steep companionway steps. All this unruffled by passing wakes. And, with an 18-inch draft, we can anchor closer to the beach than any other boat on the bay — even on the beach if we choose.

For peace of mind we reef early and often and we remind ourselves that our boat is unsinkable, with no massive bulb of lead waiting to drag us all to Davy Jones' locker. The 8,000 pound displacement means our speed through the water averages about 8 knots in 18 knots of breeze, with no discernible angle of heel. In heavy seas and at anchor we roll

Michael Beattie making bread in the galley. The length of the starboard hull, it has an 8-foot-long counter space, with 8 feet of lockers inboard. The stove has a grill and oven and it's not gimbaled.

not at all, unlike the monohulls and trawlers rockin' and rollin' nearby. Cheaper end ties in the marina don't worry us at all for the same reason.

Layne loves to cook, and in her galley, the length of the starboard hull she has an 8-foot-long counter space, with 8 feet of lockers inboard. Her stove has a grill and oven and it's not gimbaled, though she does have pot holders as the boat does bounce when hitting heavy wakes, or large waves or in a beam sea. As the boat sails flat we can use an RV-style freezer/fridge which operates on shore power or propane: silent, efficient and cheap, and it makes ice cubes too! All this, and while cooking the chef gets to look out the windows at the world passing outside her galley.

Layne's other foible is that she likes to take hot showers and the Gemini has a propane water heater that gives hot water, on demand, in the galley or the shower, which is located in the bow of the port hull. This means the engine really is an auxiliary, not needed to heat water or freeze ice, but when we do have to motor we have a three-bladed prop on the end of a outdrive unit, like those used on power boats, so when we aren't motoring the prop comes out of the water.

The Cons

As the saying goes, every paradise has its serpent, and catamarans have their drawbacks too. You can't get around the expense, for a start. There are many seaworthy, safe monohulls that are 20 years old and make excellent homes for as little as $30,000. Unfortunately, the catamaran market has only just started to grow so the only used boats tend to be expensive large boats from the charter trade or home-built wooden machines that likely won't offer the amenities you will be looking for in a modern boat. Unless you are a boat builder, you won't find much in the used catamaran market, except for early Geminis, for less than

$100,000. And if you need a bigger boat, there isn't much under $200,000, which increases your cost if you like to live aboard with a ton of stuff. All those spacious lockers on a catamaran love to get filled; we are fighting a constant struggle to stay light! Weight slows a catamaran, which is no problem unless you also like to sail, which we do.

Another disadvantage of having lots of space is that it can take a lot to keep warm in cool climates and condensation is an ever-present threat. Underway, catamarans, particularly the smaller boats, can be noisy with lots of wave slap on the hulls and bridge deck. You get used to it, but it sure sounds different if you are used to monohulls. Multihulls unhappily are still seen as a threat by "traditional" boaters who will give you lots of grief about them tipping, being difficult to maneuver under power, unable to point under sail, unsafe in heavy seas, and unable to carry a load.

Emma the Lab keeping an eye on things. Debs, the other canine aboard, is of similar size.

Most of the naysayers have never even stepped on a modern cruising catamaran. Ask them!

However, I doubt I will ever go back to a monohull, especially not as a home afloat. I love sailing and living flat. On rainy days I can sit in my saloon, or on my queen-size double bed forward and look out at the rain coming down. No more teak caves for me. Underway, at 8 or more knots, I can navigate, cook or take a shower without getting seasick, and when I reach that delightful anchorage I can cut through water 2 feet deep to the prime anchoring spot. With my beam I have lots of room for a dinghy in davits, and the dogs love to come sailing with us on a boat that doesn't sail on its ear.

If you are open minded enough to even consider living afloat, I urge you to keep that mind open wide enough to consider living on two hulls; a catamaran could substantially change your quality of life aboard. It did ours.

25 Feet of the Good Life

Leslie Woodcock

Whittaker Creek Yacht Harbor in Oriental, North Carolina, is our new home. It's hard to believe, but barely a year ago living at a marina was just a dream for the distant future. However, with a little sweat and a lot of optimism we have achieved our dream. We now call ourselves liveaboards.

For several years, my wife Dana and I read stories of couples and families who lived aboard their boats. Some lived on modest 35-foot sailboats, while others lived on 65-foot megayachts. We dreamed of the day we could move aboard. With two children though, we were concerned about getting a big enough boat. There was also a financial question. Could we afford to purchase a boat large enough on which to live? I am a stay-at-home dad and, although my wife's income supports us comfortably, we had not acquired the assets associated with either real estate ownership or stock investment. Still, we perused *Soundings* magazine each

How big is big enough? Well, Leslie and Dana Woodcock are raising two happy kids, ages 10 and 7, aboard a 25-foot Bruce Roberts motor sailer. And did we mention that their crew includes Nauticat the Siamese and Mickey the Chihuahua? Starting small enabled them to realize their dream while they renovate a 41-foot wooden ketch for future adventures.

month, but the market prices clearly indicated that it would be at least five, and probably eight, years before we could afford even a well-used boat. Six months later, however, our new home was sitting in a boatyard awaiting repairs, and we were beginning the process of greatly downsizing our lives in preparation for moving aboard our own boat. In June of 1998, my wife, two children, Siamese cat, Chihuahua and I moved onto our sailboat — all 25 feet of it!

Once people learn the size of our boat — and after the initial astonishment — they ask questions that invariably focus on how we deal with the lack of space and basic day-to-day activities. We assure them that our decision to move aboard was not made without many hours of discussion. Each family member had to be comfortable with the idea. We would not be able to simply say that we would tolerate particular adjustments in our lifestyle — such as having to walk to the bathroom in 20-degree weather. We would actually have to adopt these changes as a natural and totally acceptable part of our new lives. Now, after eight months aboard, we are still enjoying both the joys and challenges of our unique situation.

Our new home is a 1982, 25-foot Bruce Roberts motor sailer. We purchased the boat for $1,400 from a backyard boat repair business. The boat was the victim of years of neglect. Though structurally sound, it required much cosmetic work including painting, brightwork and extensive interior cleaning. We also needed to make some design changes to make it more livable.

Because of its motor sailer design, it offered us more interior volume than similarly sized boats. It would be very comfortable for a weekend retreat. My wife had other ideas however, and she enlightened me about her decision shortly after the bill of sale was signed: that is, we could live on the boat. Once I regained my composure, I decided that her idea had merit. There really was no viable reason to dismiss the possibility of living on this boat. Still, I spent several days studying and evaluating the merits of different design changes to assure myself that it truly was feasible to live on it. Aside from the space issues, we also had to consider the emotional effects associated with eliminating or separating ourselves from 80% of the possessions that we had accumulated over the last 16 years. We sold or gave away many of our belongings. The rest were entombed in a metal storage room.

My wife and I also knew that we would be dealing with people's uncertainty concerning the feasibility of four people living on such a small vessel. However, because we home school and have had to deal with similar skepticism about "socialization," we felt confident in our ability to respond to such queries. With these initial concerns addressed we then began the process of actually preparing the boat for our arrival.

Three major issues needed to be addressed. Where would we store our clothes and toys? (As far as my children were concerned, nudism was preferable to not having an adequate supply of playthings.) How could we redesign the galley so that buttering a slice of bread would not require an hour of planning? And could a 30-amp electrical system afford us enough basic comforts and luxuries to enjoy our new residence on a permanent basis?

The sleeping arrangements were never a real issue. They were dictated

Dana Woodcock and children Teague and Samantha, above, at Whittaker Creek in front of their new home. Leslie Woodcock with the kids, right, and the boat. "Admittedly," he says, "we are a cozy bunch."

by the fact that the kids needed the V-berth in order to have sufficient toy and play space. The 5-foot pilot berth on the starboard side precluded any full-grown person from enjoying a good night's sleep. My wife and I agreed upon a head-to-toe arrangement on the quarter and port berths. This has proved quite comfortable thus far. By eliminating the pilot berth and the hanging locker next to it, we were able to extend the galley 24 inches forward and add a chart table that has become an invaluable catchall area for school books, loose change and a phone. Under this table we installed electric panels for 12-volt and shore power. A small refrigerator was fit into the remaining space.

Since showering and personal hygiene would be done at the marina facilities, we decided to remove the head and shower. By adding three shelves and a tension rod in the space, we created ample room for both folded and hanging clothing. Beneath this area there is still space for a clothes hamper and a potty if necessary. We suspended wire baskets below the two access panels in the V-berth for toy storage, and the area under the V-berth accommodates the pets' needs. We also narrowed the port berth from 30 inches to 24 inches by installing a full backrest that angles upward from the berth to the hull. A hinged door allows access to the resulting space. A narrow shelf on top provides room for knick-knacks.

Onboard we have a telephone, TV for the kids, Playstation, a computer under the galley area that doubles as our TV, toaster oven, two-burner propane stove, refrigerator and enough toys for most of Oriental. At the time of this writing we also are running two ceramic heaters. With only the need to balance our electric load when running the heaters on high and simultaneously using the toaster oven, we maintain our system well below 30 amps. Our garage, *a.k.a.* dock box, is used to store laundry supplies, tools and other needed items.

Admittedly, we are a cozy bunch. There are not many places where one can lie in bed and still flip pancakes on the stove without ever moving. Care must be taken not to crush someone's foot while negotiating the descent from the hatchway into the cabin. Some creative organization is required during the change of seasons, when it is necessary to have both summer and winter clothes on board. Still, we know that we made the right decision each day as we watch the sun rise or set over the swaying masts, or when we watch our children playing in such a serene setting, or as we contemplate the madness of the rest of the world as it rushes through each day blindly groping for what we have already found — happiness. If one wonders whether or not our children are truly happy, consider the following statement my daughter made.

While waiting for some Saturday morning cartoon to begin, she was watching one of those "get rich quick" infomercials. I jokingly asked her if she was learning how to have the good life. Without any hesitation she casually responded, "We already have it, daddy." I have to agree with her.

"Give a man a boat he can sail, and his rank and wealth, his strength and health on sea nor shore shall fail."

– James Thompson

Her Name is *Amy*

John Callahan

Ilive aboard *Amy* full time. *Amy* is a 31-foot Cruise-A-Home, which is a cruising houseboat, sometimes referred to by sailors as a "Water Winnebago." She is a houseboat built on a Westport fishing boat hull. *Amy* is quite seaworthy; she has been to Alaska several times. Regrettably, I was not with her any of those times.

I bought *Amy* at the end of January. The weather in Puget Sound was so bad last winter that it took five tries before we could even go out for sea trials. She's stayed in the marina, safe from the 50-knot winds and heavy rains — one night it rained so hard that the water in the marina seemed to be boiling.

While houseboats are sometimes demeaned as the country cousins of the boating world, they offer spacious and comfortable living conditions, attributes not to be underestimated if you are living aboard full time. The Northwest-built Cruise-A-Home is also a worthy cruiser — equally at home in saltwater or on freshwater lakes.

Amy is quite roomy, by boat standards. The house is approximately 10' x 20'. She has an enclosed head, located aft, with a shower with a pull-around curtain. The stateroom, also aft, has a full-size double bed with two large drawers below. There is also a 24-inch hanging locker. The main saloon has the galley on the starboard side just aft of the lower helm. The galley has a 110-volt LPG refrigerator, a single-bowl stainless steel sink, a four-burner propane stove with oven, and not enough counter space. The appliances and sink are built-in.

The rest of the main saloon is furnished with freestanding house furniture. The furniture came from a condominium that I sold. It is all light in color to counteract the Seattle winter gloom. I have a 34" x 34" ash dining table from Denmark with 11-inch leaves that slide out from each end. There are two high-backed ash dining chairs, also from Denmark. The table is on the port side of the main saloon against the bulkhead that separates the stateroom from the main saloon. This bulkhead has a chart rack for storage of six rolled-up charts. The dining table serves as a table for meals, my desk and charts. I also have two Siesta chairs from Norway. They are made from steam-bent beech and have white leather cushions. The chairs are a very clever design. They are extremely strong, yet very light and easy to move around. In addition, I have one ash side-table from Denmark and two light, wooden folding tables from Thailand.

I have developed several configurations for the main saloon by moving around the furniture. In the office configuration, I have the leaves of the dining table extended, both Siesta chairs at the front of the saloon, and the folding tables (which are only 15" x 20") on each side of my chair for setting things upon. This arrangement gives me room to slide my chair in and out from under the table, plenty of walk-around room, and most important, clear access to the galley to make coffee.

In the leisure configuration, one of the Siesta chairs is moved to the port side of the saloon, against the port wall of the house, just forward of the dining table. The ash side table is at the left of the chair. On the table is a high-intensity desk lamp that I use for reading — the lamp is moved to the dining table for the office configuration. The other Siesta chair remains at the lower helm but is angled to face the other chair. Sometimes I pull the forward chair close enough to use it as a footrest.

The cooking configuration is, at the moment, only conceptual. I have purchased a cuttingboard from a camping store. It is backed with ScootGuard and covers the four-burner stovetop. This doubles my working counter space. I've also bought another cuttingboard that fits over the sink, again increasing the working counter space. I plan to use the two folding tables to add yet more places to put things when I am cooking.

The configuration I like best, so far, is the leisure configuration. I use it for relaxing, reading, talking to friends on the phone, writing on a notebook computer, and surfing the Internet. I have a wireline telephone installed at the slip, and I have ordered DSL (digital subscriber line) for fast Internet access. I also have a cellular phone that wouldn't work in my previous slip, but seems to work in my new one. I have a CDPD (cellular) modem for wireless e-mail and Internet access. When it works, it's pretty slow. It seems to work in the marina only at high tide. Having to drive to a hilltop to get my e-mail is very inconvenient.

Amy also has an aft deck, just aft of the stateroom, where the engine hatches are located. The aft deck, which is 5' x 11', is large enough to hold a couple of white plastic armchairs and a small table. It's a nice place to sit and sip a glass of wine in the evening. In the Northwest, even in the summer, it is normally too cold to enjoy my morning coffee there.

Amy's flybridge, where the upper helm is located, has a useable area of about 9' x 12'. There is seating that converts

John Callahan pilots Amy *out of his marina on Puget Sound.*

into a double berth, although I've never used it for sleeping. There's also enough room for a couple of other chairs (white plastic, of course) and a small table.

Amy's one shortcoming might be her range. She carries only 120 gallons of fuel. She is powered by a single 210-hp Deutz air-cooled diesel engine that burns about 4.5 gallons an hour at 10 knots. That gives her a range of just over 200 miles, with a small safety factor. That's okay around Puget Sound and the San Juan Islands, where fuel is readily available. In other places, it might not be.

Would I choose the same type boat again? Yes, probably. Like most people on boats, I spend 98 percent of my time in port, where I find *Amy* is a very comfortable liveaboard. I can't comment on *Amy* as a cruising boat, although experienced boaters who are familiar with Cruise-A-Homes have only good things to say about them. Even the marine surveyor liked her.

My significant other and I have been living aboard going on six years. We purchased a 62-foot Skipperliner Motor Yacht cruiser a year ago and we do live in luxury now. Our home port is on the Upper Mississippi River in St. Paul, Minnesota. We live aboard because we love the river and can not imagine ever moving back to a land home. Denny is a towboat pilot of 35 years on this part of the river and I am a union representative. To answer some questions, no we are not just tied to shore all the time we take her out often. We did just complete a 500-mile round trip through 22 locks and dams traveling to Dubuque, Iowa and it was a great trip! Our long range plan is to pay this boat off, retire and head down river in the winter months back to Minnesota in the summer.

— *Denny Lynch & Nola Profant,*
aboard Dream Catcher

Our boat is the *Y-Knot,* a 37' Skyline trawler with a single Perkins 6-354T, sedan model. It has a 13' beam. We live five miles up-river from Mile Marker 107 on the ICW near St. Catherine's Sound. My wife and I enjoy the barrier islands along the Georgia to South Carolina coasts, and one day look forward to parttime living aboard.

— *Al & Marilyn Hernandez,*
Richmond Hill, Georgia

How to Buy a Used Houseboat

Robert Perkins

Most folks that have contacted the Houseboat Association of America about what to look for in buying a used houseboat have neglected the very first item to consider: How and where do you plan to use the boat?

The type of area in which you intend to use your boat has a profound effect on the type of boat you should look for. If you are going to put your boat on a small inland lake where you will not be able to move off the lake without trailering, then it is overkill to buy a large full hull boat with twin powerhouse engines. The extra money you will spend on that kind of boat could buy you a lot of extra time on the water as well as other goodies.

Choose Your Hull

The next item to consider is the type of hull you want. On the small- to medium-sized lake, without navigable egress, your houseboat will probably be used more as a substitute for a beachfront cottage, with limited cruising, and weather will not be of great concern. The emphasis, most likely, will be on living space and comfort. Here the pontoon boat (or catamaran, if you will) becomes a very good choice. The advantages of the pontoon include lower cost for the same sized boat (more boat for the money), a single-level cabin, and simpler construction. This simpler construction is appealing to the boater who wants to do most of his or her own maintenance. Another advantage is the ability to power a pontoon with even small outboards. If you are just moving over to the other side of the lake, you don't need 300 horsepower!

Whether you are in the market for a new or used houseboat, here is good advice from the former president of the Houseboat Association of America and founding editor of *Houseboat News*.

Some folks also like the idea that pontoons, in almost all cases, have several watertight compartments which make them very hard to sink. In fact, one of our members had his pontoon houseboat completely turned upside down in a severe windstorm a few years ago but it didn't sink. Admittedly, the cabin was in the water hanging upside down from the pontoons but the pontoons were still floating. He did not have to raise the boat, just had to turn it right side up!

Another advantage of having two pontoons right out to the edge of the boat is stability. Now when you talk about stability you have to know the difference between at rest stability and rough water stability. When you are at anchor or underway in calm water, there is less rocking from side to side. Some people find that very welcome. The story changes when you get into really rough water. The high lifting forces on each side of the boat tend to over-compensate in really rough water, especially if waves are coming from the sides of the boat, giving rise to a really rough and possibly dangerous ride.

On the other hand, if you are planning on cruising the inland waterway or large lakes, you might want to consider a full hull. In fact, the trend seems to be toward the full hull models. There is a trend toward fancier, higher priced houseboats in the market today and fewer basic, lower cost models. There are still some available, but the demand just doesn't seem to be there anymore. Due to this trend, one of the advantages of the used, full-hull houseboat is better resale possibilities. Also, the full hull handles better in adverse weather conditions.

Because of the full hull and the keel, however minimal it may be, the wind will not affect the handling of a full hull as much as it does the pontoon boat. In addition, strange as it may seem, handling in close quarters is usually easier with the full hull. The draft of a full hull boat is less at the bow than it is at the stern, allowing the bow to swing around a little more easily than that of a pontoon boat. The pontoon boat has two (or more) pontoons which as a rule have just as much draft at the bow as they do at the stern. This makes them act as two full-length keels and keeps the bow from swinging around as easily as the full hull.

Now is a good time to correct any idea you should not use a pontoon boat anywhere but a small lake. One of our members made the complete circumnavigation of the Great Circle Route — up the East Coast, over through the Great Lakes, down the Mississippi, Ohio and Tenn-Tom Waterway back to Florida-in a pontoon boat with a single outboard. It shows it can be done, but I still would not recommend it to just anybody.

On the other hand, there are several models of full-hull boats that feature one-level layouts like pontoon boats and that can be powered with lower powered outboards. These boats generally feature low freeboards and are designed, like pontoon boats, for lake and protected water use.

What's It Made Of?

Once you have decided on the type of hull, you have to decide on the construction material. The options are steel, fiberglass, aluminum or wood. Looking at used boats, you will find that used wooden boats are practically non-existent. Only if you are building your own does wood really come into consideration, so we will ignore wood for this discussion and consider only steel, fiberglass and aluminum.

If you are going to use your boat exclusively on fresh, unpolluted water, you do not have much to worry about. Any of the above will do. If you will encounter heavily polluted or salt water, then you will probably want to stay away from steel. We once owned a steel houseboat which we had purchased to use on Lake Hartwell, a fresh water lake in upper South Carolina. It was just right for Lake Hartwell, but when we moved to Charleston and brought the boat down into salt water, it became a maintenance nightmare. When they are trying to sell you a boat, some salesmen will tell you all kinds of ways to avoid rust in salt water, such as coal tar, epoxy, etc. Don't believe them. It's true that you can avoid the rust if proper preparation was made and the coating is unbroken, but just try to maintain an unbroken coating in the marine environment. The epoxy and other finishes available today do work well in fresh water, but are entirely inadequate, in our opinion, for salt water.

Aluminum is good but needs electrolysis protection in salt or heavily polluted water. Fiberglass is the most popular choice these days for hull material. It won't rust and it won't get eaten up with stray electrical current, but it still needs regular care. Fiberglass may also be easier and cheaper to repair.

Inboard or Outboard?

The next choice to consider is power. The choice in power usually is between outboard or inboard/outboards, commonly known as stern drives, although you will find a few V-drives and conventional drives. There are even a few — very few — jet drives beginning to show up on the used market.

Conventional drives are the simplest, consisting of the engine, a transmission and the shaft to the prop. They are the cheapest to build and the easiest to maintain if you don't mind checking the stuffing box regularly. However, if you run your prop into something, you could have a major repair bill requiring hauling the boat for repairs. V-drives are much the same except that they have the engines sitting in the stern with the power take off toward the bow. Direction is reversed by a V-drive and a shaft to the prop. These two groups, with twin engines, are the easiest to maneuver.

Only if the price was a deciding factor would I consider a single screw in this configuration over a stern drive. Stern drives are probably the most popular configuration for houseboats. While a little complicated, they are fairly easily accessed, with the ability to kick up the prop out of the way like an outboard if you should happen to hit an obstruction. Therefore if you ding up a prop you generally are not tearing out the entire underwater structure and you can usually replace a prop without a major expenditure. Other advantages include easy handling of the single-engine configuration because the prop is the rudder, so whichever way you point the prop, that is the way it is going to go, in forward or reverse.

> We live fulltime aboard our Cari-Craft houseboat with an added second floor – a total of 750 sq. ft. of floor space. We have everything we had "on the hill" except the basement.
>
> *– Jimmy Vaughn,*
> *anchored out in the Gulf of Mexico*

The advantage of inboards over outboards are that they usually have a lower noise levels, better gasoline economy, and do not required oil in the gasoline, although that problem is minimized or eliminated with the newer outboards. Also, until recently, inboards have been considered to be better for the environment, but that attitude is changing due to improvements appearing in the newer outboard models.

Outboards have the advantage of being more easily removed from the boat when needing major repairs and present less risk of gasoline explosion due to their open air position. They also might cost less on the used market.

Inspecting the Condition

The next important item to check is general condition. Check the hull for condition first. If the hull is not in good condition, forget it. In aluminum or steel hulls, check carefully for electrolysis. Electrolysis can eat through a steel hull in such a way as to make numerous small pinholes which weep water into the bilge constantly, but not enough to alarm you. What it does mean is that the hull is probably unacceptably thin and can rupture at the very worst time. Check a steel or aluminum hull carefully for this problem, especially around salt water.

Check also for signs of previous damage. A hull that has been damaged is not necessarily unsuitable. It just means that you should make sure it has been

repaired properly. Steel and aluminum damage usually can be spotted by welds in unusual places or wavy plates. Fiberglass shows up in wavy lines and/or discoloration. Also look for delaminating and bubbles in fiberglass which might indicate a serious leak somewhere.

A particularly hard problem to spot for the uninitiated is rot in wooden members covered by fiberglass. This in itself is a good reason to employ the services of a surveyor. If you are going to spend thousands of dollars on a used houseboat, the cost of a surveyor can be money well spent. You can usually get the seller to defray the cost if you buy the boat, and if the surveyor keeps you from buying the boat, he has saved you from a costly mistake and his fee is money well spent.

If the boat is out of the water and you decide you might want it, condition the deal on a water trial. If it is in the water, make the deal conditional on a pull-out inspection. Again, you can usually get the seller to defray the cost of the pull-out if you buy the boat, and if you don't buy it because of what you see when it is pulled, it is again money well spent. If you do buy the boat, it is a good time to take care of any minor deficiencies or bring the bottom paint up to snuff. In any event, you will feel better knowing what is under you.

While you have it out of the water, check for corrosion around underwater fittings, the propulsion system and zincs. Look at the number of hours on the engine. If it is over 1,000, the engine should have a complete check-out including such items as a compression check. Check for corrosion in and on the exhaust system. On raw water-cooled engines, one of the most common problems is corrosion and/or salt build-up in the water cooled exhaust manifold which can restrict water flow and cause the engine to slowly overheat. It is hard to detect in the early stage because it takes quite a bit of running for the engine heat to build up.

If the boat is in the water, start the engine and listen for any strange noises. If possible, take the boat out for a test run, letting someone else do most of the piloting while you are in the engine compartment listening to the engine and the propulsion system. Yes, propulsion systems make noises, too. You may see a whipping shaft or hear a grinding noise from an outdrive, neither of which you want to find out about after you have spent your money.

Above all, do not try to impress the seller with how much you know about boats. The more inexperienced you seem, the more questions you can ask without looking silly and the more answers you will get. You will soon get a feeling as to the sellers intentions. Is he or she being truthful and helpful or is he shading the truth a bit?

Finally, take a look at the interior. A good indication of the type of upkeep the boat has had is the way the interior has been maintained. It is not a foolproof marker, but generally the type of person that will keep the interior nice and neat is usually the type that will maintain the rest of the boat. If he or she has kept the oven clean, the drapes intact, the cabin neat, chances are that the rest of the boat has had the same kind of treatment. A dealer, however, may have cleaned up the boat for a quick sale. Then you have to look for more subtle signs of poor maintenance such as scarred bulkheads and overheads, signs of leaks in the overheads, loose cabinet fittings, dirt and/or rusty bilges and various other things that do not work quite properly.

Check every lightswitch, every appliance, and every system on the boat for proper operation. It is a boring job, but it will need to be done sooner or later and it is better to do it before you spend your money. Now one word of caution. Don't expect everything to be perfect. That kind of boat is usually not available on the used market. The point is to know what is wrong and how much it is going to cost to get it right before you spend your money, then you can make an informed decision.

Some of your best bargains are from individual owners, but just because you are dealing with an individual owner, don't assume that you will get a better deal than you may be able to get from a dealer. Also, remember that when you buy directly from an owner, once you have paid your money it is yours for better or worse! When buying from a dealer some kind of warranty is usually available; but again you have to remember that a dealer warranty is no better than the dealer offering it. Therefore, when buying from a dealer, try to buy from the most reputable dealer you can find. If possible, try to talk to some of his or her former customers. If the boat you are looking at is in a marina, try to wander down to the docks and talk to some of the owners.

Still Want It?

Now, after you have found your dream boat, checked it out to the best of your ability and you are wondering if you are making the right decision, what do you do? You hope a lot, pray a little; then go ahead, make the plunge and enjoy houseboating!

Good luck!

"All I ask is a tall ship and a star to steer her by."

– John Masefield
Sea-Fever

Finding Clementine

Paula Day

When Bob came home from a bike ride with great news, I had no idea that I was being set up. He had met some terrific people down at the marina who "live aboard," and he just couldn't wait until I went with him to meet them. I had heard the term liveaboard only once before in my life and I thought that the woman was crazy for actually wanting to live on a boat full time. "Marine," for me, was a large person who trained at Quantico. But a close-up view of life aboard inspired us to seek our own boat. This story is about our search.

Objectives

We wanted a trawler. How did we know? Well we needed room, fuel economy, and we were in no hurry to "get there." Sounds like a trawler to me. Eight to nine knots, OK. Full displacement to semi-displacement hull, OK. Twin diesels that just keep on ticking, if the fuel and air are clean and the maintenance schedule is kept, OK. We did think a little about a single, but then we decided that we were people who needed the insurance/assurance of two engines and that we could live with the added expense. (About $20,000 more to buy and three to four gallons per hour instead of 1.5-two gallons per hour for a single.)

After painstaking research and time wasted kissing a few frogs, Bob and Paula Day's boat lust turned to love when they found a 43' Gulfstar, Mark II.

It's important to not go looking for just a liveaboard. The old biological adage "use it or lose it" applies to mechanical systems as well. A boat deteriorates when it's not run. That's one of the reasons we got the boat we did; the owners had not been able to take her out for two months and they were smart enough to know this wasn't good.

Size

Definitely between 36' and 43'. Bob was six feet tall and I am 5' 10". And did I mention our 76-pound Labrador retriever named Joy? We soon learned the terms LOA, length overall, and length at the waterline. If you want to compare apples to apples and oranges to oranges you need the "at the waterline" figure. It also is necessary in figuring hull speed. The reason you need the second number is to make sure the swim platform and bow pulpit are not factored in, as they are not living space and can turn 40' into 46' real fast.

The next important figure, especially in southwest Florida, is the draft, or how much water does she draw. A shallow-draft vessel means more freedom of access because the Caloosahatchee River and the ICW on the Gulf of Mexico side have some very shallow water. We realized, however, it is a trade-off on stability. The draft counter balances the swing of the fly bridge.

Floor Plan

Two cabins, galley down, sundeck or sedan. Why? The forward cabin becomes the pantry for long cruising. Galley down because it left more room in the saloon and puts the cook at the lowest level (less rock and roll), and the feeling of expansion because the floor-to-ceiling height at the interface between the galley and saloon. Sedan is nice because of the direct access from the stern deck to the saloon. Sundeck, without the hard top, was definitely our first choice but we did consider a cabin over cabin. They run about $10,000 less. The main advantage to the sundeck is the headroom it gives the aft cabin. You're still going to bend over in order to take off your T-shirt, but the soffit over the bunks is gone, making the ceiling all one height. No hardtop because it acts as a windfoil if not enclosed and we are outside people.

As far as other physical parameters, we did not want too much teak. We were lucky in this respect because she didn't have to look like a classic trawler to please us. Bob definitely did not want teak decks.

Finances

Price range $60,000 to $80,000, depending upon condition and electronics. This put us in the 20-year-old range, 1975-77, and not wood because of insurance difficulties and maintenance.

Banks, your friendly neighborhood type, will not loan on a boat which is over eight years old. So it was off to the marine finance companies, a different world. I wanted a mortgage for tax reasons while I am still working. The *Clementine* qualifies as a second home or recreational property. They wanted our last two years tax statements. I told them it was illegal. They said that they couldn't process our application without them. I dragged my feet for two months but couldn't find one marine finance company who'd cooperate, so I gave in.

Research

I call this part the "trawler litany" (or, more subjectively, the good, the bad and the ugly). Here are the boats we looked at:

1. 36' Marine Trader
2. 36' Shin Shing
3. 43' Albin
4. 43' Defever
5. Durbeck
6. 36' Gulfstar
7. Sea Nymph, Chin Wu
8. 29' Prarie, Commander CCPS
9. 42' Grand Banks
10. 36' Monk
11. 36' Mainship
12. Thompson
13. 43' Gulfstar, Mark II
14. Present

*"A life on
the ocean wave,
A home on
the rolling deep,
Where the scattered
waters rave,
And the winds
their revels keep."*

– Epes Sargent:
"A Life on the Ocean
Wave"

15. 36' Krogen Manatee
16. 43' Gulfstar, Mark I
17. Uniflight
18. 43' Gulfstar
19. 43' Newburyport
20. Various motor yachts

The Ruling Out Process

After visiting the Marine Trader that started it all, I was convinced that we were going to have to get a really big trawler. Her captain is about 5'4" and very spry. Bob Day was 6 foot and had two football knees and an artificial hip joint. Bob liked the Defever because of the stand-up engine room. I was dead set against it because it drew 5 feet. The Prairie, a very shallow-draft vessel, had only one cabin and we never got to see the bigger one. The Krogen Manatee was not a walkaround. You had to go up and over to get to the bow. Thirty-six feet was just not enough room. The Grand Banks had too much teak for us and an up galley.

The Albin and Newburyport — again too much teak. Durbeck and Kady-Krogen had pilothouses, not on our wishlist. The first Gulfstar I saw I didn't like. We were just walking through a marina and she was a Mark I (cabin over cabin), old and oxidized with a jury-rigged window air conditioner sticking out over the aft cabin roof. I did not like the "look"; to me, she looked like a fat sailboat and someone forgot the mast. How wrong can you be?

Narrowing the Choices

We were invited aboard a 43' Gulfstar, Mark II, 1976, in immaculate condition with enough room to seat six comfortably at the dinette opposite the down galley. This one had more room than anything we had seen, so we started looking into Gulfstars. They were built in St. Petersburg, Florida, from 1971-77 on a sailboat frame. After that they took the shape of a motor yacht and eventually became Vikings. Therefore she has a chine, which allowed for great storage, and the small keel, which allowed for "almost" stand-up room between the two engines while creating a center skeg for prop protection and stability. They have a very thick fiberglass hull (but are subject to osmotic blistering), Perkins diesel engines, draft 3.5 ft., beam 14 ft. and 22,000 lbs. displacement in the 43' range.

Now we were focused. We wrote to the Gulfstar Owner's Association. We went to the MTOA rendezvous at Burnt Store Marina looking for a Gulfstar. We had gone from "Is that a Gulfstar?" to "What a beautiful Gulfstar you have!"

Sea Yawl is a sailboat, a 1981 Palmer-Johnson Bounty II yawl-rigged craft that is sleek — read that as very narrow of beam. She is 40 feet overall but only 28 feet on the water line. For two people who don't really need a lot of space, nor need to own much stuff she is very well-suited for living aboard. However, the dog needs more space and one of our crew needs to own a lot of stuff like tools and spare parts so the vessel has a minimal amount of freeboard and no space for feet on the floor. Visions of a trawler have sneaked by in our daydreams periodically although our life and love is the Bounty sailboat. Who knows?

— Pat & Bill Poupore,
s/v Sea Yawl

How We Bid

You try to keep an open mind but eventually you fall in "boat love." Our first was puppy love but we didn't know it. We found a 43' Gulfstar Mark II, 1975, one owner. He bought the *Windsong* in 1975 and he was 75; there's something to be said for numerology here. He was about to "come off the water," emphasis on the word about. He liked us. He said he'd make us a fair price. We were good;

we called only once during the whole summer. In the fall he said $74,000, and I said go write the buy/sell agreement quick. It took two agonizing meetings before he would take our deposit and sign the buy/sell. He said he knew nothing about selling a boat and we said "great, we're even; all we know is what we have read." We were about to find out that brokers earn their money.

The buy/sell agreement, which I typed up myself, was very simple. It gave the parties, the price, the closing date and the "subject to's": sea trial, haul

Bob and Paula Day aboard
Clementine

and survey, engine survey, and financing. Even at that it made the seller nervous and he made us amend it to read that the subject to's were at the expense of the buyers.

We had lined up a general surveyor, a marine engine surveyor and a marine finance broker. And then the owner backed out asking us if we could wait another year. We said "no" and started looking for another boat. But as communications improved, it seemed the real catch was that he wanted the use of the boat over Christmas. We said fine and changed the closing date and we were on again. Then came the survey, our first.

The Survey

Bob said the sea trial went well but he knew something was wrong when they got her up to full throttle and the surveyor told him he'd need trim tabs to bring the nose down. This was not a trawler person. Now just in case you are not falling down laughing when you read this part, let me explain. Trawlers do not and cannot get up on plane. They have, by definition, a displacement or semi-displacement hull. No matter how much power you give them you are only going to get hull speed, which is 1.25 times the square root of the length of the hull at the waterline. And if you could even imagine trim tabs, they'd be the size of barn doors and as effective as putting them on the QE II. There are surveyors and then there are surveyors.

Hindsight is always 20/20 but there are some classic lessons here. My first mistake was not taking the day off. If I had been present I hope that I would have called off the survey, and paid for half a survey, when they found termites. Yes, termites in a fiberglass boat! You'd be surprised how much wood there is, like under the entire superstructure. (Now our big boat friends tell me they spray their dock lines regularly.) But when there was no apparent soft wood (I had gotten so I walked a deck and felt for soft spots almost as a reflex) they continued right down to the oil samples. And, $1,200 later, we had a terrible decision to make.

We bought our current boat, a 40 Endeavor and live aboard full-time. We would definitely buy another Endeavor. Our daughter is 21 months and she is one of the reasons we are living aboard preparing to cruise south. We are both working full-time and don't get to spend enough time with each other enjoying life.

– *Jen Dupree,*
aboard Nouveau Vie, *Huntington, New York*

How much to bring her up to present-day standards? That is, after getting rid of the termites and praying that they didn't damage anything we couldn't get at to see and to fix. I could go through a long list, but the major problems can be said to have been: a bulkhead separation under the sink, two Riritan direct-flush heads (which were outlawed by the EPA last October), worn cutlass bearings, and a bottom job, with repair to bad patches and blisters. So off Bob went to the marina where the haul-out inspection occurred with his list of things to be done and a grid marked "now", "later", "they do", and "we do". The bottom line turned out to be $14,000, including the fumigation. We were crushed, but Bob assured me that there were other Gulfstars out there.

The Second Search

Back to the boat ads — but I had a strict rule: "Don't read me anything but Gulfstar ads!" So why are we going to St. Petersburg to see an Invictus? It isn't even a trawler! But the broker is just doing his job — trying to keep us open-minded. She turned out to be a real fixer-upper, not for us. Then off to Daytona to see a renovated Mark I with a center queen in the aft cabin. The anchor rode wasn't even connected. This was a liveaboard, but she hadn't cruised in quite a while.

We called the broker about the local Mark I. Maybe we could be happy with a cabin over cabin? It was under contract.

Then Bob found a new ad, 43' Gulfstar 1977 Mark II for $85,000 in Marathon. Before we started a five-hour drive, we had a friend who is a retired surveyor call and ask some pointed questions. This took place on Thursday. On Saturday the three of us were in our van before sunrise headed for Marathon. Our friend was going to keep us from doing something stupid "on the rebound."

We turned off Route 1 at Key Colony and as we approached the meeting place, we saw a Gulfstar on the next canal with people walking the deck. We groaned but bought some coffee and waited for the couple to leave. Via cell phone we were directed to the dock to take our turn. The men headed for the engine room and I walked the deck for soft spots. The engine room passed; the deck passed. We sat and talked with the owner. We asked the usual questions. How long had they had her and how many long trips? The owner was forthcoming and obviously proud of his boat. I found myself wanting to join this man's team in taking care of the Gulfstar. Did he think he had the porthole problem licked? They were new, but the water stains and teak damage seemed to indicate a recurrent problem. The aft cabin hatch, which was an option we hadn't seen before, leaked but only if the canvas was off.

The only negatives were teak damage and recurrent porthole leaks. And she needed saloon curtains. The spray rails needed to be painted.

The positives were almost too many to list: a survey done within 30 days that the bank accepted, documentation of a bottom job within the last eight months, new canvas on the bridge bimini and weather wrap on the sundeck, upgraded 50-amp service with cable and access hookups on both sides, two new conforming heads, three air-conditioning units (two of which were new), two new marine kitchen refrigerators, and a Zodiac dinghy less than two years old on davits off the stern.

The equipment list was equally impressive: auto-pilot, windlass, GPS, Garmin plot planner with four carts, Raytheon swing-arm 24-mile radar, two VHF radios, two compasses, carbon monoxide detector, two inline depth finders, swivel plow anchor mounted on the bow pulpit, Danforth lashed to the bow railing, all the emergency equipment adequate and in date, and an Onan generator only three years old.

We negotiated and settled at $78,000. We had a buy/sell agreement with us and wrote a check with no hesitation for 10% to start the process again. But this time we felt sure that our ship had truly come in.

We have a Kadey-Krogen 42 Classic trawler. The boat is well suited for living aboard and traveling in the ICW and Continental waters. It has a single diesel engine and burns 2 gallons/hour and travels about 8 miles/hour. It carries 700 gallons of fuel and 360 gallons of water. It has a washer and drier and a generator. It handles well in rough water but has difficulty in beam seas because of rolling. The boat does fine but it is hard on the occupants.

We live aboard full-time and have traveled down the Mississippi from Minnesota, Tombigbee, Florida Keys, and up the East Coast to the Chesapeake.

— *Al & Sue Martens,*
aboard Northern Light

What the Survey Won't Show You

J.J. Stives

Hooray! You've found your dreamboat.

Before you hire the surveyor, before you plunk down big dollars and before you make a major mental commitment to turn this boat into your new home, consider some things that a survey won't show. Think about comfort and livability, seeing the boat not as a cruiser but as a full-time home. Usually, the surveyor's report won't show these things.

When you are looking for a good liveaboard boat, remember: A good pleasure boat may not be a good place to live full-time. Here are some things to look for when the boat you are buying will also be your home.

Systems

The fewer complex systems on the vessel, be it sail, power, barge or houseboat, the easier the maintenance. While you may embrace the idea of lots of mechanical and electronic gadgetry, try to avoid buying what you don't need. Non-vital electronics are costly, require significant time and money to install and maintain, and may not last that long.

For living aboard, the minimum you really need is a VHF radio and a portable GPS. Radar, Loran, fixed GPS, TV antennas, electrical power management systems, radar reflectors, ham or shortwave radios, weather fax equipment and electric monitors throughout the boat are very appealing devices, but not always necessary. A depth sounder, speed and relative wind indicator system (for sail), are a practical investment. The two power accessories used most are a power windlass and the autopilot. Having had both of these fail at times when they were needed, our current home has neither, but when they work, they can be very useful.

Shallow Draft

The deeper your boat extends below the waterline, the fewer the places you can go with her. The same is true about height. With the 65-foot fixed bridge limits along the Intracoastal, tall rigs are now restricted to fewer harbors. Boats drawing more than 6 or 7 feet have already been limited by the shallow depths of the ICW and many marinas. If you study charts of the areas where you think you want to cruise/live, I suggest you cut all indicated depths by at least half to get a realistic picture of the working depths you will find. Select a boat that meets your real needs: deep draft for blue water, shoal draft for shallow water.

Storage Space (Dry)

No boat ever has enough storage space. I cannot tell you how to solve this problem, but it is important enough to merit your close attention in shopping for a liveaboard vessel. What boats *do* have is a lot of niches where you can stash things and never find them again. What you need, in fact, is enough space to store what you need to live. This means using drawers and cabinets creatively and for things that cannot be placed in open storage areas.

Liveaboards are often ingenious in creating "new space" after they move aboard. One solution is to convert a smaller cabin to a storage/work room. I have seen aft cabins nicely transformed, using plastic storage bins, a telescoping bar for hanging clothes, and a small, fixed worktable for everything from a mini lathe to a sewing machine.

Remember that there is a great difference in "at rest" storage and "at sea" storage. Clothes piled neatly in a shelf over a bunk will shortly be in a wet pile on the cabin sole once you are at sea.

Consider supplementing your storage with watertight bags, including zip-lock baggies of all sizes. We use every size baggie known to mankind, up through the 3-gallon sizes for clothes, computers, cameras and food storage. Even trash bags have a use in storage for dirty clothes and bulky gear. For valuable items, we use Pelican waterproof cases. These are costly, but very much worth the price. Chris, my partner, keeps her professional cameras, Hasselblads, in a Pelican that we stow in the main cabin. In our liveaboard time, this case has worked flawlessly in saving these cameras from damp and shock damage.

Heating & Cooling Systems

Most vessels do not have any real thermal insulation. So when it gets hot or cold outside, the boat will be the same temperature inside. In colder climates, we use three heating systems: a portable propane heater that uses throwaway cylinders, a small 3,200-Btu portable electric blower/heater, and the onboard A/C's reverse-cycle heating. We have had to run all three of these while wintering over in Portsmouth, Rhode Island, and Bridgeport, Connecticut. In southern winters, the reverse-cycle system works well at dockside. On the mooring, we use the propane system for really cold nights.

In Georgia, Texas and Florida, from May to November, our onboard A/C is a true necessity for cooling. We have a Cruisair 16,000-Btu system with a condensing unit under the V-berth and two separate cooling units in lockers. This works well and is now almost 15 years old! In Florida summers, we must supplement this with awnings over the entire boat, otherwise the system runs all the time and cannot keep temperatures below 80 degrees. When water temperatures exceed 80 degrees, the efficiency of the system declines dramatically. The same is true up north when the water temp is too cold to provide any heat for the reverse-cycle system.

Water Systems

Pressurized water systems are essential on any vessel you might use for living aboard. Small, low-power pumps, accumulator tanks, flexible hoses and adequate tankage all make such systems pretty much trouble-free today. Check carefully how the system works. The best will be one that easily switches from onboard pressure to shore lines. We use a third hand/foot pump system when we are running and conserving power. Some boats may also have a system for bringing saltwater into the galley or for washing down. Anything handling saltwater needs to be closely maintained. Some years ago, I switched our single head to freshwater only. This cut maintenance dramatically, as we no longer pump any saltwater into the boat except for engine cooling.

Headroom

How much head room you have and where it is can have you, after a few months aboard, looking like the hunchback of Notre Dame. Headroom is really critical in the head, galley and saloon/living areas. Make no compromise on these or you will regret it. In sleeping quarters, headroom is not as important, but look for the ideal bunks where you will not smash your head every time you sit up or climb into a bunk in the dark on a rolling sea.

The Stives formula for headroom is as follows: The best looking boats from the outside have the least headroom on the inside. This is not a brilliant observation, but is generally true. You will find that the typical charter queens, long proven as comfortable vacation boats, tend to not be really slick looking boats. Flush decks and high freeboard make them comfortable below and reasonably safe for sailing in protected waters. The sleeker the vessel, the less likely she is to have very comfortable living space below.

Seating Arrangements

This may seem silly, but give it some attention. Consider:
- How many people can comfortably sit in one cabin?
- Can you get forward and aft if people sit in the saloon?
- Can you cook and serve a meal without climbing over your guests?
- Can someone work the nav station while you cook?
- Is there anywhere to lie down except in the sleeping areas, and do seats double as bunks?

Sleeping Quarters

It is not as important to know how many people the boat sleeps as it is *how* they sleep. Sales information will tell you *how many* can sleep aboard. Occasionally you will see the phrase, "in separate cabins." Until you actually see the quarters, take this with a grain of salt. Separate cabins does not necessarily mean privacy.

I ask "How many permanent, full-sized bunks?" This precludes the "make-up berth" engineered from dropping the tabletop or pulling out hidden shelves, as you often find in the saloon. Our Cheoy Lee Pedrick has the typical large V-berth forward, big enough for two adults of reasonable size. We also have a large, three-quarter bunk in the aft cabin, yet the literature will tell you that she "sleeps six or more." We have done that, but no one slept much. This meant two in the V-berths, one each in the pull-out bunks in the saloon — nice, wide, long berths, but no one can stay up and play Scrabble if the saloon folks want to go to bed — and three kids in the three-quarter berth. We have friends with a Pearson 42, a power vessel roughly the same LOA as ours. The book says they sleep eight to nine. But actual sleeping arrangements, despite it being a much roomier boat, are only marginally better than ours. They have an owner's suite with a queen-size bed behind the bridge. All other bunks are in the forward area below deck. These bunks are a bit roomier than ours, but dark, gloomy and poorly ventilated, a situation that is quite common.

A sensible tenet — comfortable, easty-to-use-and-repair systems outweigh glitz and chrome. Jeff Stives, Christine Ascherman and Opus, the golden retriever, live happily with this conviction.

Ventilation

This is a very, very hot topic (so to speak). Most boats do not allow adequate air movement through the boat. This is a fact of life. For a number of reasons (economics, hull integrity, space, etc.), manufacturers install sealed ports or windows, perhaps a single hatch forward, and rely on air conditioning and forward speed to keep interior temperatures in a livable range. In a slip, using shore power, this usually works, although A/C installed in northern ports may be inadequate in the south in the summer. On the hook, getting enough air through the boat in warm weather is a challenge. If you have a generator and it can handle the A/C, you may be able to solve this most of the time, allowing for noise and fuel consumption.

We live in a noise-restricted marina. Between 7 p.m. and 8 a.m., you cannot legally operate an engine or gen set. Dockside, you must use shore power for electrical equipment and on moorings you cannot run major electrical appliances after sunset. On the hook without A/C, wind scoops can be lifesavers.

Natural Lighting

This may not seem like a big issue, but how does the idea of living in the dark sound to you? To save money in construction, many boats are built with a minimum of openings. This concerns safety too. The more holes in your hull, the more places for water to enter. Ideal hull integrity would be with no holes. But openings in the deck for light and air to get in and out of the living space are very important. One of the things that makes our Cheoy Lee a fine liveaboard vessel is large hatches that admit lots of air and light. Our main cabin, galley and nav station have four 16-inch deck hatches large enough for a human to fit through. The forward cabin has a monster 24-inch hatch ideal for passing sails onto the foredeck. The aft cabin has its own 16-inch hatch, as does the head. We also have a tinted sliding hatch for the companionway. This gives us a total of eight large skylights for our living space. In summer, we cover these with screens and later with full awnings, but we have lots of light.

Look for good hatches when you buy, rather than thinking you'll upgrade later. Seaworthy hatches, made from heavy-grade aluminum and thick acrylic material, are expensive: Our 24-inch Lewmar hatch, last time I checked, would cost us over $1,000 just to buy a replacement.

Cooking Equipment & Galley Area

This takes a lot of forward planning. The meals you may cook aboard could be the same as you cook at home, but this is unlikely once you settle into the live-aboard lifestyle. Why? Because you have been massively downsized. You will be cooking and preparing meals in what could be a space no bigger than your current pantry — if you have a pantry. While most boats today have a three-burner stove, many are electric. You may think, "Great — no gas, no tanks, no safety hazards." Yes, but check to see if you can run the stove from the gen set and still have power for other appliances, like the A/C. Some boats do not have this much power. At dockside, pulling 50-amp A/C current from the shore power, you may find that the stove eats a lot of that amperage. If you run A/C, a microwave, water heater, refrigerator and lights, you may not have enough electricity. Electric stoves will free you from the gas demons: propane and compressed natural gas (CNG), both of which have dangers, but which can be operated anywhere. I have cooked on all three and frankly prefer the CNG, but I know this is a debatable topic. I do suggest that you consider the cooking equipment carefully before you buy a liveaboard, unless you plan to eat ashore all the time.

Cooking Fuel

A few words here about fuels. There was a time when we cooked onboard with alcohol, God forbid. Hundreds of accidents, fires and some considerable progress later, most boats went to propane. Today, there is a balance of about 50 percent propane, 35 percent electric and 15 percent other fuels, including compressed natural gas. But CNG stations are hard to find. We have never had to go without, but on more than one occasion I have had to drive a round-trip of more than 100 miles to get the fuel. CNG is cheap and safer than propane because it will not settle into the bilge, creating a fire hazard, but it is stored in heavy, high-pressure tanks. Propane is easier to use and find. Make sure you have adequate safe storage for the tanks.

We also carry a tiny backpacker's butane stove for emergencies and ashore when camping. I recommend this backup stove and have found it extremely useful for quick heating on deck or in the cockpit in hot weather. The canisters should be stored in a safe, above-deck location where any leakage will not enter the hull spaces.

Heads & Showers

If you are going to live aboard, you need to think carefully about sanitation. Modern recreational vessels do not feature modern American plumbing. The head can be the single most annoying facility on your boat, so it is worth some detailed examination before you buy. Myth versus reality is important here:

Myth: Modern heads are trouble-free.

Reality: Modern heads are complex systems and subject to high maintenance because of failure to apply common sense, regulatory issues, saltwater usage and holding tank limitations.

Myth: A head is just a toilet.

Reality: A head is part of a Marine Sanitation System. There's quite a difference. What you may want is the simplest system possible and to keep it spotlessly clean. Nothing turns anyone's stomach faster than a smelly head, and keeping yours odor free is, believe me, a challenge. Vacuum, electric and chemical heads are contemporary options to consider. Each has advantages and disadvantages.

Myth: Old hand-pump units are obsolete.

Reality: Only if you're talking to someone who sells fancier units. If costs and doing your own maintenance are high on your list, avoid anything other than a plain-Jane hand-pump head with a simple, easy-to-get-to, lockable Y-valve. Many areas require a locked system, and you will be cited and fined if boarded in these areas and found to have the Y-valve set to discharge anywhere but into the holding tank. We solved this problem years ago by simply disconnecting the overboard plumbing. Our head sewage can only go into the holding tank. There is no other option.

Check out your boat's shower area. Can you stand up in it and operate the water controls? Is there a seat? Does the head have a separate area for the shower? Is the floor safe when wet? Is there storage? On our 41-footer, the answer to all of these is "yes." This makes the shower a true pleasure to use. I know of others on larger boats that are not.

The Last Word

Your surveyor will help you spot structural and functional concerns on a new or used boat and that is very important. However, he probably will not be thinking about how it will function as a liveaboard boat, and that is also very important. Living aboard full-time, I have found that being comfortable and having systems that are easy to use and repair outweigh glitz and chrome.

Had I Known I'd Have Named Her *Woman's Work*

Shellie Taylor, captain of POP *(Pile of Parts)*

I moved aboard a 1972 Kaiser 38 ketch named *Pincoya*, upon whom I've spent an obscene amount of money so far just making dry rot and cracked swedges and broken wires and dead electronics and leaking plumbing and frozen thru-hulls go away. But what the hey — I fell in love on the sea trial (I was only infatuated before that) and everybody knows boat lust is not a rational state. Besides, she needed to be saved, she's pretty and I'm a sucker for projects. I've never lived aboard before, I've never rewired a boat before, I recognize plumbing only because most of it looks like garden hoses, but here are a dozen Newbie observations:

OK, you've fallen in love, you've found the perfect boat. You'll live happily ever after, right? Right!

1. When I moved aboard, I started using all of the (mostly 25-year-old) systems much harder than they've ever been used before.

2. A significant number of them have broken. The rest have given me notice.

3. My fuel feed system consists of several valves, a maze of hoses, two fuel filters, a voodoo doll, and an on-call demon. None of which work the way the pencil diagram on the wall says they do. Only the demon understands it, and he requires live sacrifices.

4. It is better if my water runs out in the middle of the dishes than in the middle of a shower.

5. Radio Shack speaker wire must be cheap. Most of my boat is wired with it. Well, the part I haven't already rewired, anyway.

6. Electrical books are not in English. And they're user-hostile.

7. Cast-off garden hose must be cheap too.

8. If ducks were any dumber they'd have chlorophyll.

9. New halyards stretch in the rain. They wait until 3 in the morning.

10. The leak is not coming from where you think it is coming from.

11. Boats dissolve in water. Slowly but steadily.

12. The leftover piece of wire is ³/₄" too short. There's more wire, but none of it is black.

- 3 -

MONEY TALKS
Affording the Dream

Once the dream of living aboard begins to take shape, reality intrudes with the question, "What will it cost?" One answer is, "How much do you have?" It can cost as much to live on a boat as it does to live on land — it all depends on your lifestyle. Some people cheerfully eat macaroni and cheese, others won't leave the dock without a pasta maker. Some live for a month on what it takes another to pay his cell phone bill.

Living Aboard surveys show that most full time liveaboards have retirement or investment income; others, however, choose to begin enjoying their boats while still working, keeping their jobs on land and commuting from their boat. A select few move their office or business aboard. And some take their retirement in pieces, cruising until the money runs low and then dropping anchor and obtaining temporary jobs to refill the cruising kitty.

While we can't answer the question of what it costs; nor advise you as to whether or not you can afford to live your dream, we can tell you how other people have done it. Here are the stories of those who figured out how to make moving aboard financially feasible. Their experience may raise the real question: "What is a dream worth?"

Sure, money talks, but as the song reminds us "it don't sing and it don't dance . . ."

Moving Toward Freedom

Clyde Hancock

Four years ago I had a house (with mortgage), a new pickup and a two-year-old car — all owned by the bank. One morning I woke up, realized that the pressure of having to come up with $1,500 a month (after taxes) just to keep the major stuff I had, plus more money for living expenses, was something I didn't like anymore. I also felt trapped into one town (that I didn't really like) and one job (that I didn't really like). I began the slow process of getting out from under it. I changed jobs (moving to Colorado) which got rid of the house (took a loss and we moved to an apartment), then I sold both vehicles (taking losses, but stopping the bleeding). I bought a truck with 185,000 miles on it for $1,000 and drove that for three years.

Removing financial restraints is the first step to gaining personal freedom.

About 2½ years ago I reached the "debt-free" point. I was never unfortunate enough to have large credit card bills — that was one pitfall I avoided.

After the financial weight was lifted I was free to think about lifestyles. I seek adventure, as does my wife, and we love to meet people and generally enjoy life. I decided that being a computer programmer wasn't the kind of existence I wanted. I do enjoy the work, but don't want to do it 8 x 5 or more and I never wanted to see a beeper again, at least the one that was hooked onto my pants!

Michelle's and my first task was to get out of Colorado and by the ocean. Since I had no financial weights it was an easy thing to do. I just found another job here by the Chesapeake Bay and we moved to an apartment in Richmond, Virginia. Then we began the task of replacing our 23-footer with a boat that would be large enough (plenty of room for argument here) to live on and, just as importantly, one we could afford. We had managed to save about $20,000 in the past two years so that was our budget. Two weeks ago we bought our 1979 Catalina 30, which is the boat that will be our home and carry us on our adventure. Last weekend we sailed her from Annapolis down to Deltaville, which is where we will live aboard until we depart the Bay around the end of next summer. Her name is *Delfina*. The remaining months until we go cruising will be spent saving and spending to get her equipped with cruising related items — dink, motor, EPIRB, etc.

The freedom and adventure that is offered by living aboard and traveling wherever one decides to go via water is the exciting part. We love meeting people through sailing and have met so many terrific people that we would not have met otherwise. We have several friends that we met since our arrival here who are already out cruising and we will probably run into them sometime.

The main point is that it is the lifestyle that draws people in. The idea of not worrying about traffic, mortgage, etc. Many people can't do it because of jobs, family and all the usual reasons. These are powerful reasons and I would never tell someone they should just throw it all away to do this, because in a sense that is what you have to do. Our contact with our families will be minimal, basically they won't easily be able to get in touch with us in the event of an emergency.

You can live the lifestyle in high style or frugal style, either way it is essentially the same lifestyle. We will do it frugally because we have to. If I had more money I would spend more, but it is also important to me that the amount of money tied up in boat and gear isn't such a huge sum that I constantly worry about something happening to it. Then I am a prisoner to our boat, the boat isn't our servant and companion. Our situation is such that the amount of money lost, if she went down with all our stuff, is only two or three years worth of savings. I can live with that and won't worry every time we leave her at anchor to go exploring.

Because of our financial limits (no debt is acceptable) we were limited in the type of boat we could buy which also limits our cruising waters (due to safety concerns). I don't want to take a Catalina 30 around the Horn, and won't ever attempt it. That is just my preference; I suppose some people would do it. If they truly know what they are doing, then they are braver than I. The places in between — like the Caribbean or from the Florida Keys across the Gulf to Mexico — are decisions that we will make later. Right now we are sure we will go to the Bahamas.

The point is, it is the lifestyle that draws people and the most important feature of that lifestyle is freedom. To me the second most important is adventure. You can do it with lots of money or a little money, both will work. Doing it requires abandoning the other way of life to a great degree. It requires financial freedom or I should just say the financial ability to leave the land-based lifestyle. It requires that you truly like whomever the person or people are who will share the cramped living conditions with you. Loving isn't enough, but it is certainly a benefit. It doesn't have to be and usually isn't forever. People can do it for a year or two and decide they have enjoyed it but are now ready to get a place on the land to live.

Michelle and I are going to learn and live a lot in the next few years. We are looking forward to it and anticipate good and bad times. We will get through them all and meet a lot of people. Some of whom will prove to be our friends for many years. We may meet up with some of you "out there." I hope so.

Financing the Liveaboard Life

Robert D. Reib

Afavorite topic of discussion among people seeking to join the liveaboard life is how to finance a boat large enough to live on if you don't have $50,000 to $250,000 to pay for one. Let me start by saying I believe that those figures are very accurate for a 35' to 50' boat on which you can live and cruise comfortably. We have lived aboard and cruised for seven years and met thousands of others doing the same. Most of us are older (50-65) and our families are grown and on their own. We were able to finance our own dream boat by selling our land home and using the proceeds to buy a boat (our new water home).

Along the way, we've met people who have been able to buy their

It is fair to say that a boat large enough to live on can cost from $50,000 to $250,000 or more. Finding that sort of money might seem like an impossible dream, but don't give up. Skipper Bob offers five examples of people who have done it for less — in some cases, a lot less.

boat out of savings and keep their home or rent it out. On this more affluent side of the scale, we have also met those who were able to buy a new boat and paid $350,000 to $500,000. Rest assured though, these liveaboard boaters do not represent the majority. From my experience, most of the liveaboard cruisers paid between $50,000 and $250,000 for their new "home" and in fact did not have to finance the boat. For most of us who are retired, financing a boat is simply not an option.

So how do you go about living aboard comfortably when you don't have the money reserves to spend on a boat? First, and foremost, you must address the question of what you plan on doing with your new boat. Will you live aboard in one area and continue to work? Or will you cruise full-time and not work at all? In between, you have those folks who want to live aboard a truly comfortable boat and are willing to work in one location to pay for it.

The bottom line is that there are many unique personal needs and complex situations which will dictate the best solution for you. To illustrate my point, I offer here five examples of people we have met who are now liveaboard boaters enjoying the good life.

Beth was a single mother in her mid-40s. When her husband died, she had only a few thousand dollars left from his insurance. She needed a home and a job to support her daughter. Beth bought an older sailboat in terrible condition in Florida for $3,500. It was 32 feet long, had an engine which needed major work if it was ever to run again, and sails which would have to be replaced. The outside was in terrible condition, with badly faded fiberglass and teak trim which would make you want to cry.

The boat was in a "do-it-yourself" yard. Beth did not know much about boat maintenance, but she was willing to work and learn. She and her daughter moved aboard a boat which essentially could not move under its own power and then she went to work. First she cleaned up the outside of her "new" boat. She immediately began to hire out to help boaters working on their boat in the yard while she made money and learned the boat repair business. As she became more proficient, she could charge more for her services. We would stop and talk to her each year as we moved north and south. After three years, she still doesn't have the engine running in her little boat. It is clean and neat to look at. With no sails and no engine, she isn't going anywhere. However, she has crewed on two boat deliveries to the Bahamas and she is becoming more experienced and knowledgeable each year. Meanwhile, she lives aboard, enjoys her lifestyle and watches the sun set over her stern while manatees play in the water behind her boat.

Mark and Carol lived and worked in Michigan. They loved boating and wanted to move aboard, however, they didn't feel Michigan was the place to do this. It gets just too cold in the winter. They bought a 28-foot sailboat with an outboard motor for $15,000. They quit their jobs and headed off around the world with a couple of thousand dollars in the bank.

By the time they got to Florida, reality set in and they decided they needed a bigger boat. Both of them went to work (in the computer field) and continued to live on their boat while they banked as much of their joint paychecks as they could. Six years later when we saw them again, they owned two sailboats — their original, but still used, 28-foot sailboat and larger 36-foot sailboat which they were outfitting. They plan on leaving Florida within a year, as soon as the older boat sells, and cruising around the world. I hope they make it.

Doug knew next to nothing about boats. He was in his early 60s and ready to retire, but had not built up much of a nest egg during his life. On a trip to the Bahamas to see friends, he saw a 42-foot powerboat for sale. The engines were ruined, as was the generator. The boat leaked and the outside was in terrible condition. The helm station was a mess. He bought it for $5,000. Doug put the boat in a marina in the Bahamas, cleaned up the outside and inside, and moved aboard. Over the next five years that we saw Doug, he cleaned and painted the boat, fixed most of the leaks and truly began to enjoy his life aboard. To this day, whenever we are near, we stop by for a drink and talk to Doug. We have been privileged to bring him replacement appliances from time to time, as well as ships stores. Doug is now talking about selling his "home" in the Bahamas and buying a trawler to cruise and live on.

Bob lived aboard a 37-foot Owens wooden boat. In the last few years, he had the engines overhauled, installed a new generator, and made his boat look great. However, with dual gas engines, this boat is not built for cruising. The cost of fuel would be too high. Six months ago, he bought an old, wooden 50-foot trawler. He has fixed it up the way he wants it and is ready to take off. Now he must sell his Owens. He is asking $12,500 for the boat. It would make a fine liveaboard home for one or two people, is in good shape and could be had for a very reasonable fee. However — and this is important — it would not be used

"Our liquid assets include a fund of experience, a stock of knowledge, a bond with the Bahamas, and a wealth of sand dollars."

– Carolyn Corbett aboard *Bifrost*, a Morgan 41

for extensive cruising because gas boats simply cost too much to operate over long distances.

Dudley and Carol were literally the first two cruisers we met when we started cruising. They had been cruising on their smaller 32-foot sailboat and realized they needed something bigger to be comfortable. They had just bought a 42-foot motorsailer when we met them in 1992. The proud owners of two boats, they were in the process of working to pay for the new boat and selling their older, smaller boat. They paid $72,000 for the motorsailer. With what they expected to get from their sailboat, they planned to work for five years to pay their new boat off and be able to go cruising again. Each year as we passed through Annapolis, we would stop and see how they were doing. In 1997, we received a note from them on the Trent-Severn Canal; they were cruising again and traveling the Great Circle Route.

The point of each of these stories is to illustrate that even if you don't have $50,000 to $250,000 to buy a boat, you can still move aboard. The boat you buy may not have the capability to go cruising, and it certainly will not be as comfortable as a $250,000 fiberglass trawler with dual staterooms, icemaker, refrigerator, bow thruster, air conditioning, etc., but you will be able to live aboard and begin to work toward the boat you really want. After all, most of us living aboard have some larger, more comfortable boat in mind that we will eventually get when we hit the lottery. ☙

A small boat and a suitcase full of cash beats a 40-footer tied to the bank any day.

– Rick Kennerly aboard Xapic, Westsail 32

Money Matters

Karen Dodd

When my husband and I first considered the idea of retiring and moving aboard, money was one of the primary issues. We broached the subject by deciding to live aboard at least a month or two every year for a few years. This helped us get an idea of how often we like to treat ourselves with a meal ashore and how fancy a wardrobe we needed and what kind of lifestyle we enjoyed. I recommend this approach.

We have found we can live nicely on my husband's retirement pension along with his social security. However, we socked away a nest egg to cover inflation and the unexpected. We also draw yearly from our investment fund to purchase additions for the boat and pay for major repairs and haul outs.

Since I was a practicing financial planner, I am able to run our financial plan a variety of ways showing different end results. While there are computer programs available that can offer you the capability of doing this yourself, I recommend that if you are serious about your goals you should seek professional advice.

> Karen Dodd, a retired financial planner, keeps careful track of her budget and her investments. Karen and her husband "practiced" living aboard before actually making the move in order to get a realistic idea of what it would cost once they were living on their boat full-time.

How to Analyze your Finances

I used a 4% inflation factor and ran the numbers showing what it would take for us to — (a) live aboard and (b) cruise for five years and then move back ashore. I also calculated what my position would be if I were a widow. A financial planner will charge you about $300 to do these kinds of calculations.

We use Quicken to track our expenses before and during retirement. That way we keep an eye on those ATM dollars and watch how often unexpected expenses come up. I use TurboTax to prepare our income return and project the next year's estimated taxes. I have to say I'm looking forward to claiming residency for eight months in Florida this year to be relieved of a part of out North Carolina state income taxes.

Financing the Dream

If you are planning on living aboard and haven't yet made the big step there are several ways you can finance your dream: You can move aboard and continue to work-full time saving for later years when you can take that extended cruise. You can sell your home and use that money, supplementing your income as needed with part-time jobs on the move. You can keep the house and rent it out. Be wary, however, about describing your house as your primary residence if you are claiming it as rental property.

Without the additional expense of a house, you probably won't have many more expenses living aboard than ashore, and, in fact they may be less. Most dock rents are lower than apartment rentals. We rent our home while we are away. It supplements our income and goes into the savings or investment kitty depending on the level of our cash reserves. We are depreciating our house each tax year which lowers our total basis in the house. Fortunately, we still have the one-time exclusion on sale of primary residence if we decide to sell. Otherwise the house assumes a new basis at our death for our heirs.

Whether or not you decide to keep your house, I encourage you to examine your overall financial position. A few hints: You should be saving 10% of your total earnings. Your primary cash reserves should be three times your monthly living expenses. Cash reserves are emergency monies for repairs, trips, new purchases, medical needs. You, in effect, borrow from yourself to cover short-term expenses that can be overcome by time and continued saving.

You need to get rid of as much outside debt as possible. As you pay off a bill or get a raise or unexpected amount of money comes in — save one half of it. Whatever the amount is, save half — it does add up over the long run. At the end of the year, you should be worth more than you were at the beginning, with your savings and investments greater than your prior year's. There are a few exceptions, but in general the base rules apply. Learn to save. Build up cash reserves. Then you don't have to use that bank card and run up another debt because you don't have any short-term money.

If you decide to sell your house, consider carefully before deciding to invest all of your house money into "the boat." After a couple of years of searching for the perfect boat, my husband and I decided the best boat was the one that was paid for — ours! We sank some bucks into her. We changed the inside a bit and went for roller furling and fancy dodger and bimini to give us a bigger "back porch." We had water hookup added as well as some major changes in the galley. The icebox had to go as far as I was concerned, but we had no room or inclination for the installed refrigeration. An AC/DC/propane cooler that even makes ice was the happy median. (I can now keep pots, pans and an electric frying pan where we once stored huge chunks of ice.) If you don't know what your boat's potential can be, seek out someone who has a boat similar to yours and ask for advice, look at magazines and go to boat shows. I enjoy visiting other people's boats. I get all kinds of useful ideas, and I've never met anyone who denied answering a sincere question about living aboard. The majority of cruising boats are bigger than our 32', but after just adding Sta-Loks to our standing rigging I cringe to think about the price of hardware on larger boats.

Where to Invest Savings

A big question is how to invest. I would sooner tell you what kind of boat you should live on than offer advice on your portfolio (although I do recommend you buy low and sell high!). However you invest, shop around for the services. Do they offer direct toll-free phone access to a real person who can buy and sell and bank transfer? Does the tax and record information help you do taxes and

"I enjoy visiting other people's boats. I get all kinds of useful ideas, and I've never met anyone who denied answering a sincere question about living aboard."

keep up with your basis all the time? I have 24-hour access to all my account information and the quarterly reports are very user friendly. Lots of companies are out there, but you live on a boat and want help, you don't want to be put on hold or find yourself in a never-ending telephone cycle. The phone booth is usually too hot and I don't like to use up my cell phone minutes being on hold.

My age is 50 and my husband is 66; therefore, we are primarily invested in good blue-chip and large-cap growth stocks. Those are portfolios which are professionally managed and primarily invested in large corporations with proven records and performance. The fund directors have a growth vision. If you look up mutual funds in a magazine look for "growth and income funds" and "large-cap stock funds." We also have about 15% invested in small-capital and aggressive growth including international funds. I like the variety, and having experience in this field I know what to expect in the down market.

I like to dollar cost average, so we invest a bit every month into various funds. I watch a fund and read the prospectus and somewhere there is a record of the NAV (net asset value) price for several years going. I often sell half of a large holding when it reaches the apex of prior years, then I turn around and dollar cost average it back into the same or similar funds. These past few years have been phenomenal for the market. A more conservative stance would be to go with balanced funds. They invest half in stocks and half in bonds — a good place to be if this market is making you queasy.

One thing that a lot of people don't know is that you can get to your IRA monies or rollovers (qualified monies) before you are $59\frac{1}{2}$ without penalty. This is called a SEPP Systematic Equal Periodic Payment plan. I have several IRAs. If I wanted to supplement our income without penalty, I must take a specified amount of money out each year and that amount can't change until I am $59\frac{1}{2}$ or for five years — whichever is greater. Again there are computer programs that calculate this amount and give you very flexible options. You can use one or several IRA's to calculate this. Again talk to an advisor if you have questions.

Another payout option for some old annuities is to annuitize them with a percentage in variable payout. That way some or all of you money stays in the market during your lifetime payout. Also if you are considering the IRA payout plan then if your IRA is large enough break it into several then just draw on the amount you need. I also recommend not investing all your living money into funds. It s possible to invest your money in funds that pay you out a specific amount periodically. The idea is to not take out more than it earns including capital gains. Again find out what its total growth has been for ten years. I'd like to hope all our investments could pay us 10% per year if we needed it over the long run. If this is your plan then don't put all your money initially into your growth and income stocks. Keep out what you will need for a year and have it systematically paid out to you each month from either a revolving CD or high-yield money market. Why pay a sales charge to buy and or sell something you will need in the first year?

I also suggest staggering certificates of deposit so that they mature every quarter. If the market is down and you find you need a new engine or the hull painted, you could schedule it for when that next CD matures. Obviously when you use up one you need to shift some money before the year is out.

Most of the people I meet on the waterway planned their "retirement." They didn't inherit their wealth — they did save and make sacrifices to afford their lifestyle. Living aboard is worth it.

Working Stiffs
Can Live Aboard Too!

Marge Ziegler

When I get up in the morning my routine is just like those of all other working people. I wake to the obnoxious alarm and complain to no one in particular how much I hate getting up to go to work. Ugh! I take my shower in my nice large shower stall on the boat and yes, I have plenty of hot water. I put on the nicely pressed business suit and silk blouse. (It took a bit of ingenuity for me to figure out how to iron some of my blouses. I use a regular iron and a carefully folded towel slipped inside the blouse in the specific area I want to press. I found that this works great for getting out the wrinkles without having to stow an ironing board on the boat.)

You need not wait until you retire to enjoy your boat full-time. You'll have to do things a bit differently, but, really, the biggest problem of living aboard while working ashore may lie in getting the boss to believe you when you call in sick.

Next I fuss with my hair, which is ritually cut short for the summer. My hairstylist knows that I need something easy and simple to maintain. He hasn't disappointed me yet.

And then I do all the other last minute things, just like all the other working people do. But from there it's different. I open the door, step out on the "back veranda" and just breathe the sea air, taking time to "smell the flowers." I look around at either a duck passing by or a fish jumping out of the water I embrace the usually beautiful early morning sky, something I don't like to see on weekends when I can sleep late! After I take this small, special, quiet moment to realize where I really am, I hike up my skirt, jump to the dock and by the time I get to my car my hair is a mess!

I find it very important to wear sneakers with my skirt. It makes it easier to get safely out of the boat and down the dock to my car. In my car, one can find an assortment of business jackets and about seven pairs of shoes: heels, flats and sneakers. Did I mention the three purses I have there just to match the heels? Our old boat doesn't have enough closet space for all my work clothes, especially the dresses. I guess if I thought about it, I really could do without all those shoes but I don't want to sacrifice my business attire. I think this is the biggest problem I have with living on the boat and still being a part of the working class. Attention boatmakers: Bigger closets please! Maybe we should start looking for a bigger boat.

Lucky for me, the large corporation I work for has just relaxed its dress code. Business casual or in their words, "contemporary" is now in order unless you deal directly with the outside customer. This has helped immensely as far as being on the boat. Now I can wear my dress slacks (and forget about hiking up that skirt!) and just toss on one of those suit jackets I keep hanging in the back of the car.

I always carry a semi-large bag. (It also doubles as extra weight to keep me from blowing off the dock on those windy days!) In this bag are all the things I have found I have needed close at hand now that I live aboard: my calendar (so I know where I am and where I'm supposed to be), my makeup bag, a cellular phone, a couple of books and/or magazines that I am currently reading, a toothbrush and toothpaste, lotion, and shorts and matching top for the days I "stay in the city" longer than normal. Well, you get the idea.

In this useful bag I also have my breakfast. Traveling an hour to work in the morning is a little bothersome at times. I need something (other than driving) to help pass the time, so I have my coffee with a bagel or dry cereal and listen to classical music. What a great way to start a morning if one really must go to work.

My boyfriend carries his briefcase for the same purposes and more. He is in business for himself, so he carries a "traveling office" of his customer order book, telephone listings, notepads, paper clips, paper, and a calculator. This mode of operation took Tim a while to devise but now works just great for him. If you really want to do something as crazy as living on a boat, you learn to improvise. Tim still keeps his file cabinets at "home base" and just brings specific folders home to the boat. In the evenings, Tim spends his time with followup telephone calls, arranging appointments for the next day and other business activities. His cellular phone comes in handy for this. He also has his telephone calls automatically forwarded to the cellular. This allows his customers to get in touch with him in the evenings and they don't have to remember yet another phone number.

Now that I think about it, there is another problem I have working and living aboard. Calling in sick is hard. Nobody believes you! Just getting into the right frame of mind to force yourself off that boat and to work some days is enough to make one sick! It's best not to tell too many coworkers about your living on a boat. You will probably sacrifice any hope of getting sympathy when you finally do return, though you've been moping around the boat for days trying to determine if it's really your stomach that's making you nauseous or if it's the boat rocking in the waves that's making you feel so sick

Sometimes I'm lucky enough to borrow a laptop from work. It's very compact and folds up small enough to fit in a closet. And it's very easy to bring out when required. The laptop can be plugged in or allowed to run on its own battery. If I am really swamped at work, I can bring assignments home and work right on the boat. I also like to keep my personal stuff on disk. I can keep recipes, lists of items stored on the boat, addresses and phone numbers, etc. Having the laptop at home gives me the freedom to update my lists. If I need to print, I just copy my work onto a disk and I'm off to work the next day for printing.

I haven't had the nerve yet to ask my boss about pursuing an alternative work environment. I really could work from the boat; I'd just plug the laptop into the telephone line and dial up into the main computers at work right from my "back veranda." I really would work, but I might have a hard time selling that idea. The problem is similar to calling in sick.

I am taking Fridays off in the summertime as vacation days. I try to knock out all my running around, shopping and weekend prep, like extra cooking, getting salads made, etc. Using these Fridays the way I do allows me to enjoy the weekend. It also gives us an extra day to cruise if we want to get away for the weekend. And remember, if you live aboard there is no extra packing! We just untie our home and off we go.

Storage, of course, is something we have come to love and appreciate. There were no empty shelves on board available for paperwork; books, dictionary, magazines, and the like, so I store them all in a large wicker basket. The oblong basket is approximately 30 inches long. I have arranged the books so it is easy to see the titles and that also makes them free to grab. I keep the basket tucked in the corner on the galley floor. It is out of the way but can be moved around by the handle easily. This has worked out great. It allows us to keep books aboard without the hassle of finding extra storage compartments. This sturdy basket doubles as a doorstop too!

Tim's routine is a little different from mine. He is not one to wake up early. Therefore, when he opens the door to the "back veranda" he just keeps walking. Off the boat, down the dock and into the car. Intent only on driving the short distance to the local coffee shop for that first dose of caffeine. Tim does, however, have a difficult time when the sun gets hot in the afternoon. It just makes him sick to know it's so nice out and his "ship" is sitting out on that water all by itself. He swears it just calls him. And you guessed it: he answers! You can be assured he heads out early on those days to be one with his boat.

The things we've gained – a closeness to nature, the ability to move our home, and especially the time to enjoy life on board our boat – far outweigh what we gave up to make this dream come true.

– Nancy Mills, aboard Summer School

For us Sunday nights are the best. That's when all the other "working stiffs" are packing it up. They make many trips back and forth from their boats to their cars. Pillows, extra blankets, clothes, boat toys, food. Many times it's the same things that not just two days ago they carted from their cars to their boats! And they do this every weekend. Sundays find these landlubbers somberly preparing for their trip home. No thanks. Not having to pack everything and sadly go home is wonderful!

Living on board our 38-foot Chris Craft Roamer is just like living at home. Tim's only other complaint is not having a washer and dryer on board. He hates to drag those heavy laundry bags down that long dock. We have most of the standard living conveniences and much, much more. So if you too have a nice cruiser and want to enjoy the great things life on the water has to offer, go for it! Enjoy, and take time to smell the flowers.

You Can Bank On It

Living Aboard Is Great

I have been living year-round aboard a 31-foot Island Packet sailboat for the past five years, and am employed as a senior vice president of a bank on Nantucket Island. Nantucket is 30 miles off the coast of Cape Cod, Massachusetts.

I had been planning this move for several years and worked out a system that would be compatible to my career as well as my boating activity.

The solution was to have a clothes closet at work. I purchased a wooden wardrobe closet and placed it inside a storage room in the basement of the bank. This is where I keep all my dress suits, shirts, ties and shoes. All my casual clothes remain on the boat in lockers or Rubbermaid storage containers.

I am an early riser and my routine is as follows:
- awake at 5 a.m., dress casual – khakis, sweater, boat shoes (jacket in the winter);
- arrive at the community pool at 5:30 a.m., swim until 7 a.m.;
- shower and shave at the pool (backup is marina and my shower on board);
- arrive at bank at 7:30, dress – suit, shirt, tie, shoes, etc.;
- behind desk at 7:45 until whenever the day ends;
- after work change clothes, return to boat wearing casual clothes.

Because Nantucket is a small island, I have no commute – I'm only minutes from my boat. If I have a situation at night that requires me to dress up, I just return to the bank and get dressed.

The cabin design on the Island Packet is such that books store behind the settee on both sides of the cabin. I place the books on top of two pieces of strapping which allows air to circulate under the books and when I sail there are railings that keep the books in place. Since I work with computers all day I have not found it necessary to install one on board at the present time. I use a cellular phone for personal use and while in a slip it is charged using AC.

Because our marina gets busy and expensive in July and August, I move out onto my own private mooring. My routine stays the same, except that I then use an inflatable to get back and forth. Since I am then on DC power for two months, I keep extra battery packs for my cellular phone. They are charged in my office along with electric shavers and cordless drill packs. Even though I have the capability of TV, cable and VCR, I choose not to watch TV.

Since July and August are the times I do most of my sailing, I remove all incidental items like lamps and knickknacks and stow most of the things that would get in the way when I take the boat out. The boat is usually ready to sail within 15 minutes, after I get out of work.

If you really want to be a liveaboard, you learn to make do with only those things that are absolutely essential. The word "clutter" is a no-no in a live-aboard life. It doesn't take too many items laying around to create total havoc; therefore, I spend a good deal of time thinking and organizing where things are going to be put. Just as the America's Cup yachts need a tender to take on all the extra equipment, I also need something on shore to store seasonal items or maintenance items that are currently not needed. This is accomplished by boxing things up and storing them in a friend's basement or a rental storage locker. I take advantage of my situation at the bank and store items that are not currently needed at the office. I have a beautiful credenza in my office – if only people knew what was in it. To this day, my secretary wonders why I give her all my files for her to keep.

The other major consideration was that I wanted my living conditions to be as good as if I were living on land. One issue is the dryness of the boat. My boat is extremely dry. I work very hard at keeping the boat smelling fresh and dry. I have as many as five or six canisters of damp-rid opened and all going at one time. I picked up a hint from one of the mega-yachts visiting Nantucket several years ago, and that was to use fabric softener sheets in between the cushions, in between my towels and sweaters, in all compartments and in all Rubbermaid containers and lockers.

— Daniel P. Neath, aboard Oh Danny Boy,
Nantucket, Massachusetts

Working Aboard

Establishing a Boat-Based Business

Louise Coulson

Every morning I roll out of my bunk by 6:30, make a 30-second commute to a cluttered desk, turn the computer on, and start the teapot. I am ready to go to work. With the huge increase in home-based businesses, it is only logical that those of us who live aboard are also working aboard. We have all of the typical problems associated with working from home along with some particular to living on a boat. If you're lucky enough to both live aboard and cruise, working aboard can present even more challenges. On the other hand, living and working aboard your boat can be such a treat that the compensations far surpass the problems.

Could you run your business from aboard your boat? More to the point, should you? Is it worth it? Louise Coulson says, "Absolutely!" There are many compensations, including those financial.

Boat-Based Business Problems
- Credibility
- Communications
- Space
- Separating work from your home life
- Discipline
- Isolation
- Moisture
- Networking
- Meeting with clients

Credibility

Its difficult to be taken seriously when you work from home, and when home is a boat, it can be even more challenging. Your printed materials enhance your company image. When you're at home, you may work in your bathrobe, but when you meet clients, dress the part of a professional. Having a separate phone line and mailing address establishes your business credibility.

Should you let your clients know you work from your boat? Our own business concerns the marine industry, so most of our clients are rather interested and pleased that we work aboard. This is probably a question you should pose for yourself. Consider your credibility and make your own decision.

Communications

The marina setting can pose problems with your business lifeline — the telephone. Some local phone companies offer "ring-mate" service so you can appear to have a business phone line. You answer your ring-mate line with your business name during business hours.

An answering service or "call answering" — which is offered by some local phone companies — allows your business to work for you even while you are underway. If you travel constantly, your answering service can "beep" you anywhere. Skytel is one of the companies that provides this solution for traveling communication problems.

A toll-free number shouldn't cost extra, but if you have "long distance" clients it can add to your credibility as a business. The extra advantage to a toll-free number is that it can usually be moved with you from state to state.

"The address" is sometimes difficult for liveaboards, and can be even more of a problem for a boat-based business. Our own solution is a local mailbox service that can forward mail as we are cruising. A land-based business partner or a family member can be valuable as a constant contact also.

E-mail has opened a world of communications for everyone who has access to a phone line at least once in a while. Many local providers have made toll-free numbers available for Internet access while traveling.

Other communication resources are available, and the field is growing constantly. These advances in communications will help those of us with boat-based businesses.

Space

Those of us who work with computers have the "space advantage." If your work requires large equipment or space-consuming supplies, you may be able to redesign your methods or store infrequently used materials and equipment at a remote location. If you are cruising, you will need access to shipping or storage aboard. Storage solutions are the key to keeping the work equipment and supplies from taking over your living space.

Louise Coulson runs Caper CanvasWorks, a company that provides custom-made canvas products for the boating community, from her office aboard the Caper *in Gloucester, Massachusetts.*

Separating Work

Physically separating work from home may be almost impossible. Whatever you can put out of sight will help with that division, but your best chance at work/home separation will be time assignment. Keep your work hours and don't work after hours except in an extreme emergency. Don't be afraid to tell a client to call back during business hours. Would they take a business call at 7:30 pm on a Saturday evening?

Discipline

Self-discipline isn't too difficult if you are really enjoying the work — in fact, it is sometimes more difficult to stop working than to keep yourself working. Again, time is your ally. Set your work hours and let family, friends and business associates know what those hours are.

Distractions abound at a marina. I always think I have to run and look out the window to see what boat is going by. Summer at a marina or anchorage can be such fun that you will probably want to get out and socialize. Starting your work very early can allow you to quit a little earlier so you can join the fun.

Isolation

Some people don't enjoy being alone for most of the day. The marina setting can offer more chances for interaction than the typical neighborhood home-based business. Just because you work from your boat doesn't mean you must work on board your boat all of the time. You might consider a business that will take you off the boat and into an environment with other people at least part of the time.

Moisture & Moving

Here is a problem that land-based businesses don't face: your equipment and supplies need to be protected from bouncing around and moisture. It won't be a shock that you need to fasten things down and pack them away. Plastic bags and boxes along with silica packs have great value in keeping things dry. Computers don't like water and a printer won't like damp paper. Protect your expensive equipment and supplies from mildew, dampness and any leaks.

A Dozen Tips for Marketing a Boat-Based Business

- Network with local groups to meet prospective clients.
- Write columns and articles to position yourself a credible resource – send a press release.
- Develop relationships with media by offering information.
- Have a logo that people will always associate with your business.
- Be sure your business name relates to what you actually do.
- Present an award to a prominent person in your field – send a press release.
- Position yourself or your competition will.
- Offer a newsletter as a marketing/informational piece.
- Always follow up every contact or request for information.
- Tune up your marketing materials.
- Teach a seminar – send a press release.
- Consider press releases for any newsworthy company event.

Meeting with Clients

Having clients moving to and from your boat is extremely risky due to liability. This can eliminate the idea of something like a boat-based tutoring business or create problems when meeting with clients. You might ask your local library director about using a space in the library for tutoring. Temporary or "on-demand" office space can sometimes be rented in under-utilized office buildings. Look into insurance coverage for visitors to the building to see where your liabilities lie.

If you live in a marina, keeping your boat-based business reasonably low-profile is probably the best policy unless you have permission from your marina management to publicize the business on the premises.

Compensations

Is it worth the extra work involved in working aboard? Absolutely. Being productive aboard your boat is truly the very best of both worlds. Freedom, flexibility, lower stress and lower business costs — office space, clothes, commuting — are just a few of the advantages of working and living aboard your boat. Through organization, thorough checking of legal issues, motivation and discipline, you should be able to enjoy a productive and interesting experience.

John Coulson, son of Louise Coulson, lives on his 34' John Alden yawl, Zephyr, that he has been rebuilding for 2 ½ years. He works from his boat as a ship's carpenter when he is not commercial fishing out of Gloucester, Massachusetts. He's building a new rudder in this picture.

Hot Ideas

Marlene Parry

The waves are gently rolling in, the sun is peeking out behind the clouds, and the dolphins are surfacing for some air. What a view for a business office! It is 7 a.m. and J.J. Hollis is already on his cellular phone tracking down the location of his latest hot sauce shipment. "Who says you can't run a successful business from your home?," grins J.J., who lives aboard a 41-foot Gulfstar anchored in Melbourne, Florida and named after his company, *Hot Idea.*

J.J.'s energy is non-stop even after his bout with cancer. Indeed, there are several occasions during any day where you will spot J.J. talking on two cellular phones at the same time.

Inspired by his love of the sea – and the need to vary his cruising diet – this sailor turned a hot idea into a successful business venture, one he can run from his boat.

Pepper plants line the deck of his sailboat for home usage. Both J.J. and his fiancee, Beth, have a green thumb for growing these plants. My eyes were fixated on one particular plant on which the small peppers were colors of light purple, dark purple, and mature red pepper. "It's like a Christmas tree," Beth said with a gleam in her eye. I nodded in agreement and in awe of the simplistic beauty of this plant, which bloomed and gave Beth and J.J. the joy of Christmas colors all year round.

J.J.'s love of hot sauces and his keen business sense made it an easy transition to start his own business. "Most hot sauces on the market are just hot and lack any real flavor," says J.J. "I put the flavor back in my recipes." J.J.'s hot sauce varieties encompass mild, hot, extra hot, and for the really daring captain, hot-as-fire. He markets his products to restaurants throughout Florida. J.J. is involved in every aspect of his product right down to designing the labels. His love of the sea and nautical history has found its way to his sauce labels which depict pirates peering into a treasure chest filled with — what else? — bottles of hot sauce. To distinguish his hot-as-fire sauce, the label also includes a skull and crossbones.

J.J. and Beth spent several months in their galley cooking up their hot sauce and experimenting with various ingredients until he had refined the product. "Once the taste was right, I found a chemist, the building for mass production, and was ready for the market," states J.J. "I enjoy people and enjoy marketing a product with all natural ingredients."

While spending six months last year cruising the Bahamas, Beth and J.J. caught fish every day for dinner. "I love fish, but after a daily diet of fish, you start looking for ways to enhance, but not drown the fish flavor, and the hot sauce gave the ordinary an extra zest," said J.J. "From conch chowder to chicken wings, everything tastes better."

Favorite Recipes
from s/v *Hot Idea*

Shrimp Bisque
1 10$\frac{1}{2}$-oz. can of condensed cream of celery soup
1$\frac{1}{2}$ cup of milk
1 5-oz. can of shrimp
$\frac{1}{4}$ cup chopped green pepper
4 or more drops of J.J.'s Bayou Juice

Dilute soup with milk in saucepan. Chop shrimp, reserving some whole shrimp for garnish. Add shrimp, green pepper, and J.J.'s Bayou Juice to soup. Heat and pour into soup bowls. Makes 6 servings.

Brunswick Stew
1 medium onion chopped
1 green pepper, chopped
1 cup chopped celery
$\frac{1}{4}$ cup of butter
1 1-lb. can mixed vegetables
1 8-oz. can cut okra
1 1-lb. can cream-style corn
1 6-oz. can tomato paste
1 tbsp. Worcestershire sauce
1 tbsp. J.J.'s Extra Hot Sauce
1$\frac{1}{2}$ tsp. salt
$\frac{1}{2}$ tsp. black pepper
1 12-oz. can roast beef
1 cup fine bread crumbs

Saute onion, green pepper and celery in butter over low heat until just tender. Mix in remaining ingredients, except meat and crumbs. Add meat; cover and cook over low heat 30 minutes. Stir in crumbs just before serving. Makes 6 to 8 servings.

Buffalo Wings
12 chicken wings
2 tablespoons of J.J.'s Hot Sauce
   (your choice, hot, extra hot, or hot-as-fire)
2 tablespoons of margarine or butter

In 1-quart saucepan over medium heat, heat hot pepper sauce and margarine until melted, stirring occasionally. Drizzle over wings and arrange wings on rack in broiler pan. Broil 6 inches from heat, 25 minutes or until chicken is no longer pink and juices run clear, turning and basting occasionally.

J.J. Hollis, the "sailor with the hot touch," shows off some of the peppers he grows aboard the boat.

J.J. was born and raised in Florida and has been a commercial fisherman and is a licensed scuba dive master. So, whether he is in the water or on the water, he's at home. Beth, on the other hand, hails from Cleveland, but it did not take long for her to become acclimated to the warm Florida weather where she can tend to her pepper plants all year long. This couple, along with their cat, Tommy, have found a way to live their dream, run a business, and fund the cruising kitty. J.J. Hollis is definitely the "sailor with the hot touch" and with a true enjoyment of life. So, if you cross paths with a boat stocked with pepper plants, most likely it will be *Hot Idea*.

Worth Every Penny

Steve Madden

Last fall my wife and I analyzed our financial situation and came to the conclusion that money was not slipping through our fingers fast enough. Somehow we had fallen into the habit of living within our means and we didn't even realize it. Shocked, we knew that something had to be done before others started following our example and we would be blamed for a massive slowdown in the economy. So, we bought a houseboat.

Sure enough, that solved the problem. There is nothing like boat ownership for eliminating those pesky worries about such things as savings accounts or Roth IRAs. Not only that, but we'll never end a month by saying, "Where did all the money go?" When one owns a boat, one already knows where all the money has gone.

No grass to cut, no hedge to trim, no yard to be re-seeded,
No weeds to pull, no leaves to rake, no fertilizer needed.
No trees to prune, no mulch to spread, no shrubbery to clip,
No wonder we like "yard work" now . . .
    we just hose down the slip

No better form of sleeping aid than water's gentle motion,
No place more peaceful to call home than river, lake or ocean.
No second thoughts now that we've cut dry land's umbilical cord.
No way we'll ever turn back now . . .
    we're hooked on living aboard.

– Steve Madden

I'm not saying that's all bad. For instance, creating an annual budget has become much simpler. With only two categories, "boat" and "whatever is left," it takes only a few minutes to put it down on paper. In fact, with direct deposit, life couldn't be simpler. All our income is deposited directly into the marina owner's account, and if he needs more, we just cash in another certificate of deposit.

On the other hand, boat ownership offers many opportunities to expand one's base of knowledge. My wife and I have learned many interesting things during our tenure as yachtsmen — hey, it sounds better than "boat people" — and I would like to share some of them with you.

- Carrots float, pagers don't.
- When people say, "If you ever want to sell that, let me know," they really hope you never want to sell it.
- "Heave, Ho!" is not a good thing to yell when your wife is about to drop the anchor overboard.
- The quieter the cove, the quicker it attracts contenders for a "Loudest Marine Stereo" contest.

- The smoothness of your docking is inversely proportional to the number of people watching you dock.
- Someday, God is going to say, "Enough, already!" and reach down with a giant fly swatter to flatten every JetSki and Wave Runner He (or She) can find.
- Neutral is your friend.
- Seven-dollar K-Mart sunglasses will cling to a swim-ladder practically forever, but $200 prescription glasses will jump to their watery death without hesitation.
- If you want to get rich, figure out how to make grass grow as fast, thick and green as algae on a boat bottom.
- Straight lines knot themselves, knots untie themselves.
- One's next boat is always going to be one's "last boat."
- Getting an accurate forecast from the Weather Channel and winning the state lottery have similar odds.
- The bungee cord is a more useful invention than the telephone.
- Sometimes an anchor just refuses to anch.
- Stick the word "marine" on anything and it doubles in price automatically.
- Some boats should have blinkers.
- The sun is not obligated to appear even on a day called Sunday.

These are but a few of the bits of tid (*a.k.a.* tidbits) that we have come to learn while enjoying our houseboat. Surely we will learn more in the years to come.

I hope that this information is helpful. While it is being provided free of charge, donations will be accepted. Make your check payable to The Bottomless Pit Fund. Or, in lieu of a check, you may choose to play a game called Virtual Houseboat Owner. It's really quite simple. Just go to the nearest toilet, drop in some sizable wads of cash (no coins) and pull the flush handle. There, now you know just how it feels to own a houseboat.

But, with the possible exception of having to replace that sunken pager, it's been worth every penny.

- 4 -

MAKING THE MOVE

Sure You Can Have It All –
You Just Can't Keep It on the Boat.

Making the decision to trade life on land for life on the water is the easy part. The real work comes after you've worked out a budget, bought the boat, and informed your boss. How will you pack a 30-year accumulation of stuff filling a 3,000-square-foot house into a 300-square-foot boat? What will you tell your friends and family? And what will you do with the stuff you can't bear to part with but can't take onto the boat?

Some people do it in stages, moving from a house to an apartment before making the final move onto their boat. Others rent storage spaces in which to keep the things they want to keep, although more than one person has reported being seriously annoyed about paying good money to store stuff they never looked at again. However you do it, however hard it is, the payoff is an exhilarating sense of freedom and lightness of being.

From time to time we receive notice that one of our readers has done it — made the move and is now living aboard. Of these messages, one of my favorites was simply a change of address card with these handwritten words: "We did it!" Those three, simple words convey the exhilaration of starting a new adventure. Many people have written longer messages giving details about the final stages of planning as they made the move, and, importantly, telling us how they feel about leaving their life on land. These letters are compelling and an inspiration to those not quite ready to untangle their ties to shore. In fact, we consider such letters important enough to dedicate a regular feature to them in a section of the magazine called "We Did It." Here we offer a few of the best stories of those who "did it."

The lesson we can learn from their experience is that, painful though the process of downsizing may be, the best thing to own is your own life.

We Did It!

No Jobs, No Cars, No House, No Bills

Susan Davison

We retired, quit, sold or gave away everything we owned. It's just my husband, Rich, myself and our 37' Irwin. We did it. We're official liveaboards, sailing our way to paradise. It wasn't always easy getting to this point but it was always interesting.

Buying the Boat

We started three years ago with the purchase of our boat. After five intense days, 3,500 miles and looking at a vast array of boats, we found our dream. We wanted a center cockpit for the large aft cabin. Two sails were enough for us to handle, putting a sloop rig on our wish list. A full shoal keel for coastal cruising was deemed necessary. After researching the market we decided to try locating an Irwin Mark IV. We considered ourselves lucky to find a bristol one in Florida. We had it hauled home to Indiana.

Leaving your land-based home is a big step and, for those who plan to cruise extensively, it is just the first step. Since moving aboard, Rich and Sue Davison have been fulltime cruisers.

Maybe We Ought To . . .

We plain couldn't resist customizing the boat — just a little! Hearing from three other Irwin owners that they had a chain plate break was enough to fire us up to replace ours. Grinding fiberglass inside your own boat is not for the faint of heart. Let's just say three years later we are still finding fiberglass dust. It was worth doing as we found the starboard forward one was broken. That same year we sanded the bottom to the gel coat (oops, and a little beyond) repaired the sanding errors, sanded and painted the top deck. Over the next two years we replaced the cabin sole, added new upholstery, larger holding tanks, replaced or rebuilt engine parts, made a new table for the main saloon and replaced all our windows. There were a host of other homey touches. Every project lead into another one. Our days off became consumed with working on the boat. We began to plan the great escape.

What to Take and How to Store It

In a true fashion I thought we should take as many items from home as we could shove, stow and hide on board. Little did I know Rich was masterminding the same for the tool shed. He was just as willing to get rid of my stuff as I was to get rid of his. We began to guard our treasures, hiding things we wanted to keep. Our children and friends learned to lock their cars when they came over because we'd load them up with stuff we wanted to ditch. Rich and I had the perfect plan. I distract them with food and Rich would stuff their cars to overflowing. The ones who owned trucks got fed the most. Finally we admitted that getting rid of years of treasures was tough to do. If you can't bear to part with it, find a way to store it somewhere. Rich's parents agreed to store the things we couldn't give up. For us, it was important to take certain comfy things with us. I wanted my computer and all my cooking spices and Rich wanted a host of tools. We built a pantry under the largest settee we have. I'm amazed at what I can fit in there. Taking things out of packages and storing them in Ziploc bags saved a lot of room. I also used a few crates to hold food groups together. Be sure to label everything and take the cooking directions. We cut a door in the side area under the aft berth. Most of the tools can be stored in there, out of sight. We keep a large hanging cloth tool rack in the aft head with the most used hand tools in it.

Taking Care of Business

We had to decide how to pay insurance, phone bills, credit card bills, and anything else that might come up. We set up our regular bills to be paid directly from our bank and we use a debit card for everything else. Our retirement checks are direct deposit. Although there are mail services that will handle your mail, we use a post office box with Rich's parents monitoring it. We have our mail forwarded when we know we'll be in a port for a few days. We also use his parent's address for people who insist we must have a land-based address. We've given up explaining that we live on our boat and don't have an address and just give them what they want. With ATMs, direct deposit and phone cards, our paperwork is minimal. Because we sold everything, our bills are almost non-existent. Someone once said that if you have more than one key on your key ring, life is too complicated. We agree.

Medical Needs

We keep extra prescriptions with us for our medicines. We also use a nationwide pharmacy that has a computer database. Knowing that any pharmacy can call another and transfer your prescription makes it simple — for a small fee, of course. Make sure your doctor has a notation in your chart to authorize refills in case the doctor is on vacation when you need something. We keep a full medical kit onboard and we both know CPR. A book we found useful and easy to read is *The Onboard Medical Handbook* by Paul G. Gill, Jr., M.D. There is a list in our record book with our medical history. My biggest concern is knowing what to do in an emergency. We have a friend that works in the medical field who came on board and give us in-service advice. We took notes and periodically review it.

Get Organized

My idea for being organized is to have everything in bags, baskets, drawers, and crates with everything labeled, and an inventory on the computer. Rich's idea of being organized is to have it onboard, somewhere. We had to compromise. Compromising in our case means I usually know where everything is and he asks me where to find it. All my stuff is accessible and I can find whatever is needed. Rich's stuff is, well, it's on board. Living in limited space, means if you

And with some sweet oblivious antidote Cleanse the bosom of that perilous stuff Which weighs upon the heart.

– Shakespeare;
Macbeth V.iii

take it out you put it back, today. One thing I could not live without is Ziploc bags in sandwich and gallon size. I have to confess to being a cheapskate and washing them out for reuse. We also have a Seal-a-Meal on board. We have a cold plate freezer under our nav station. It can hold about a month's worth of meat and we always have a bag of ice in there. Because I repackage everything for the freezer, I can buy meats in bulk. That saves money too. Where things are today are not always where they started out. As you spend more time living aboard you'll become more organized. We discovered we took too many clothes. It looks like we'll be sending stuff to Rich's parents.

Saying Goodbye

It's bittersweet saying good-bye to family and friends. We'll see our family again but you know some friends are gone forever. While well-intentioned, most friends really won't visit. It was hard leaving our children and grandchildren. Rich and I each have one son, one daughter and one grandchild. Our grandchildren are one month apart in age. Keeping in mind that a lot of parents/grandparents have long-distance relationships with their family made it easier. We call, send little gifts in the mail, and make video tapes. The grandkids love receiving tapes of us reading them a story, and we send the book with it. Remember, you're not leaving forever, just taking a really long vacation.

Keeping in Touch

For us, e-mail is the only answer. Our Internet server allows us to pre-type our mail, then we can send and receive when we log on. We are using an acoustic coupler which sometimes refuses to connect on a pay phone. Most marinas are very good about letting us use their phone line to do our mail. We've even seen marinas that are set up with computer rooms, or at least a separate computer line. We carry enough phone line, with male and female plugs to run to a pole if we're lucky enough to be in a marina that offers dockside phones. We also carry coaxial cable for the television. Before we left, each member of our families got a list of everyone's name, addresses, phone numbers, and e-mail addresses. Also included was a description of the boat and how to call the Coast Guard in case of an emergency. I write a lot of letters to our friends who are without e-mail, call our parents once a week, and e-mail newsletters about every 10 days. As I'm typing this on the computer, we are underway on the Erie Canal. There is a 300-watt inverter connected to a battery that I'm plugged into. Pretty spoiled, aren't I?

What Do You Do All Day?

The days fly by and each day is different. We can plan on sailing for a day and the wind is either from the wrong direction or there is no wind at all. Each night we chart our course, picking two or three ports to head to. Where we end up depends on the weather. Because we are not on a timetable, we're able to layover in port as long as we want. Living on a boat means everything takes twice as long to get ready. By the time I get in the pantry, get my food out for dinner, start preparing, go back into the panty for the forgotten item, it can take an hour for a normal 15-minute recipe. We call it being on island time. "No hurry, mon." Some days are spent sailing, some doing work on the boat and some just playing. Personally, I like the playing days the best. If we're in port we'll work around the boat until noon and then go hiking, fishing, swimming, snorkeling, sightseeing or picnic on the beach. We've met people in port who are doing the same thing and we'll get together on each other's boats. Entertaining is a big part of our social life. We keep plenty of snacks with us to serve to company.

Going from the fast-paced working world to living aboard can be startling. Appreciation of nature has entered our thinking. Seeing different sights, watching the way people live, and enjoying our environment has lead to a fulfillment that was unexpected. Now we both realize the preparation we did was worth it. The anxiety wasn't. If I could offer one piece of advice for anyone considering living aboard, just do it. You'll wonder what took you so long.

Tick, tick, tick . . . Gave my landlord 30 days' notice this morning. Gulp! Oh God, oh God, what am I going to do with all the STUFF that seemed so important when I bought it? Aaarrrggghhh! I've taken about, oh, I don't know, two percent of it aboard and somehow I don't feel deprived at all. One the other hand, I finally have an excuse to throw out all the old socks whose mates I keep believing are going to mysteriously reappear after mumble years . . . can I also please have everyone's permission to throw out every article of clothing I hate but about which my mother would say, "There's still years of use in that, if you throw it away the day will come when you wish you had it."?

Can I now quit pretending I make omelets and give away the omelet pan? Bet I only need one salad/mixing/serving/emergency leak-catcher bowl, too. And this thing that I not only don't remember why I ever wanted it, I don't even have a clue what it IS! Old, ratty sheets – GONE! Old, ratty bath towels, too. Wheee! This is fun!

— Shellie, who needs a dumpster and
can't imagine why she moved any of this stuff even once,
let alone carted it around all these years, Alameda, California

Verbs, Not Nouns

Marilyn R.P. Morgan

I've always admired the characters on *Star Trek.* Not just for their bold exploration of strange new worlds, but also because they know how to travel light. When you see them being transferred to another ship or beaming down to a research station, they're never carrying anything bigger than a briefcase. No moving vans full of cardboard boxes for them. The only personal possession Captain Kirk seems to have is the case he keeps his service medals in.

A glossy magazine dedicated to "simple living" exhorts its readers to "Do less, have more." But as Marilyn Morgan explains, it's doing things, not having things that rules liveaboard lives.

Maybe it's not so much a lack of materialism as it is the constraints of television production that keep Starfleet traveling so light. Maybe that sort of thing is more difficult to pull off in real life than it is in science fiction, but I envy that lifestyle just the same.

I've been in graduate school for five years now — six if you count the year I spent away from campus on a cooperative education assignment, and I've moved six times and lived in four states during that time. Each move has been to a smaller set of living quarters, starting out in a two-bedroom apartment (I still miss my sewing room) and ending up, for now, in a furnished rented room with a tiny shared kitchen. Each time I've failed to get rid of quite enough stuff, and always there's a pile of unopened boxes left stashed in some corner or closet that I don't have room to unpack. This is one tradition that's going to stop — I've taken a vow. Besides, although I'm landlocked at the moment, living aboard lies somewhere in my future, and rumor has it that there isn't much storage space on a sailboat.

I've been doing my own personal form of downsizing for years, even before the first subversive thought of living on a sailboat entered my mind. As a recovering packrat, I don't find this downsizing easy, but it is satisfying.

"Good! You're learning to let go," a sailor friend said when I told him I'd spent the weekend hauling stuff down to Goodwill. He's right — it is good. I don't need stuff anymore. I want experience instead.

I refer to myself as a "recovering" packrat to remind myself that it's a state that requires constant vigilance to maintain. Less so since I quit my job and went back to school — poverty does have its compensations — but temptation lurks around every corner of my world just the same. For me, it isn't shopping malls that are the problem. I can shop for hours with friends and be the only one still empty-handed at the end of the day. Bookstores, though, are another matter. As a professional scholar, I'm supposed to love books, right? I have a built-in, socially acceptable excuse for my bibliophilic excesses. I suspect some of *Living Aboard*'s other readers may have similar problems with discount marine stores.

So I try to stay out of bookstores (and away from the book sections of discount marine stores), but that's not enough because the thing about junk is, it breeds. Or perhaps it comes into existence by spontaneous generation when the conditions are right: that is, in dark, cardboard-enclosed spaces like moving boxes. Every time I've moved I've gotten rid of every last bit of junk I owned and packed only the good and useful things up in boxes to ship. Funnily enough, when I get where I'm going and I unpack the boxes, they're always full of junk. Next time I'm going to skip the shipping part and just pack the boxes and then toss them out back in the trash before I leave. I could have saved a lot of money in moving costs if only I'd known to do that from the beginning.

Right now I have eight boxes left piled in a corner of my room. Those eight boxes are my own personal *bête noire*, my Moriarty, my Everest. What's in those last eight boxes is the most difficult stuff to deal with: all the ceramic art my mother made for me over the years. Parting with those pieces feels disloyal, and besides, they're beautiful and I like having them. If I had room I'd still have them on display. I think, though, every time I check the boxes for breakage from the latest round of moving, that my mother could have chosen a more portable art form. I lose a few pieces every time I move, so eventually the problem will solve itself even if I don't do anything about it. There's a lesson in there, too, I think: We can't hang on forever even if we want to.

My mother gave me other things besides ceramics. Yesterday I sat going through a file box full of recipes clipped out of magazines and newspapers, throwing some away, setting others aside to try. In a way, my mother gave them to me; she passed on to me her habit of collecting recipes and taking pleasure in trying them out. I can't throw that gift away, nor does it take up storage space. It won't mildew, rust, or chafe, and I live it every day. These are the kinds of gifts we can and should hang onto.

So I'm packing up another box of stuff to donate to my current landlady's church's rummage sale. She's generously offered me some storage space in her garage, but I told her not to give me any excuse for not dealing with my remaining stuff. It's time for some tough love, as in "It's tough, but I love my liveaboard dream, and this stuff has got to go."

Last week I dumped 15 years worth of personal journals in the trash. It's not easy for a writer to let go of her words, but I'm curiously the stronger for it in a way that's hard to define. It has something to do with the thought that, "That's one less thing I'll have to worry about where I'm going to keep on the boat." But I think it has more to do with the fact that owning things is a reciprocal arrangement. You own the things, but the things also own you. You have to move them, store them, protect them, repair them, dust them, and, in the case of my journals, worry about who will see them when you're not around. When you get rid of stuff, you simplify your life and gain mental breathing space along with your physical breathing space.

The simplification of my life is still in progress, but as it's gone on I've discovered some things that make the transition from weighed-down packrat to footloose vagabond easier. Here are some things that have helped me along the way:

But I think it has more to do with the fact that owning things is a reciprocal arrangement. You own the things, but the things own you.

A *library card.* Keep it handy when you weed out your personal library to remind you that there are other ways to enjoy books than owning them.

A *trash can or recycling bin.* Drop all those glossy mail-order catalogs in it the moment they hit your mailbox. Don't look at them first, not even the covers. Just toss 'em. For packrats, they're deadly — much worse than shopping malls.

A *camera.* Photographs are as good as the original objects for things you want to remember, and they're much easier to ship and store. Once you get used to not having the things you photographed and got rid of, then sometimes you can get rid of the photographs, too.

A *garage sale kit, complete with signs and newspaper advertising.* Nothing kills the pain of parting with your stuff better than being able to turn around and buy that new winch you want with the proceeds.

A *charity rummage sale, Goodwill dropoff box, or other worthy cause that will accept your donation of the stuff that doesn't sell in your garage sale.* If you have to part with it, it feels better to know that someone else will get some good out of it.

Friends who will tell you that you are doing the right thing when you call them in a panic as the garbage truck comes down the street, bearing down on all those beloved treasures you put out in the cans last night. If you suspect your friends might not know to tell you that on their own, tell them in advance that's what you'll want to hear when you call.

Your birthday and holiday gift list. Call everyone on it and propose that you stop exchanging gifts. A card conveys the fact that you're thinking about them just as well as some object does. I made this agreement with my family last year and I don't regret it. If gifts are important to your family and they won't accept the cards-only option, suggest that they make donations in your name to a favorite charity, or give things like gourmet food baskets that will be used up and disappear. Don't save the basket afterwards. (I only add that last bit of advice because I know from personal experience — don't ask for the details — that some of us will be tempted.)

Finally, most important of all, is a firm commitment to the idea that experiences are better than objects, and doing things is better than having things. Maybe we don't have to stop being packrats if we're willing simply to change what it is we collect. Collect memories, not artifacts. Make a difference, not a pile. Stuff the lockers of your life with verbs, not nouns. ✑

Making the Move

Two Kids, a Dog, a Parrot, a Cockatoo & All . . .

Louise Coulson

Every month for ten years we read the boat-for-sale ads in our favorite boating magazines. We wanted a boat to live on, and constantly studied the hull design, deck space, systems and interior space on boats. Many were tempting, but there was always something that held us back until my husband showed me the ad for *Caper*. The ad was only about five lines with a small picture of a large custom-built Harpswell trawler cruiser with only 230 hours on the big, single diesel. I fell in love immediately and urged him to call the builder. After some negotiations and a survey, we were the excited owners of a 48' boat that we figured we could fix up with a few coats of paint. After 10 years of planning, hard labor and heavy expenses, we're still fixing and loving it.

Our children were just getting ready to leave home, so thought we'd work on the boat and move onboard within two years. The lure of the boat was irresistible, and we were living aboard full time within three months — kids, old English sheepdog, a parrot, a cockatoo and all.

It took them ten years to figure it out, but once they found the right boat Don, Louise, Amy and John Coulson took their old English sheepdog, their parrot and their cat and moved aboard a 48' Harpswell trawler. They just did it and never looked back. Now, ten years later, Don and Louise are preparing to cruise and the kids each have their own boats. Moving aboard was the right choice for this family.

How do you move six tons of belongings, four people, and three animals aboard a 48' boat? First, we took everything we thought we needed and could fit comfortably onboard the boat. Every possible empty space was filled to capacity. Our clothes, personal belongings, tools and books were all settled, though not necessarily easily accessible.

Extra tools, my wool (I am a knitter and handspinner), some keepsakes and many books went into a horse trailer that I'd rented for storage. Of course it rained and I found bugs in the trailer and moved everything to a much more expensive storage unit that was weather and varmint tight.

Long-term storage is a very expensive proposition and we don't like to think of what we've spent for storage over the past six years. I can tell you that all of the "stuff" in storage isn't worth a year's rent on the storage building. Our only excuse is that we are rebuilding and maintaining three boats out of the shed — *Caper*, our son's 1947 John Alden and our daughter's 27' Buccaneer. My goal is to someday eliminate the storage building, but I don't think the others in the family share that goal.

Once we loaded the boat and put things in storage, everything — I do mean everything — at the house had a price marked on it. We put an ad into the paper telling everyone that we were moving aboard and were having a gigantic

yard sale. Everything would go. We had to empty a three-bedroom house with all of the appliances, furnishings, junk, etc. that you might expect. We put as much as possible in the garage and left the rest in the house so we could take people inside to see merchandise. We made a poster with a listing of items for sale inside the house — furniture, tools and appliances.

Caper, *a 48' Harpswell trawler, before (above) and after.*

On that Saturday morning when I opened the garage door 60 cars were parked in front of my house. I must admit to two minutes of sheer terror and shock. We were inundated with buyers. People would ask, "Do you have a _____?" Sometimes we would. Right now I couldn't list ten items that we sold that day.

By noon the next day, all we had left fit into the pickup and was taken to the Salvation Army to start another life. All was done, and, within a month, I couldn't have told you what the couch looked like because we were busy working on *Caper*. We lived with no head for five months; we carried water in five-gallon jugs for that first difficult winter in a very cold Gloucester, Massachusetts; moved the galley twice, installed a new electrical system, and more.

That was 10 years ago, and we never looked back. The kids have gone on to live on their own boats, and the old English sheepdog went to doggie heaven, but we're still here. Much of the "stuff" we thought we needed has been discarded or sold so we have some moving-around space.

Good luck to those of you taking the step, I believe it is a matter of attitude. All we seem to keep with us through our cleaning binges are family pictures. People mean more than "stuff" and the boxes we keep it in.

When people see the before and after photos of the *Caper*, they frequently say we had tremendous vision. Looking at the pictures I think you would agree with me that it wasn't a vision, but an hallucination.

Monday Morning is Different Now

Retired Postal Worker Sets Sail for Easy Living

Tom Murphy

I had been reading *Living Aboard* on and off for quite a few years. One of the thoughts I had for retirement was to live on a boat. I've had several small sailboats over the years, from 8 to 18 feet, but I was not much of a sailor.

Well, the post office set me free in October '92 and I bought a 30' Bristol sloop in September '93. I named the boat *Monday Morning* since, now that I'm retired, Monday morning is different. I moved aboard dur-

> Conventional wisdom decrees that you should plan carefully when making a major move. But Tom Murphy just "did it" and figured it out as he went along. So far, so good. Ten years later Tom is still living aboard and cruising the East Coast.

ing the next two or three months. I had been living in a rented apartment so I didn't have any problems about getting rid of a house. My daughter took some of my furniture and what was left ended up in my mother's cellar.

The boat I bought was over 20 years old, but was in reasonable condition. I would say that I've taken the poor man's route to living aboard. My moving aboard was not carefully planned: I just did it and fixed my mistakes as I went. When I read articles about how carefully people plan their moves onto boats and how many pitfalls there are, I become paralyzed with how overwhelming everything is. I just did it and didn't seem to make any horrible mistakes.

My first winter was probably as bad as it could be. One time the thermometer dropped below zero for a whole week. Did you know how G.D. Fahrenheit set zero? The freezing point of sea water. I had five inches of not-so-soft sea ice around the boat for some time. Since I hadn't yet figured out how to heat the boat properly, I had some not-too-warm nights.

I lived in a marina in east Boston for two full years, occasionally going on short cruises. Then I moved across the harbor to the Charlestown Navy Yard for another winter. The best thing that happened to me that winter was that someone hit my little pickup truck head-on during a snowstorm. Best thing? Yeah, cuz the truck was totaled and I didn't have to go about selling it. I was free to cruise!

I took the Intracoastal Waterway down the East Coast in the summer of '96. For a couple of months one friend traveled with me from New York City to Charleston, South Carolina, but most of the time I traveled alone. Everyone says they'd love to go with you, but somehow no one ever seems to be able to. My girlfriend stayed in Boston, so the two of us had to visit back and forth with each other.

I stayed mostly at anchor. Some friends live in the Palm Beach area and that led me to living at anchor in Lake Worth in North Palm Beach for a couple of months. I think I prefer to anchor rather than go into a marina . . . even aside from being a cheapskate.

The most useful book I had on the way was *Anchorages Along the Intracoastal Waterway* (available from Skipper Bob, 802 7th Street, East Rochester, PA 15074) This loose-leaf packet rates hundreds of anchorages and cheap (less than 75 cents/foot) marinas. It also lists do-it-yourself boatyards. As for charts, I used Better Boating's Chart Kits. You can get them discounted for approximately $110 each and it takes four to cover the East Coast from Cape Cod to the Keys.

I came back up to Boston to visit last fall and stayed there for the winter — not too bright. It was cold! Many marinas here welcome liveaboards and the one I'm in now has about 50. It's a short walk from downtown Boston for the poor souls who have to work there. Just past the last raft in the marina is the U.S.S. Constitution, so, it's a pretty interesting area.

Tom Murphy lives aboard, but is never too far from a bustling city port for too long.

Some things that I've found useful for peace of mind . . .

I signed up with a forwarding service instead of asking friends to take care of my mail. The one I'm using is Voyagers' in Islamorada, Florida. I'm quite satisfied with them. They charge a flat fee per year plus postage and will cull your junk mail if you want. I usually call their 800 number once or twice a month and have them send me a packet. It almost always fits (junk mail included) into an all-you-can-stuff priority mail envelope. I have not had any problem with general delivery in any of the post offices I've used. Once in a while, I've had them send it UPS or FedEx to a marina or such.

For a voting address, I used my mother's home in Dorchester, Massachusetts. The voter registration clerk at Boston City Hall is easy to get along with. He is quite understanding about people who cruise. I use this address for my "domicile," my official residence.

I had a cellular phone on the boat in Boston and kept it just to keep the same number. It doesn't make much difference where I sign up for cellular service, because I'm more often than not "roaming." Most of my calls are made from pay phones with a credit card, anyhow. But having the cell phone with its voice mail is good for peace of mind.

I have four credit cards and buy almost everything with them (though I'm going to dump American Express, which costs too much). I have them set up to be paid automatically from my credit union checking account. Of course, I can easily check on the balances by phone, but I log all of my purchases anyhow. My retirement check is zapped to my checking account every month. It's like magic — zap! I'm rich! Well, unpoor.

Tom Murphy keeps a cellular phone for peace of mind, but staying in touch with the mainland doesn't trouble him very much.

My credit union offers an ATM card that has no use limits, so I can get cash most anywhere. In the Northeast, ATMs are free to use, but I was shocked to find that from Maryland south those money grubbing banks charged an extra fee in addition to the fee the ATM systems charge your home bank to use their machines. Luckily, you can almost always find ATMs that don't charge extra. Credit unions are a good bet; they still hold some of the old populist notions of banking. In Florida, I use the ATMs at Publix markets. They don't charge any fees. Publix wins 'cuz now I do all my shopping there.

In July, or maybe even June, I'm planning to head south again. I'll probably arrive in Florida in November. I intend to stay in various cities along the way. I am a city boy, and though I enjoy the quiet anchorage as I travel, I like to spend time in real cities with libraries and movies and buses and bookstores and such. In New York City, the moorings at the West 79th Street Marina cost $10 per day. I can afford that! And in Baltimore Harbor, the anchorage in the Inner Harbor is free. I can really afford that! I know I'll spend some time in Charleston. It's really convenient to a cruiser on foot. It has a compact downtown and good bus service. When I get to Florida, I think I'll spend some time in the anchorage at Miami Beach before I go on to the Keys.

If anyone reading this is interested in spending some low-quality time with me, I'm always happy to have company . . . well, almost always. You can pick the time or pick the place, but not both 'cuz I don't know when I'll be where. ✐

Choosing the Right Marina

Philip Lange

Marilyn and I live and cruise aboard our Searunner 37 trimaran and usually spend our time on the hook. We value privacy and quiet. There are two of the reasons we chose to live on a boat. But there are times when shore-side facilities become important. When those times come, we select our tie-up carefully. We would like to share with you some of what we find important and a little of how we go about looking for it.

When you move aboard, your marina will not only be where you keep your boat, it will be your neighborhood. Like land-based neighborhoods, marinas offer a variety of lifestyles, from low key and laid back to upscale and highly social. It pays to shop around to find the one that's right for you.

First, of course, select the area. After that, read the guides and the ads, they're a good place to start, but do not neglect the phone book. The local yellow pages will sometimes reveal a tie-up that does not show in your guide. Word of mouth from fellow cruisers can also be revealing. After you have made a list of the facilities in the area, plan to visit them. What follows is some of what you might look for.

Cost

I bring this up first, not because it is the most important, but because it is so subjective. For some it is our biggest consideration; for others, within reason, the least. You don't always get what you pay for. What you have to spend in addition to dockage such as insurance, transportation and utilities should be factored into the overall cost of your stay. Often we find a bargain in an older, but well-maintained, facility with nearby shopping. For some of us, being able to go out for a day cruise is important. Sometimes lower prices will be found way up the creek past a draw that only opens with 24 hours notice.

The Friendliness Factor

This cannot be underestimated! Do you belong to a cruising club? Are there other members at the marina? Does the mix of power and sail suit you? Many cruisers and liveaboards return to the same marina year after year and form long-lasting friendships at the dock. While it is hard to judge this right off the bat, sometimes chatting up the residents while inspecting the piers will help you get a feel for the place as well as discovering any adjustments you may need to make.

The attitude of management can greatly affect the tenor and tone of every one at the marina. Can you easily talk with the folks in charge? If you called ahead by telephone, what was your impression? If they are not accommodating and helpful when you first arrive, don't expect it to be any better after your have committed for a stay. Some questions you might ask are:

- How accessible will management be at odd hours? Does the dockmaster or their assistant live aboard? (It's a plus if they do.)
- Mail and packages? How are they handled? Are they in a secure place?
- Does the management encourage potlucks and get-togethers?
- How will personal messages be handled by the dock office? Will you find out that your day sailing guest, who called two days before, won't arrive, after you have made all the preparations?
- Will you be able to do those on-deck projects you want to accomplish? Some places will not allow work of any kind, others require only that you use contractors supplied through the marina office. Some just request that you abide by the "good neighbor policy." Ask before you sign up if this is important to you.

While you're at it, ask about oil recycling. Oil changes are a fact of life for all boats. It's no fun looking for a place to dump your used oil. Most marinas I have visited have facilities for recycling.

Ambience

Are the grounds maintained to your standards? Are the docks lighted at night? Do the prevailing breezes blow through, or is it in a pocket of dead air? How about industrial stink and noise? Ask about mosquitoes and no-see-ums if you like to sit on deck in the evenings. Is there a common meeting place or recreation room? How is the bulletin board?

The Pay Phone

Is it in the broiling sun with no place to set a notepad? Can it be called back to from the outside? Not all do. The accessibility of a fax machine might be of concern to you, so check it out.

Protection

How protected is the marina? I have seen some that get downright dangerous during storm winds. Will you have to leave your slip if a hurricane threatens? Where will you go? Will everyone else be there too? In what condition are the pilings? Some apparently stout timbers waste away to broomstick diameter between the tides. I have seen pilings supported by the docks they were supposedly supporting.

Depth

Is it sufficient? Many marinas really do not know for certain the depth at the slip you will be put in. Allow for extreme spring tides or you will find yourself resting on the bottom. Some will also offer a discount if you can fit into a spot where no one else can float.

Noise

Does a charter fleet of headboats blast through at sunrise on a daily basis? Will commercial fisherman fire up their dry stack Jimmies in the pre-dawn hours? How about a ferry that churns up a killer wake on a regular schedule? If in doubt ask.

Security

Does the marina allow unmonitored access to the marina docks? How is it enforced? By a dead word sign? Or by the marina staff? If there is a restaurant or other public facility in the marina there will be lots of gawkers walking by. It also creates a situation where unsavory types can hide in the general flow while they check out your boat.

Pets

Are leash laws enforced? What do you do if your neighbor has a dog that barks all day long? Do cats roam and kill every bird and insect-eating lizard they can find? If you have a dog on board, where will you walk it?

Electricity

Some charge a flat rate, others meter. If you are a high user, the flat-rate method may appeal to you, but if not, you will be paying a premium for the comforting hum of your neighbors air conditioning. Is the service enough for you? Will your plugs fit or will you have to buy adaptors? What is the voltage? I have seen marinas where the end-of-the-line voltage drops low enough to cause serious problems. Ask — and if it's important to you, make sure with a voltmeter. It takes less time than replacing a burned out air conditioner.

Telephone & Cable Access

Sometimes an apparently close phone box or cable outlet is full or otherwise unusable and extra cost will be incurred. Make sure the marina will guarantee that hookups are usable. Also check with the local phone and cable company and find out their installation fees. You are going to have to contact them anyway, so find out now. The fees vary and some are quite high. At the least you will know what you are getting into.

Water

Not all potable water is drinkable. Just because it meets "safety standards" does not mean it's tasty. A simple sip and sniff will tell. Try it at air temperature out of the tap by your prospective slip, if you really want to know.

While we are on the subject, if you're in northern climes, will the water be running throughout the winter? If not, how will you fill your tanks? And how about the water you'll be floating in? Is it likely to freeze?

Privacy

Will your boat be slipped next to another liveaboard? If so, cockpit privacy will be severely compromised. In some marinas liveaboards are slipped chock-a-block and have less "air space" than most inner city dwellers. If your neighbor likes his television, music or conversations louder than you would like, your serenity may be taxed.

Head & Showers

I have seen them range from those you would not want to walk into dirty to those you felt dirtier after walking out. A spot check will reveal a lot. If you plan on using them on a regular basis, is there sufficient number of stalls for the population? How far will you have to walk to the head? Holding tanks are the rule in most inland U.S. waters and using the shore facilities in all but inclement weather will reduce holding tank bloat. What provisions does the marina have for pump-outs? Do they come to the boat? Or do you have to move the boat to the pump? How much is charged for this service?

Access to Shopping

Where are the nearest supermarket and hardware stores? Will you have to buy a car, bike it, or can you walk? Some marinas offer a courtesy car or run a regular shuttle for shopping. Some cities actually have decent public transport. Check it out and figure this in to the cost of your stay.

Laundry

Do the machines appear to be well maintained? A ragged out-of-order sign is a tip to make note of. Is the space clean? How pricey are they? Do they require tokens? Tokens discourage the general public from using them.

Vermin

In the islands they are known as "mahogany birds;" in Florida they're referred to as "palmetto bugs;" up north they're called "roaches." Rodents can also be a problem. From my experience I know any of the above can wreak havoc with the provisions. When your furry little guest uses shreds of your spinnaker or gennie to make its nest, it will cost you big bucks. If your boat is going to be near a field of rarely mowed grass or a poorly managed trash facility, you're likely to have the patter of little feet disturb your slumber. The closer you are, the better your chances of acquiring these pets. Screening can help, but pie plates on your lines are a joke. To some species a leap of couple of feet is nothing when the hungry critter is looking for a home.

I've probably left out some things important to you. Add them to the list. Very rarely will you find a marina that fits all your needs — we never have — but some will come close. Expect to compromise. The friendliness factor will cover a lot of faults. If you have investigated, at the very least you will know what you are buying. When you plunk down your bucks for a tie-up you are the consumer. You are buying more than a tie-up, you are buying safety, comfort and convenience. *Caveat emptor* — let the buyer "be aware"!

"Just do it! Life's too short to wait until everything is perfect. Living aboard makes you realize what living is all about."

– Chris Caldwell

These are a Few of our Favorite Things

Jay Knoll

Making the transition from weekender/vacationer to full-time liveaboard cruiser involves a lot of change, not only to the boat, but yourself as well. Too often in our preparation we focus on those things we have to do to the yacht to make it seaworthy and comfortable. While these preparations are certainly necessary, they will only assure you a safe and uneventful trip. As you prepare to cast off you should not overlook those non-boating items which can ease and enhance life afloat. In many instances we all "make do" when our only sailing is weekends and vacation. We want our boats to be as simple as possible to maintain so we can maximize our time on the water. Lugging extra gear between home and boat is a drag when time is a premium. However, your perspective will change when your boat becomes your fulltime home.

You may have revised your budget and planned for a simpler way of life, but frugal doesn't have to mean spartan and simple doesn't have to mean uncomfortable. Living aboard means having fewer things, but those things should be chosen well, to satisfy, please and last. Here Jay Knoll describes how he and his wife, Linda, turned their boat from a weekend camper into a fulltime home.

Unfortunately, as all of us with disappearing waterlines know, space onboard is limited. We can't take along everything. The presence of certain "favorite things" can ease the mind, soothe the spirit and enhance your cruising experience while you are away from home port.

What then, are those favorite things we bring along on *Simple Gifts* as we head south? We've grouped them in certain broad categories to stimulate your own thinking, it is unlikely that what is important to us will be important to you. But, here's *our* list!

Home

Bedspread

The forepeak looks a bit more colorful and "pulled together" when the double bunk is made up with our favorite lightweight quilt. Not only does it provide a home-like look, its light weight makes it the perfect alternative to a blanket when the nighttime temperatures fall into the range when a sheet isn't enough and a blanket is too warm. Be careful with your selection. We brought along a favorite handmade quilt. It was beautiful and fit our requirements perfectly, except that its all cotton construction meant that it attracted moisture. Even with frequent airing out, it began to smell musty and we feared an onslaught of mildew. After sending it home for cleaning and storage, we made a duvet cover out of two colorful sheets. Now we can vary the spread's insulating value according to the temperature. In warm climes we use it empty, in cooler weather a lightweight blanket goes inside, and for cold fall and winter nights an unzipped sleeping bag turns it into a wonderful comforter.

Cabin pillows

Boat berths are notorious for poor seating. The seats are often too deep to provide comfort when eating at the table and the rigid backs are unforgiving when one is cabin bound for prolonged periods. Our solution is four colorful throw pillows chosen to contrast with our upholstery. Not only do they provide greater comfort when seated, but they provide a welcome splash of color below. We are so pleased with them that we are thinking of making several additional bolsters with zippers to use for storing our out of season sleeping bags and sweaters. This will provide additional seating flexibility plus free up locker storage space.

Wall-to-wall carpeting

Our cabin sole, a teak and holly plywood common on many boats, was a joy to behold, but previous cruising experience taught us that is could be slippery in wet weather and cold when the air/sea temperature dropped below 50°. Our solution was to purchase a neutral, tight-weave olefin remnant which the salesperson assured us could be impervious to a high-humidity environment. We cut a paper pattern of the cabin sole and trimmed the remnant to fit. An application of seam sealer assured that the edges wouldn't unravel. Since the carpet fits tightly against all bulkheads it is impossible for it to slip; no further fastening is necessary. We made two smaller rugs from the same remnant which we placed in the galley and at the foot of the companionway ladder. These bear the brunt of the high traffic/spill area and are easily removed for shaking over the side. Several strips of Velcro (hook side) assure that they don't slip. Not only have we warmed the cabin in cold weather, the light color (almost sand) brightens up the cabin and improves the acoustics. We are delighted with the effect, as was one of our cruising friends who cautioned us to guard against the carpet becoming laden with salt from the sea air and then wicking water out of the humid air. We haven't seen this happen yet, but we will be on our guard and will remove it occasionally hose it down and let it dry in the sun before replacing it.

Holiday decorations

Holidays away from home and family can be difficult, in spite of gatherings with newfound cruising friends. We brought along a few treasured holiday decorations which helped us maintain the "specialness" of the holiday season. Our stockings, formerly hung on the mantel at home, graced the bulkhead alongside our cabin heater. A few yards of ribbon and several handfuls of decorations yielded a garland which brightened the cabin when it was hung from port to port. A friend surprised us with a set of battery operated lights which we used to light up the miniature tree we found along the way. Sharing Christmas celebrations with our new friends was wonderful, and it became more special when we saw how festive the boat looked. Similarly, tucking two Halloween masks aboard gave us the opportunity to go trick or treating by dinghy, and causing squeals of laughter when we popped out of the hatch when a handful of kids came by in their dinghy.

Galley

For us, food takes on a greater significance than, perhaps, it did when we lived ashore. Not only do you do more cooking aboard, but getting together with other cruisers is an important element of socializing on the water. So, careful additions to the galley equipment can enhance the dining experience.

Stovetop toaster

Breakfast isn't complete without a good piece of toast or a nicely browned English muffin. Unfortunately, stovetop toasters are hardly known for the effectiveness. After many tries with various sheet-metal versions, and a most unsatisfactory attempt to make toast in the frying pan, a cruising friend introduced us

to our current toaster. It's a simple contraption consisting of a square cast iron base and a rack which sits above. Once the unit is heated (about two minutes on high) you can turn out a piece of toast in a shorter time than the electric version at home. You don't have to collapse it for storage, and it's small (4 x 4 x $\frac{1}{2}$) making stowing a cinch. We haven't seen one in a store for years, but a careful examination of ours indicates that the manufacturer was H.E. Bremer Mfg., Milwaukee, Wisconsin.

Stoneware dishes/wine glasses

Plastic has its place on a boat, especially in rough weather and when dining in the cockpit or on the beach. However, for most of our meals we prefer eating off stoneware dishes and drinking wine from glass goblets. Not only does the food stay warmer (especially when the dishes have been warmed) but the whole dining experience is enhanced when the dishes are like those at home. We had a special storage rack built for them and have never had a breakage problem, other than an occasional wine glass fatality. Now, we don't bring glassware above decks.

Waffle iron

A simple way to make an elegant breakfast is to have a waffle iron aboard! We found a stovetop version in a kitchen shop several years ago. Its small size allows us to slip it in the back of a locker, where it is easily accessible for impromptu entertaining. Inviting cruising friends over for breakfast is a welcome change from the cocktail party/potluck beach dinner circuit. Our guests get quite a kick out of something which is so simple, but out of the ordinary.

Entertainment

Television

Yep, we admit it, there are programs on television we enjoy. So, we brought along a small TV which will work on 12 volts. We find that we use it when we are in port and are tired of socializing or reading. And, if you are concerned about the weather, you can often find a weather summary for pilots broadcast on the public broadcasting channel early in the morning which is much more detailed than anything you will get on the regular television channels.

CD player

We purchased a car CD player and installed it in place of a weary cassette player we had aboard. The CDs are not damaged by the salt air (or the saltwater in one unfortunate circumstance) and take up less space than cassettes — especially if you use the CD holders which allow you to leave the plastic jewel boxes behind. Music adds that "special touch" in many occasions.

Touring

Even though we are sailing, we don't want to miss the attractions on land. Bringing along a few "land-based" items can make the trip more interesting.

Atlas/almanac

Nautical charts don't give enough detail for you to understand what's going on past the shoreline. We brought along a road atlas on our cruise. Not only did it give us better detail of the cities we visited, but helped us plan some interior "land cruises" when we rented a car. We also brought along an almanac to help answer those crazy questions that occur when you are sitting around the cockpit discussing life and the world at large.

Dressy clothes

Most of the time, your sailing clothes will suffice in any social situation you are likely to encounter, but there are times when you will want to look your best. Or, a special dressy event will arise and you won't be able to attend unless you've got the proper wardrobe. Just slip a blue blazer, a couple of dress shirts, and a tie

The question of how to minimize reminded me of my pre-living aboard days. While on a visit, my mother helped with laundry and ironed my shirts. Upon completion she exclaimed, "Do you know you have 27 shirts here?" to which I replied, "The rest must be at the dry cleaners."

That was over three years ago and while my current job requires me to dress in business attire, I have reduced my wardrobe considerably. Still, suits do take up more room than jeans and T-shirts. I tend to leave clothes with the dry cleaners for longer periods of time rather than squeezing freshly pressed items into a full locker. Casual days (known as "beans for jeans" day on which my employer allows casual attire on Fridays in exchange for bringing in canned goods for local charities) helps reduce clothing as well as the galley storage.

Actually, you'd be surprisd how quickly you prioritize when you have limited space. I have a laptop computer with a laptop printer. I sold all three of my TVs and both of my VCRs and purchased a small TV/VCR combination unit. I can't save all my magazines as I used to, which forces me to read more quickly or toss – *Living Aboard* exempted, of course. My only excess is compact disks. I just couldn't part with all my music variation and as such will put up with the ribbing I receive from other boaters about such decadence.

I also must admit that I still rent a storage area which holds furniture, coats, toys, and much miscellaneous "just in case" I changed my mind. I'm getting ready to liquidate nearly all the contents in yet another garage sale, so if anyone wants a good deal on some clean shirts . . .

– *Stephanie Strong,*
aboard Airhead,
Philadelphia, Pennsylvania

or two in a zippered clothing bag and tuck it in the hanging locker. The first mate can slip in a dress or two, and you've got it made! We were glad we had our "fancy duds" aboard when a friend offered to take us to dinner at the Bahamian Club in Nassau — if I hadn't had a coat and tie, we would not have been admitted to the restaurant.

So, when you are planning your cruise, take a break from the boat equipment catalogs and look around your home. Take along a few special things of your own. Making your boat more like your home will make your cruise more enjoyable. And you can bask in your friends' admiration as they say how comfortable your boat feels as they come below.

Our First Year Aboard

We Did It – But It Wasn't Easy

John Mason

We have just completed our first year of living aboard our Fast Passage 39 sailboat *Wanderstar*.

We had been planning a multi-year cruise, possibly including a circumnavigation, for several years. I had every intention of retiring at the first possible moment — June 1995, when I turned 55 — but ended up working an extra year for my company's convenience. I retired and we moved aboard, giving up our shore residence, on the same day: June 30, 1996.

Change of any kind can be difficult, and moving onto a boat is no exception. It was a big adjustment and took some time, but John Mason eventually came to appreciate the special pleasures of living aboard.

Background

Our background is we are reasonably experienced cruising sailors with a little racing experience. We owned a 1969 Swan 36 for 14 years, which we cruised through the Caribbean and the Panama Canal to Los Angeles, and extensively in southern California. Prior to that I owned a Columbia Challenger 24' sloop which I cruised around southern California for several years. We moved the Swan to the Chesapeake by truck in 1985, and cruised there for awhile. We sold the Swan in 1988 and had not sailed until we purchased *Wanderstar*.

We purchased our boat in 1995 as a "turnkey" boat, ready to set sail for bluewater ports immediately. A few practical factors intruded, causing us to delay the bluewater part for a year. These factors were: one, adapting to the liveaboard lifestyle took more time than expected; two, the boat was not truly ready to go; and three, we had a lot to learn about our boat.

Adapting to the Lifestyle

Stepping aboard our relatively new (to us) boat and setting out did not happen quite like we planned. We had problems to solve. There were far too many possessions still in hand (aboard, in a storage shed, and in vehicles); we needed to work out certain living processes (home address, taxes, mail, finances and "household living"), and we had to learn to operate our new boat while living aboard.

Possessions Panic

A boat of any reasonable size for a two-person crew has a very limited volume. We all know this, but our abrupt transition from house to boat was not smooth. We had already downscaled when we sold our house in northern Virginia and moved to a smaller, rented house in Stafford, Virginia. Prior to my retirement, I think we disposed of about 70% (by weight) of our possessions, and put the bulk of the remaining treasures into commercial storage. We also rented a small room in an outbuilding from my sister in Pensacola, Florida, which we use for unwanted boat gear and items which did not make it into the commercial storage.

John and Diane Mason

Before moving aboard we stashed stuff everywhere. The boat was chock full, totally inoperable. We rented a storage shed in Deltaville, Virginia, where the boat was berthed, and this was full to the roof. We still had two vehicles, one a full-size pickup truck, and these were full too. It took us two months to solve this by trashing treasures, donating items to charity, and selling the bigger items (we had four dinghies, for example). By the end of August we were able to get rid of the storage shed and operate the boat. We later sold the truck.

Living Aboard

We established two home addresses — an official tax home using my sister's address for IRS, ham license, driver's licenses, etc., and a mailing address using Voyager's Services in Islamorada, Florida (providing excellent service, by the way). We did not want to burden my sister with the mail and we find Voyager's Services to be ideal for this. We became legal Florida residents in Santa Rosa County and pay all applicable Florida taxes including boat registrations and intangibles tax, but no income tax.

It takes awhile to get used to living in the small space. Cooking, sleeping, and maintenance all take on a new (tight) dimension. Stowage is a big problem; knowing where you stowed an item is another. Some facts of life become clear though. There is never enough room on a boat for the things you want and need. Even the smallest job will create a colossal mess. Anything you want is behind or under three layers of other things, or you took it off to save space. The "list" always grows — a very good day is when more comes off than goes on it. You are never completely ready. Tasks, however small in appearance, grow to vast proportions as you have to uncover things, find things, move things, order things. Murphy is alive and well. We are still working on this, and will be for years.

Finances

Everyone has their own approach and their own limitations. Like many cruisers, we are living on investments. We do not plan to work. We have several cash and credit cards intended to cover all situations. I track all our expenditures very carefully with a series of spreadsheets, and project our budget for three years ahead. So far so good.

Cost is a function of mode. I would characterize our mode so far as relatively infrequent moves (every few months) between long stays in marinas. We have worked our way down the East Coast from Virginia to Titusville, Florida, but did not get away to the southern Caribbean as planned.

I tracked costs in 16 categories: personal costs, boat repairs and maintenance, food, transportation, boat capital improvements, boat accessories, taxes (non-boat), dockage, boat taxes and fees, boat insurance, medical, communications, information, tools, fuel and oil, and propane.

Our largest cost category was the category I termed "personal" — costs associated with ourselves including clothing, scuba gear, cameras, computers, film, entertainment, motel fees, etc. (but not including food or medical). Our second costliest item was boat repairs and maintenance; the third largest was food; fourth was transportation (vehicle maintenance, insurance, gasoline, air fares, taxi, car rentals, etc.); fifth was boat capital improvements (new attachments such as a watermaker, additional battery bank, etc.); and sixth was boat and cruise accessories (binoculars, hand-held radios, etc.).

Boat costs are highly specific to the boat in question. We had a high initial "pulse" of costs associated with capital improvements (things added and attached to the boat such as a watermaker, new sails, sail cover, etc.) and accessories (things not attached such as hand-held GPS, VHF, binoculars, etc.). Later we had a pulse of repair costs. Diesel fuel and propane have been negligible costs so far. I expect — and depend on — our costs to drop considerably when we finally dispose of the remaining car and get away from the continental United States.

Operating the Boat

Our biggest impediment to sailing the boat was and is the stowage problem.

Once this was somewhat under control, inertia got in the way. To leave a comfortable slip requires yet more stowage, finding the sailing gear, and unplugging water, power, phone, TV cable, etc. In Deltaville we found the tides another hindrance; the water was so shallow we only had narrow windows for movement. You have to force yourself to get the boat moving, because you must learn the boat and shake it down. This is a cruising issue, not a liveaboard issue.

Another issue to contend with was our learning the boat, personal readiness. We purchased an unfamiliar boat, somewhat larger and more complex than boats we had owned before, and were rusty with regard to our sailing skills. Those of you who cruise on a boat you have owned for years will not have this problem, but a lot of people we have met along the way started as we did with an unfamiliar boat.

Boat handling of our 28,000 lb. (as weighed; design displacement is 22,000 lbs.) 39-footer is much different than was our 14,000-lb. 36-foot Swan. Switching from the tiller on the Swan to a wheel added another discomfort. In fact, I still dislike wheel steering. The cutter rig added a new dimension (no more fast tacking; the cutter stay interferes with the jib), as did the new-to-us roller reefing and aft-led halyards. The boat has a number of systems we had to learn (radar, depth sounder, wind instruments, GPS, Loran, SSB, below-decks autopilot, steering vane, and manual alternator control). The engine controls on

"All I have found out that I couldn't get rid of was family pictures. People mean more than 'stuff' and the boxes we keep it in."

– Louise, aboard Caper

the pedestal were unfamiliar, with throttle and shift feeling and looking alike causing me some short-term confusion as to which was which. Even ordinary systems such as stove, lights and pumps had to be checked out and learned before we could cruise in confidence. The engine had to be operated for awhile to learn what was a normal sound and what was not. I had to get through periodic maintenance items such as filter changes and fuel system bleeding. The bottom line is we had to sail, power, and otherwise operate the boat and all its gear for quite a few hours before we felt we could trust it and ourselves for the more ambitious passages. After one year, many miles of waterway motoring, and one 300-mile offshore sailing passage, we are comfortable with the boat and ready for our next step.

This low-profile operational phase was also necessary to flush out problems with the boat.

Life has been one long vacation since we moved aboard. We've had a few mishaps (Mr. Kitty, Buddy, Farberware, and the cell phone have all fallen into the water at least once) but for the most part it's been an adventure. Here are our most frequently asked questions:

- Why did you move on board? (A better question would be "why not?")

- Are you both working? (So far.)

- How do you sleep/cook/eat with all that rocking? (It doesn't rock except when it's underway.)

- To Tom: How did you convince your wife to move aboard? (Actually, she convinced him.)

- What does Justin think of it? (In his words – "cooool.")

- What did you do with your house and all your stuff? (We rented the house and most of our belongings were either stored or given away.)

- Isn't the boat too small? (A boat is always too small.)

- Will you be buying a bigger boat? (Most definitely.)

- What about the dog and cat? (They love it here – we have great neighbors that watch them when we're away.)

- What do you do when it rains? (The same thing you do – stay indoors.)

- Does it get cold? (Outside yes, inside we just turn on the heater.)

- Will you be moving back to your house? (No.)

- What's the hardest thing about living on your boat? (Leaving it.)

- What's the best thing about living on your boat? (The view – we never tire of the sunrises, wildlife and sunsets.)

– The Bambergs . . . Tom, Cecilia, Justin, Buddy & Mr. Kitty, aboard *Justavacation*, Huntington Beach, California

Boat Readiness

We purchased our boat as a turnkey item. The boat had been lovingly maintained by the previous owners and the survey revealed no real flaws. A few items slipped by — a failed pump for the diesel heater, a bad wire to a spreader light, and a really out-of-bed pitch setting on the Max-Prop — but on the whole everything worked. This boat had been extensively cruised throughout the Caribbean by the previous owners, but had been lightly used for the last few years. When we moved aboard and began using everything daily, we flushed out a lot of incipient failures (most aggravating were leaks from the engine fuel injection pump and a leak in the exhaust system).

We also identified a number of changes and improvements we wanted such as new batteries, a different battery charge setup, a different bilge pump arrangement, and a total redo of the waste system. The preceding is hardly a complete list of the over 100 action items identified and worked, or of the 50 or so left! Most were individually very small tasks — adding five Hella fans, adding lights, rewiring systems — but in the aggregate they were, and continue to be, a lot of work. At the moment I judge the boat ready for limited cruising in the Caribbean, but not for a Panama to Marquesas passage. We continue to work.

Our Overall Assessment

One key question about this lifestyle is "do you like it?" My wife took all of 20 minutes to adapt and never looked back. I had a few more problems with it. About six weeks into living aboard — after suffering through Hurricane Bertha, living in a non-air-conditioned boat in the hot and humid Chesapeake summer, and having my head down in the stowage and maintenance problems — I would have done anything to return to shorebound normalcy. We had not sailed even one day at this point, and it was not fun.

But with time the expected benefits of the lifestyle appeared. Once we began sailing the Chesapeake and moving down the ICW we could enjoy the boating, and we began to meet the really great people of the water world. We have found there is no better way to see the aquatic life, wild and otherwise, than to live on a boat. By the time we reached Titusville the boat problems were under control and I was really enjoying myself. We are both looking forward to some bluewater cruising after the current hurricane season ends; in the meantime we will stay in Titusville and just "live aboard."

That First Day

Rita Burton

Let me introduce myself. I'm the new kid on the dock. (I use the term "kid" loosely.) I am another woman who has succumbed to her husband's dream of living aboard a sailboat with the intent of travel and adventure. You could easily recognize me on the dock that first day. I was the one who looked a little green. I was also the one who said my prayers continuously as I walked the two board plank back and forth onto our 36-foot tri-cabin Morgan. The prayers weren't all because of my anxiety. I had great grievance and question as to why I was present in Texas, on a boat, in the beginning of winter. My husband was the natural target of this grievance. I knew God could forgive him, but I wasn't sure I could.

Will you make it through the first days of living aboard?

Sure – and you may even come to forgive your mate.

Like everyone else who begins the "boat" adventure, choosing the right name was as important to us as naming our first child. Theater, art and music have played an important role in our early courtship and marriage of thirty-four years. We chose the name *My Fair Lady*. We even found our own Mr. (Joe) Higgins in our broker here at Watergate Yacht Center in Clear Lake Shores, Houston.

Winters are relatively mild in the Houston area. The first night onboard was calm. We had heaters going so the aft cabin was comfortable. The second night wasn't bad either. But then initiation day arrived and we had one of those "northerlies" with winds around twenty-five miles per hour. It rained five inches on our third night onboard. We leaked some, but nothing compared to other boats around us. I was beginning to trust our new home.

However, we had another taste of bitter winds that brought low tide. The hardest day for me yet, severe north winds arrived on the day of the Christmas boat parade. Winds were gusting up to thirty-five miles an hour. Temperatures were down in the thirties. The water in our boat slip had decreased by four to five feet. I felt like a chimpanzee as I groped, balanced, prayed and climbed off and on our "Lady." Hal, my husband, says I have become much more agile since then.

I would be remiss if I didn't say that more than once I shared the same vision with my husband for the same adventure — and travel. Travel will come a little later when we've completed some upgrading on our "Lady." First things first, however, and for now living aboard is in the first order of things. At least today I can breath more comfortably. The winds are quiet at dockside. The temperatures are in the fifties. I've taken that first step of moving onboard. I've forgiven my husband. I've lived through that first day!

We have a "head specialist" at Watergate Yacht Center. The boss and his wife/assistant shuttle around the marina in *Pee Wee*. Proudly they fly their banner which bears the image of a skunk and their motto, "We'll take all . . . you have!" Coast Guard law states we cannot pour waste overboard. This is how it should be. We don't have our holding tanks installed yet, so we have to use the marina heads — (bathrooms.) To have good thoughts on one of my many trips to the local "head" is an accomplishment.

Still, while returning from one of those trips, I am enchanted with the notion that I belong in this environment. The winds aren't up to the usual thirty- or forty-mile-per-hour torrents they have been over the last couple of weeks. The gusts now are down to fifteen to twenty-five miles an hour, although the temperature must be dropping to freezing. As I look out over the marina, boats bob and halyards clank against their mast. Most liveaboards here are up at the restaurant-bar watching the Super Bowl. If I were to fall overboard, no one would notice. They are engrossed in the big game. It's a lonely round-trip up to "ye old head." Yet, for the first time I could believe my thoughts: "I belong here; this is my environment." We've begun the transition.

It is strange what joy little accomplishments can give. During this past month I purchased twenty-six checkered placemats with attached napkins. I found these on sale for a dollar each: red and white checks for the saloon (dining area) and blue and white checks for the after cabin. I hand stitched them; pleated them; then, joyfully hung them as curtains over all the port holes. With the addition of a red and white checkered tablecloth our saloon looks like a little Italian Restaurant! This is appropriate as we always sought out such hideaways in our travels through the years. We are also having carpentry done in the aft cabin to give us more storage. At the Big Sur Waterbed display we found a full-sized bed that measured seventy-two inches long and fifty-four inches wide. With some adjustment to our after cabin, this mattress will fit. We will insert the waveless water tubes. After some weeks onboard we decided we can go a little longer without a refrigerator and in its place have a good bed.

Some boats are velvet; ours is gingham. This thirty-six-foot Morgan Out Islander is a most practical boat for a couple who want to live aboard. At first glance she isn't luxurious. She is inviting and comfortable. We continue to find many little nooks and hiding places for storage. The forward V-berth has become just as inviting for rest as the after cabin. The Out Islander was designed for charter in the Bahamas. The thirty-six foot was eventually considered a little small for two couples. Thus, the forty-one foot became the popular choice for charter companies. However, this thirty-six foot gem is suitable for us.

Every decision we make in life has a price. We pay, either willingly or as a by-product of our choices. A part of our choice to live aboard included giving up home and a type of security. I recall the beauty of our condo, but, I also recall the passive environment that encompassed our life. Our choices there were really a reaction to the choices others around us made. We bent and complied so as to not disrupt our lives. Our greatest hold was family and that is our greatest price. We no longer offer our children a "home base." We offer them, instead, a part of our great adventure.

A man there was, Though some would think him mad, The more he cast away, The more he had.

– Pilgrim's Progress

The winds are still blowing. The marina appears abandoned. I sit alone in our cozy saloon draped in gingham and I feel at home. The winter is almost over. Tomorrow brings the promise of spring. I can look back over the past few weeks and believe that the hardest times are past.

- 5 -

FAMILY MATTERS
Living Aboard with Kids & Pets

Moving aboard is a big decision for anyone, but things really get complicated when children are involved. Parents who are faced with that decision have many questions: What will the kids miss? What will they gain? Will closer family ties compensate for leaving behind that best friend? And what about their education? Will college admissions officers understand that the kid who studied biology on a boat has firsthand knowledge that can't be learned in a lab?

Families who raise children aboard swear there is no other way to do it. These "boat-schooled" kids learn to be curious, independent, responsible, and above all they're not addicted to television. Furthermore, a 1999 study by the Home School Legal Defense Association revealed that homeschooled children score well above the national median on standardized tests. Experts attribute the home-schoolers' success in large part to their family situations. We would add that boat-schooled children have the extra advantage of the rich experiences that come with living aboard.

Family pets are another issue. Cats generally do very well and, in fact, cats aboard ships are a time-honored tradition. Dogs, however, take some special accommodation, which, if you are cruising, may be a mild understatement. Michael Beattie and his wife, Layne Goldman, cruise with their dogs, Emma and Debs, and he says that there are days when he wants to send the pair of them right off the planet. But most of the time Emma and Debs enrich their lives and their cruise. So who among us could leave behind their best friend and loyal member of the family? Not me, and I bet not you either.

In this section experienced liveaboards share what they have learned about the complicated matter of family life aboard a boat.

The Family
That Sails Together . . .

Lisa Odaffer

You live on a boat?! How can you possibly do that with children? Aren't you afraid that they'll drown? How do you all get along in such a small space? My husband and I with our three sons — Alex (age 11), Jamie (age 21 months), and John (age 8 months) — live aboard our Hardin 45 ketch *Blue Heaven* at Fortman Marina in Alameda, California. We have been living aboard since the kids were born; they have never known any other home. As a stay-at-home mom, keeping our children safe and happy is my top priority every day.

Living aboard seems to bring families closer to each other. That's been the experience of Lisa Odaffer and her family, and this stay-at-home mom wouldn't have it any other way. Here she offers tips on keeping children safe and happy while living aboard.

One of the very first things we dealt with was how to keep the children safe on deck, whether we were underway or at the dock. Babes in arms are okay, but only in the cockpit or down below. This works only when you have enough crew to devote one adult to the full-time holding of the baby. This means no line handling, lunch making, or taking responsibility for more than one child. When this isn't possible, we secure the carseat under the dodger. The baby is OK with this as long as he can see us and has some toys attached to his seat.

All of this goes out the window, of course, when they learn to walk. At first we tried to keep our toddler in a life jacket whenever he was on deck, but we had a hard time finding one that didn't choke him when it was put on correctly. Besides, the extra weight made him so top-heavy that he was always falling over and bumping himself on the head. We finally found our answer in a child-size sailing harness made by West Marine Products. The harness hooks to a 6-foot tether (sold separately) that we attach to the binnacle. This gives him just enough lead to throw his toys, our keys, etc. into the water, but not enough to jump in after them. Obviously, there is no way we can leave him unattended. My husband and I take turns being responsible for him when he is hooked up; usually, it's whoever isn't steering. If one of us needs to go forward or down below, we look the other in the eye and say "I am leaving, you have the baby watch." The correct response is "I hear you, I have the baby watch." We can never afford to misunderstand who is supposed to be watching the little ones. They are irreplaceable.

Our 11-year-old is a strong swimmer, so we no longer worry about him as long as we are tied to the dock. The main mast makes the world's greatest jungle gym. He loves to have his dad hoist him up in the bosun's chair where he can swing around and watch the world go by. In the summertime, he and his friends use the bowsprit as a diving board and swing Tarzan-style from the main halyard into the water. However, when we are underway he must always wear his life jacket, and in bad weather he gets his own 6-foot tether that hooks from the back of his PFD to wherever on the boat he wants to be. After all, my husband reasons, if we lose him, it's a long time until the next one is old enough to take out the trash.

Down below we have two cabins plus two additional pilot's berths on either side of the main saloon. At first we thought about converting the forward cabin to hold three bunks, but then decided that our oldest son would soon be getting to an age where he would really need his privacy. Having his own room means that Alex has a place to go when he wants to be alone, where he can listen to his own music on his stereo (as loud as he wants — as long as he is wearing his headphones), where he can do his homework in peace, read, and just keep his stuff safe from the ever growing grasp of destructo-toddler.

Keeping the saloon and galley a safe place for Jamie to play was far more challenging. We decided early on (against the predictions of dire consequences from our land-dwelling friends) to teach him to climb up and down the ladder to the main hatch. Blocking it effectively was just too difficult since we ourselves had to go up and down several times a day. When he was smaller, I let him play in the cockpit while I watched because the high seats made an effective playpen barrier. Later, I had to lock the hatch from the inside because he had figured how to climb out. Now the stairs are so ho-hum that he never even bothers with them unless he wants to go somewhere with us.

To keep him in his bed at night, I purchased two Safety 1st brand toddler bedrails. I chose this particular brand because they adjust to two different lengths. One at the long setting and one at the short setting, connected together securely with wire ties so that he wouldn't get pinched between them, were just the right length to make a crib rail that covered the length of his bunk.

His other avenue of escape from bed was over the interior bulkhead that divides the saloon from the galley and into the sink. We solved this problem by having a piece of Lexan cut to extend the wall up to the ceiling of the cabin. This cost us about $50. I suppose this could have been done more cheaply with a piece of sanded plywood, but this way we can still see what he is doing, he can see us and the interior of the boat keeps its airy, open feeling.

Our next problem was his love affair with the galley and everything in it. It didn't take him long to figure out the devices designed to keep the cabinets from flying open while you are underway. So, I spent a couple of days installing those toddler-safe cabinet hooks. If you have kids who won't take no for an answer, be sure to get the two hook kind. A determined toddler can yank the single hook kind open if you give them time enough to work on the problem. This makes me believe that they wouldn't stand up to the kind of shake up your galley will take in bad weather. Do your best to leave at least one locker free for toys and things your kids can play with, preferably as far away from the galley as possible.

No doubt you will also have to watch children swinging about the rigging like monkeys. Your heart may miss a beat or two, but it can rejoice in the knowledge that they are growing up with physical self-confidence, freedom, health and strength.

– Clare Allcard,
The Intricate Art of Living Afloat

One last word about the galley. Even though we have a propane cutoff switch, I was getting nervous about Jamie trying to climb up on the stove. What would happen if one day he did it while the fire was on and my back was turned? There are dozens of companies out there that make baby safety gates of all shapes and sizes. Don't think that just because it's made for a house that you can't find one

that will help to keep your child safe inside your boat. The inconvenience of stepping over the darn thing or of constantly latching and unlatching it is far outweighed by your peace of mind where your child is concerned.

Our current boat has custom cut, wall-to-wall, indoor/outdoor carpeting. I will never go back to bare floors again. It's true that I have to vacuum them almost every day, but the benefits outweigh the work involved. They cushion the inevitable falls, protect the cabin sole from banging toys, soften loud noises, and are much kinder to bare feet. About once a month I drag them up on deck and give them a good scrubbing with a bucket of dish soap and hot water. They take a full sunny afternoon hanging off the booms to dry. At the current rate of wear, I anticipate that we will probably get about three years of use out of them before they need to be replaced. I don't think we will be able to afford to have them custom made, so I plan to take the old ones as patterns to a carpet store where I'll try to buy remnants. Whoever made these used a sewing machine to put a bias tape around the edges of each piece so that the carpet wouldn't fray. I think I can probably get a canvasmaker or sailmaker to sew edges for me for a reasonable price.

I highly recommend either a 12-volt TV/VCR or an inverter to run a standard one when you are away from shore power. I'm not saying that this should serve as an all-purpose babysitter, but if you're away from shore power for an extended period, a video in the afternoon can keep the kids from killing each other. Of course, you should stuff every nook and cranny on board with novels and picture books (paperback seems to resist mildew longer and are cheaper to replace when they finally succumb), art supplies, card games (keep these in Ziploc bags to keep out dampness) and any other diversion that your kids show an interest in.

One drawback to living aboard is that no matter how you try, your kids are never going to have enough room to have as much stuff as the other kids at school have. Every trip to the toy store for Christmas or birthdays has me constantly thinking, "If I buy this, where will I put it? What can I get rid of so that I can find room for this?" The way our family has dealt with this problem is to keep toys to a minimum and spend most of our gift money on things that we do together. We take a trip somewhere fun every Christmas and host a great big birthday party every year (not on the boat) and invite all of Alex's friends and classmates. For example, last year we rented the party room at the local ice skating rink. My husband takes lots and lots of pictures and I get them into an album as quickly as possible. The kids like looking at the albums and remembering all of our fun times together more than they ever would have played with a room full of battery-operated, overpriced toys, and our family is closer in the bargain.

We have been planning and saving for a long time. By next fall, we expect to untie the dock lines for good and take our children with us to see the world. As I sit here typing it is raining outside; my husband is working across the table from me. I have our youngest boy on my lap and the other two are alternately wrestling on the floor and watching the Disney Channel (shop around and do your best to find a marina with cable). We are warm and safe and all is well. I wouldn't trade my life for any other.

Baby on Board

Barbara Baur

My husband Lary and I have lived aboard for six years, first on a 27-foot sailboat and now on a 42-foot sailboat. Until we bought the larger boat we really didn't even consider having children, although I have heard of families living on even smaller boats.

We first spent nearly two years trying to adopt an older child. It was frustrating because very few social workers were open to the idea of a child growing up safely on a boat. So we did research in books, articles, letters to editors, etc. We were very close to trying a private adoption when we started a home-based business and adoption was put on the back burner for a while. Not long after that, we were pregnant. But it was worthwhile to spend some time getting together our business. I am very fortunate to be working out of our home, which enables me to spend all day with Wendy, our baby, while working.

Barb and Lary Baur were living aboard when they started their family. They soon learned that with a baby on board they had to "think different."

Be Creative

Just as with any other challenge of living aboard, parents need to enjoy problem solving and using a little creative thinking with children on board. For instance, just because people use highchairs to feed babies in houses doesn't mean you have to have one on board. On a similar note, most people in houses wouldn't even consider hanging a swing in their living room, but they also don't have grab rails on the ceiling for easy attachment and detachment. "Think different" is the phrase of the day.

Our daughter Wendy is 14 months old and we have made a few adjustments to the boat since her arrival. We use a wooden portacrib instead of a regular-size crib. Some advantages of the portacrib are that sheet sizes are readily available and it folds up easily to move or clean. We set up Wendy's crib in the middle of our bed and we sleep on either side. In a Whitby 42, the bed in the aft cabin is quite large allowing this setup. This arrangement worked well for us because we were always aware of the temperature in her room, and were very close for when she awoke at night. A portacrib takes up considerably less room than a full-size crib and the legs do not have to be extended at all.

In the main saloon of our boat, the dinette area converts to a double bed with walls on three sides. I leave this pulled out most of the time and I have constructed a fourth side of fabric and netting to make this bed into a large playpen. The netting is held in place by a solid pole that attaches to the bulkheads on either side. It is very sturdy and large enough that my husband and I also lounge in the playpen to watch television in the evenings. Wendy certainly enjoys the company in her little private world.

Feeding

The advantages of nursing your baby are many and very well documented. In my opinion nursing is the best option for feeding a baby on board. No bottles to mess with, no worrying about sterile nipples, temperature, or water quality. When Wendy cried at night, her needs were met almost instantly. If she needed to be fed, no matter where we were, I could feed her with very little fuss. We exhibit at boat shows sometimes because of our business and it worked out very well not to have to pack bottles, worry about refrigeration, etc. Working mothers have to consider pumping versus formula, but I think that it's worth the extra time and effort to give your baby the only food in the world that is specially designed just for him or her.

Of course nursing doesn't last long and as soon as Wendy showed an interest in solid food, I started grinding food for her. A small hand-operated baby food grinder avoids having to buy canned baby food. There are several types of grinders on the market. I avoided ones with metal parts that might rust. I found it easy to make as little or as much as needed. I also found that if you have a pressure cooker, using it to cook vegetables makes them soft enough to grind very easily in a short time. I also make most of our meals in the pressure cooker — it cooks them quicker and you know there are no extra additives that you may find in canned or instant food.

Helpful Accessories

There are several items that have made our life with Wendy particularly convenient. I suggest looking carefully in catalogs and baby stores. There are many innovative designs these days. I especially like things that have multiple uses.

One is a backpack that can also be used as a stroller. Made by Evenflo, it's called a Hike-N-Roll. It's compact design can be used in the cockpit or below. It's perfect for quick little excursions to the post office or walking the dog. It's light to carry, takes a second to fold or unfold, and even has a pocket in the back for an extra diaper or jacket. When strapped into the stroller, Wendy sits in an upright position that allows her to see everything that's going on. It has two wheels, which allow it to be pulled like a luggage carrier or pushed like a stroller, but it won't roll on its own if just sitting upright. Of course, she prefers to be carried in the backpack. Squealing with laughter and waving her arms, Wendy loves to see everything from her elevated vantage point. The Hike-N-Roll is light, can easily be handed in and out of a dinghy, fits well in overhead compartments in planes. The Hike-N-Roll certainly makes my life easier.

Another amazing item I found is a dishwasher-safe, adjustable plastic chair by First Years. Because it has no legs, it is designed to be secured to a normal kitchen chair with several straps. The chair is easily disassembled for cleaning or storage. It sits securely in the playpen area or on a settee for feeding with an adjustable tray. We don't have a separate shower stall, so now that Wendy's outgrown her baby bathtub (of which we had a lovely folding model made by Safety 1st that I used in the galley) the plastic feeding chair then gets strapped onto the toilet in the head and we take our showers together. I set up the chair, take my shower, then go get Wendy, strap her into the seat and give her a shower. Naturally I make sure all her clean clothes and new diaper are ready before I start my shower. Having a baby certainly has made me start to think ahead a little bit, especially when planning for little things like taking a shower. For instance, I always check the water tank level and make sure the hot water heater has been on for a while.

Safety

The rule on our boat is that children are not permitted on deck without a life jacket. Some parents may consider this extreme, but on our boat our rules apply to everyone on board. I suggest that even boaters who do not have children of their own should keep a medium-size child's lifejacket on board for guests. I plan to have the inflatable harness-type suspenders before Wendy is permitted to do much walking on deck while underway. This past season she couldn't walk yet and was either in her playpen below or strapped into her backpack secured in the cockpit. The coming summer poses more of a challenge as she will be wearing a harness and life jacket and will not be permitted to leave the cockpit.

The design and layout of the boat is very important. It is important that parents realize the strengths and weaknesses of their particular boat and modify accordingly. We have a center-cockpit ketch, but it is, by no means, the only type of boat a child can live

Wendy laughs as her father Lary marks the mast to show how tall she is around the time of her first birthday.

on. It's good for privacy, but parents need to ensure somehow that children stay below deck at night because of multiple hatches.

Playtime

But children need to have fun, not just rules. We usually keep a couple of fishing rods on board for children as well as items to go crabbing. The dinghy is indispensable as an entertainment center and a good place for kids to start to learn about handling a boat. Help your child set up the dinghy and take it out within sight. They can learn responsibility as well as have fun. A small sailboat or windsurfer can start a child on the basics of sailing, too.

Let the kids take turns steering while the boat is underway (supervised of course), get their opinions on sail trim, and picking destinations. If you have a spare set of charts, let the kids navigate with them. I think an extra set of binoculars is essential with children. They can learn how to respect the tools needed to navigate, as well as identify birds, boats, and faroff points in the distance. The fun and learning experiences possible when boating are really unlimited and most kids will let you know where their interests lie.

Something we started this year and plan to continue is taking a picture of Wendy on her birthday standing on deck next to the main mast. We also marked the mast with a permanent marker to record her growth. We're pretty sure she won't grow past its height of 55 feet off the water.

There are many people who just don't understand the attraction of living aboard, let alone raising a child onboard, and will let you know in so many words. However, parenting is about doing what you feel is best for your child. There are safety concerns whenever children are involved in any environment — on land or water. We can't imagine any other life for ourselves or our child. Wendy doesn't know any other life and we feel she'll have a better attitude toward the world and its limited resources as a result of her upbringing. Sure, it's a little crowded, but I think our boat would feel empty without Wendy on board. ✍

Once Wendy learned to stand, she started to climb. The companionway ladder offered the best hand and foot holds for her little body.

Keeping Vigil on the 'Wendy Watch'

Barbara Baur

When our bouncing baby girl arrived just 20 months before our long-anticipated cruising D-day, many of our family thought we would put the whole crazy idea of cruising behind us. They were wrong. When September 1998 came, we left on time, but with different plans. Our new crew-member rearranged our plans from cruising to the Pacific for the new millennium to cruising the East Coast of the United States for a few years. We knew that Pacific cruising would be a once-in-a-lifetime trip, and we wanted our daughter, Wendy, to have that experience when she was old enough to remember it.

> As Wendy grew from baby to toddler, her needs changed and Barb and Lary adjusted their plans accordingly. By preparing well and taking it slow, cruising with their toddler turned out to be a wonderful experience for everyone.

The first thing we secured was a live-in baby-sitter. Our nephew Joshua had been planning to do at least part of the trip with us long before Wendy ever arrived on the scene. His graduation from high school in June left him flexible for a few months before starting college. Josh was a great extra hand while Lary and I were still working out our cruising rhythm. His main duties were helping with Wendy, but he also stood watches and helped with other boat chores.

We left Toms River, New Jersey, briefly cruised the Chesapeake Bay, made our way down the ICW to the Keys, and arrived in Tampa Bay, Florida, in time for Thanksgiving. Josh went home shortly after Christmas, but along the way, he and Wendy forged a real bond. Wendy still talks about "My Josh," and I think Josh is the only 20-year-old I know who really has a friend that is 3 years old.

But the live-in baby-sitter was only a temporary help. Comparing notes with other cruisers, we have found that cruising with a toddler does change things. For instance, we prefer not to do overnight passages. We've done them but have found that if we are both tired from standing watch all night, neither of us is very alert to keep "Wendy watch." However, we've talked with other cruising parents who prefer night passages while the children are asleep, so it depends on what you are comfortable with.

Keeping your toddler safe while on board is the most important thing, of course, but a toddler's happiness is only slightly less important. If they aren't playing happily, everyone's well-being can be in jeopardy. I know I can't think straight with a 2-year-old screaming in the background. This is a time in a child's life when they learn by play, and if a toddler is cruising, it's also a great opportunity for parents to interact with their child. Consider that when you are cruising, it's all quality time. The little one can see Mom and Dad working together side by side, running the boat as well as spending some time with him or her.

Before you get too far, you have to face one grim fact — your pristine, Bristol-fashion yacht is going to become a playground. Better get used to it. I've put off recovering my interior cushions for a few years yet, thanks to Wendy. Toddlers are notoriously messy eaters, and accidents do happen. During the day when we are underway, the main saloon is Wendy's area, and it's usually ankle deep in toys. Definitely not shipshape, but it keeps her happy. She is blockaded into this area with a collapsible Graco netting baby gate, and for the most part, we try to keep the mess confined with her.

When in her "side," as she calls it, Wendy is pretty contented most of the time; she has all her toys and books, and at selected times, she can watch TV, either children's programs on a local PBS station or one of her videotapes. She has a few toy boxes, which are transformed by her imagination into all kinds of things, like bathtubs, boats, tables, bridges, tents and chairs, especially when used in conjunction with the built-in furniture and movable cushions. We have a small collection of musical instruments we reserve as special toys for times when we don't mind the noise.

When underway, Wendy enjoys the ride, cozy and secure in her car seat.

But you can't keep a toddler in one place all the time, and Wendy loves to be on deck, which means the full attention of one parent. We have lifeline netting in place all around the boat as extra security for both Wendy and our small dog, Sounder, but we never consider the netting a substitute for our diligence. If the boat is at anchor or tied up, Wendy is allowed to walk on deck in a life jacket or stay in the cockpit without it. If we are underway, a harness or life jacket is required in the cockpit, and walking on deck is not permitted at all. We also have the option of securing Wendy into her car seat, which frees both of us to do things. This is usually what we do when under sail, due to the main and jib sheets in the cockpit.

Wendy loves to just walk on deck and look at the ever-changing scenery around us. We learned the hard way that baby-proofing a deck also means not leaving within her reach any items you don't want overboard. Fortunately, we were able to improvise a replacement for the windlass handle that Wendy threw over the side one morning. Now we're sure to pick up everything before we let Wendy loose.

Sometimes we set up additional activities on deck. We keep a beat-up pair of binoculars in the cockpit and have slowly taught Wendy the proper use of these. She also has a working toy pair of her own. A nice gift from a family member was a toddler swing that we can attach to the mizzen or main boom to give her a nice ride. If it's warm and we're in a calm anchorage, that's the perfect time to set up Wendy's pool on the foredeck. It's one of those inflatable ones with a few

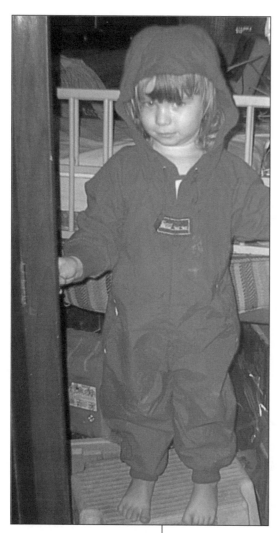

Standing on the steps to her room, the vee berth, Wendy suits up for inclement weather outside.

blow-up toys, perfect for a true water baby. If it's not very calm or we're underway, she can play in the cockpit with some selected toys in a bucket of seawater — it's kept her amused for hours at a time.

We mostly anchor out, which means using the dinghy. Wendy always wears a life jacket and can nearly climb in and out of the dinghy herself. We have found the handle on her life jacket very valuable at these times. A full rainsuit has also been a great investment in keeping her dry and warm on long dinghy rides in any kind of chop. Anything but the most compact umbrella stroller can be very cumbersome in a dinghy along with three people. Besides the umbrella stroller, we keep a larger stroller with a sunshade and built-in basket for longer walks ashore when we might want to carry some supplies, but that usually involves two trips in our small inflatable.

The messiness has been mentioned, but are there any other disadvantages to cruising with a toddler?

Forget About Going Anywhere Fast

A slower place is easier for the whole family; taking care of a small child and running a boat is a lot of work, so there's no point in pushing things and trying to make unreasonable schedules. Try to see the world through your child's eyes and you'll start to like the slower pace, too. Remember what a great opportunity this is for both of you, enjoy it.

Stopping More Often for Supplies

Potty training is still on the horizon, so disposable diapers are still a necessary staple on board. I just can't even imagine trying to wash cloth diapers on board, let alone how much water it would use. Fresh fruit and milk are important, too. We also use the room-temperature concentrated juice mixes, which means using extra water.

Toddlers Use Power, Too

I mostly refer to running the VCR, TV and lights. Sure, you could try to live without them, but if you are coming into a tricky entrance that requires your full attention, it's nice to keep the child quiet for a half hour with a videotape while you get the boat safe. Don't worry, cruising kids watch much less TV than "land children," and exactly how much is entirely up to you. Then there are lights. When Wendy first started sleeping by herself in the forward cabin, we had to leave on the fluorescent light in her room all night or she would wake up crying. You may be ready to sleep just as the sun goes down, but not your active little crew member, who had a nap while you were thrashing with the sails on deck. You'll be lucky if you can get him or her to just settle in with a book, but in any case, you'll need the lights on.

Constant Diligence

We take turns steering and navigating. The person navigating is on watch with Wendy as well as keeping an eye on the electronics below. This isn't a hard job, but it means keeping her clean, fed and safe, whether she is above or below. Sometimes we play with her or read her a book, sometimes we work on other things while letting her play with her toys or watch TV. For the one on "Wendy watch," Wendy's welfare is the top priority. We take turns so neither of us gets stuck with all the dirty diapers or all the steering in the rain. It's also good for her to see both of us running the boat equally and to know that both her parents can care for her.

The toddler stage is a fun time in a child's life, one in which they are absorbing information at an incredible pace. What better way to give your child a broad view of the world than to take him or her cruising? Any family lucky enough to consider cruising with a child in the toddler stage should prepare well, take it slow and enjoy this wonderful experience. That's what we've done and we don't regret a moment.

We live on a boat, have four kids and home school them. I wouldn't change anything.

We cruised the San Juan Islands twice. Once in a 36' sailboat with a one- and three-year old. Because of the currents, the living space and the rain, we decided if we ever did it again we would do it on a powerboat. So, in 1996 we took our four boys and cruised it in a 50' powerboat. We were there July until January.

The months of November, December and January we were on a dock in La Conner (Washington). It was the year of the horrible snowfall. We went on the free buses to the huge book store in Mt. Vernon. We got involved with a church. The local thrift store let us help work in the store. We had a life off of the boat. My children are very high energy – I let them rollerblade to town. I rollerbladed along with them. The library knew us well.

Big families have very little privacy. I think we all need a balance of alone time, people time and family time. I have made sure that this boat gives each boy his space. The quality and quantity of school work is increased and the bickering is decreased.

It is always good in America to live with less. But make sure the less is practical. Legos never fail. Battery toys do. As do other cruisers, we trade books, clothes and toys. If we were staying in one place, I would rent a pasture and get a pony.

I find my children bring in their own ideas. I follow them up. One of my boys has his own line off the mast. He swings off of it daily. Another boy has a keyboard – he composes music. Within reason, I let them pursue their interests. Children are wonderfully active and that needs to be accommodated.

My boys are now 19, 16, 14, and 7. They love cruising. We are now in the Caribbean.

– *Debra Woolworth, Salinas, Puerto Rico*

Education at Sea
Creating a Floating Classroom

Nellie K. Symm-Gruender & Zachary S. Symm

As the crew of *Rainbow Chaser* began to plan for cruising we realized there were about a million things to consider. With one of the crew members being our son Zachary, 10, soon to be 11, make that 2 million. Zachary's education was high on my list of "tasks to be completed." There were so many things to consider. What homeschool curricula were available? What would the cost be? Would the curriculum be accepted if and when we did return to "regular school"? How could we best transition Zach to homeschool?

Homeschooling requires a big commitment from both the teacher/parent and the student/child. It is a study in dedication and patience. But Nellie Symm-Gruender and Zach Symm agree that it was a gratifying part of their cruising experience.

Zach: *When we first talked about the fact that I would be going to homeschool, I had a hard time imagining how we could have a classroom on the boat. I wondered if I would have to do homework, and how much. My biggest concern was, "would I get recess?"*

At the beginning of Zach's fourth grade year at St. Paul Lutheran School in Austin, Texas, I sat down with his teacher, Ms. Lange, and talked about our plans, and my desire to have this year be a year of transition for both Zach and his class. I hoped to get the entire class involved in our adventure. I next talked to Ms. Tienert who would have been Zach's fifth grade teacher if he remained at the school. I shared with her that I wanted Zach to be an unofficial member of the class through letters, post cards, and video tapes. She agreed that this would be a wonderful opportunity for both the class and Zach.

As I began to investigate schools, one name seemed to consistently come up, the Calvert School in Baltimore, Maryland. One of our friends, Richard Kilgore, had attended Calvert when his family was in South America. Then Gene talked to a young lady while on a plane trip who had never attended "regular school." Her family owned a carnival, and as they traveled from city to city she attended Calvert. Both she and Richard said that they found they were consistently far ahead of the kids who had attended regular school. I then read that Supreme Court Justice Sandra Day O'Connor had attended Calvert. It seemed that I had some pretty good references for the school.

Zach: *When I told my friends that we were planning to live on the boat and sail all over the world, they all said, "Way Cool!" My best friend Damon Faulkner kept ask-*

ing if we would adopt him. Then one day everyone realized that I wouldn't be there for school every day, and we all got sort of sad. We decided we would really miss each other.

Nellie Symm-Gruender and her son and pupil, Zach.

I was soon corresponding with Calvert, and had literature about how the homeschool program worked. As I read the material, it began to sink in just how important an undertaking this was. During my 25 years as a nurse I had taught a trauma nursing class at the college level, and I have lectured nationally on domestic violence. Both, however, were much different than teaching a fifth grade curriculum. I had a handle on the concepts of adult learning, but for elementary school, well, I wasn't so sure. I began to consider the impact that this might have on Zach for the rest of his life, and feelings of inadequacy began to creep into the back of my mind.

Zach: *My mom seemed a whole lot more concerned about being my teacher than I was about having her for a teacher. I thought it was neat that we could be together every day, and that she would be teaching me. One thing was for sure: I wouldn't have to wait very long with my hand up to get a question answered by the teacher.*

In reviewing the literature from Calvert, my questions, and some of my concerns, were answered. The cost would be around $750 a year. This included the curriculum, all books, all supplies, shipping, and enrollment in the Advisory Teacher Program. By having an advisory teacher, Zach would be assigned a single teacher that would grade his progress through the year, give feedback as work was sent in, and offer advice as I needed it. (Advice was the clincher — I knew I'd need it.) With passing grades, Zach would receive a statement of completing the fifth grade at the end of the year. Since the cost was less than the private school tuition we were presently paying, it seemed like a bargain.

The literature stated that the home teacher would have daily plans of what the pupil was to be taught each day, and there were notes on the important aspects of each subject. As Zach and I looked over the plan we saw that he would be studying the same subjects as "regular school." The time needed each day was between four to five hours, and offered a great deal of flexibility. With references, and the promise of advice, I wrote the check, and mailed it in. Zach was enrolled.

Zach: *When I saw what I would be studying, I thought great — "normal" subjects. I knew that when my friends found out I had to only go to school for four hours a day they would really be jealous. Mom decided that she would add Spanish to the lessons* *so we could learn a foreign language together. The kids at my school couldn't start foreign language until the seventh grade.*

To get Zach's class involved in our plans I went to his class as a speaker. We talked about living on the boat, the routes we planned to take, and how Zach would go to school. The kids all took a great interest in what we were going to do. Our next step was to invite Zach's class to the boat for their end-of-the-year trip. We had lunch at the marina and took groups of kids on a sail. Zach got to do tours of the boat, show everyone his berth, and demonstrate his skills as a sailor. The kids were impressed with both the boat and Zach. At the end of the year Zach said many sad good-byes to his friends with promises to write and keep in touch.

Zach: *Saying good-bye to all my friends was the hardest part. I knew I would miss them, even if we did write. I wasn't sure if I would get to make good friends again. I had been with this class since first grade, played basketball with them, and gone to camp with them.*

Fast forward . . . six months of homeschool has been a learning experience for both of us . . .

Zach: *Even in homeschool, some things don't change. I don't like math, reading and science, but I've learned to love history, geography and art. Being the only student in the class is good and bad. Good because you get all the attention, bad because I'm the only person to get called on. I do still miss my friends, but I keep in touch through e-mail and postcards. They sent me a birthday card, and everyone in the class signed it. They also e-mailed me about what each person was doing for the science fair. In homeschool we study things, and I get to see them in real life. When we studied invertebrates, we picked up a cabbagehead (a kind of jelly fish) and looked at it. When we studied latitude and longitude, I looked at the maps we navigate from, and I could help with the navigation. Before we went to each port I studied about the area so I could have background information about it.*

Homeschool is a study in dedication and patience. The general plan is to get up in the morning and do our four to five hours of homeschool. The dedication comes in trying to stick to that. It's hard when the sailing conditions just aren't conducive to sitting or writing — try writing a composition when the toe rail is under water. There's also the call of the outdoors. It can be hard to spend the morning talking about congruent figures when there is turquoise water to swim in, iguanas to see, or reefs to be snorkeled over. We quickly found that it was ever so easy to get behind, with the consequences of doing double work for several days to catch up, or gasp . . . going to school on Saturday.

Patience comes in when either Zach or I lose touch with the teacher/pupil relationship, and slip into the mother/son relationship. Zach, on several occasions has said, "Mooooom, do you have to give me so much homework?" My reply was "I'm your teacher. I only look like your mother." However, being ever the mother, I've been heard to say, "Zach, don't you think it would be better if you did it this way?" ("Better" being my way). So much for independent thinking. I had to learn to allow Zach the opportunity to explore options. On several occasions, Gene, "the principal," as Zach likes to call him in this role, had to intervene. I'm pleased to say that while I did hit some real highs of frustration I never got to the point of throwing the books overboard as one mother did.

In George Town, Bahamas, there were many cruising kids, and we found that most had chosen the Calvert school. One family was using its own curriculum, and another was using material provided by the Canadian government. One mother faced the same challenges we did with the parent vs. teacher problem. In a fit of frustration she enrolled her kids in the local school in George Town just to remind them of what land school was like.

Zach made one especially good friend, David Higgs, from Royal Lion while in George Town. David is from Canada and shares Zach's love of Legos. To keep things simple David's mom Joyce and I would coordinate what time we planned to end school each day. This helped us maintain each child's attention without the interruption of that call on the VHF about what time everyone was meeting at the beach. Since Joyce also has two girls, Jennifer and Susan, she had triple school to do each day.

I am pleased that I have had the opportunity to participate in Zach's education. Despite my initial fears, with the help of a well-written curriculum I feel I have succeeded. Only once when we were studying a new-new math concept did I have to e-mail the school for advice. The answer was returned by e-mail within 24 hours, and we all then understood. I feel as though I have a firm grasp of Zach's many strong points, and the few weak points that need extra attention. A positive aspect of homeschooling is that the flexibility allows us to spend time working on the weaker points. A real benefit that comes from traveling is that real-life experiences go far to enhance the formal education. Seeing other cultures, talking to people from all over the world, and being in constant contact with nature is an education in itself. Zach gets to see science, geography, and math up close and personal.

Zach: *Overall I like homeschool. In regular school I never got a break to go and watch the dolphins play, or see a huge cargo ship passing by. I think I learn more because I don't have to compete with 24 other kids for attention. The other big part of homeschool is going to different places and doing different things. I've gotten to go to the Salvador Dali Museum, see what a conch looks like alive, swim with all kinds of fish, and I got to meet a famous scientist who saves sea turtles. Most kids I know don't know how to operate a dinghy, a single-side band radio, or a VHF radio. I learn something new almost everyday and a lot of it doesn't come from a book!*

As we continue to sail, education at sea has become a gratifying aspect of our traveling. With dedication and a large dose of patience, I think we've done fine. Zach got straight A's on his last report card, and Mom got a big hug from her star pupil.

Here's the "reality" of living aboard with children: *Don't do it!* I yelled that just in case you have a teenager — the time when nailing his/her feet to the bedroom floor is the only rational response. Aside from the difficulty of maneuvering around teenagers nailed in place, what are you going to do with all the stuff they collect for "when I have my own place?" They don't take it with them when they go! They take your good stuff, if, in fact, you have any left. Now, think about teenagers. They travel in droves. There are either none or twenty-five. I suppose you could dedicate a very large dinghy as the "visiting room", but the storage of snacks alone will require another boat. Last, but most importantly, living aboard is far too romantic. You may be home schooling your children, but I don't think that's the kind of education you had in mind.

We started telling our kids years ago, "September 1, we are moving aboard. We will send you postcards: Just left Port Townsend. Had a wonderful time. Not sure where we're going next." And even though we truly thought it would never happen, that summer, at ages 21, 20, and 18, they all grew up and left home. We were aboard by the 1st of October but it took another month to get rid of all the stuff in our five-bedroom house. We love our kids and they're wonderful people, but they all know the spare bedroom is the dinghy. We've successfully done our part in stopping the boomerang generation.

Again, DON'T DO IT! It's way too much fun and if you don't immediately stop exposing your children to the fantastics of boat life, you will find yourself moored across the dock from one of them in their own boat!

Good luck!

– Dione Murray & Thom Permenter
aboard Mine II, *28' Tollycraft*

A Family Affair

Susan Burke

"Mom! There's a mattress in the water right in the middle of the ocean! No, it's a fish! Do you think it's a whale, Dad?"

We were heading toward mainland Mexico out of the Gulf of California, and right at the demarcation line where the Sea of Cortez meets the Pacific Ocean were what we later learned were two huge, basking sharks, placidly "grazing." As we maneuvered our 35-foot Lord Nelson next to one of them, we found they were just about as long as our boat, and we could have touched them if our arms had been long enough. What a wonderful way to learn marine biology — school is fun when it's learning about what's going on all around you.

Ask anyone who lives aboard: Boating families are together families. And you don't have to wait until the kids are out of school – living aboard and cruising is a valuable learning experience.

We have found learning is definitely a family affair, and have used what's been going on all around us as the springboard for our homeschool curriculum as we cruise around with our two children, Tim, 10 and Debbie, 8. We studied Spanish as a family when we traveled around Central America and we learned something about each country we visited. We learned all about how the Panama Canal was built, and how politics and geography contributed to the experience we had going through the canal in the spring of 1991. We read books on the Revolutionary and Civil Wars and the beginnings of our country when we traveled up and down the East Coast and visited many historic sites. We open up the fish we catch before we prepare them for the skillet to see what they've eaten — once we found a seahorse! Almost everything turns out to be a learning experience when you have kids on board.

Neither Brian nor I had any formal teacher training when we set out to go cruising with our kids, then 4 and 6 — I had been an R.N. and Brian is a retired fire captain from Sacramento, California — but we both had a love of learning and a willingness to experience new things (as cruisers do who love this lifestyle); that is surely the basis for success in teaching your kids anywhere.

There is a wealth of material available to anyone wishing to teach children of any age, so that you never have to feel you are on your own or unprepared. We chose not to use a fully prepared curriculum, but there are many fine ones being used by cruising families, especially those who are doing it for only a year or two and want their young ones to fit right back into their peer group grade-level when they return. We used several grade-level workbooks and textbooks for such basic subjects as math and English, but really, the world was our classroom and impetus for learning.

One of our cruising necessities, occupying the place of pride on our dining table, is the Webster's Encyclopedia Unabridged Dictionary. Even in rough weather it rarely gets put away, as we are always using it to look up something or another. Are you making a rather long, boring passage where there's not much to do and you've already had breakfast, and lunch? Get out your Brain Quest question and answer card games and see if the adults can beat the kids at the fifth grade level.

Tim with his dockside friend.

One thing cruising will do for your kids is foster reading. Our kids devour books and often it can be a problem keeping enough books on board (of course there are always those favorites to read over and over). They like popular fiction such as the Hardy Boys and Babysitter's Club series and biographies and classics like *Black Beauty* and *Treasure Island* and *20,000 Leagues Under the Sea.* When we arrive at a new town we always look for these three things: a grocery store, a laundromat and a used bookstore. One of the best we found was in the little town of LaBelle, Florida. Used bookstores are wonderful; you can trade in your old books, saving both money and that precious space your boat limits you to.

Libraries are very good places to relax, to read periodicals and use reference works and computers. The one in Coconut Grove, Florida, had a computer in its children's section with some educational software programs, and we spent a lot of time there because the library was right across the street from the sailing club where we were staying. We would also find school supply stores on our travels — there's an especially good one in Panama City, Florida, within walking distance of the city docks.

In our cruising experience, we were always meeting up with other cruising families with kids, and it didn't really matter what ages they were, there were usually instant friendships. Often we would buddy-boat for awhile with another boat with kids on board. People often ask our kids if they miss not having friends around all the time, but we've found one of the advantages of cruising is that our kids are not so dependent on peer relationships and are able to enjoy people of all ages, both young and old. One of our kid's best friends during our Mexico experience was a retired Canadian single-hander, so don't use this as an excuse not to take your children with you.

The family is more of a unit as you cruise around; you relate to other families and people together almost all the time. You work together and play together, as well as learn together. Our kids get to see Mom and Dad working together as a team as we navigate the waters we pass through, instead of Dad going off to his job, and usually Mom going off to her job, too. The learning they get in cooperative family living is one of the most valuable benefits of cruising your children can have.

Tim and Debbie also have their jobs to do about the boat, and know that they are a vital part of running the boat when we are anchoring, coming in to a dock, etc.; they are able to do more and more as they get older. And even if they're not able to join soccer teams and ride around their neighborhood on bicycles as other kids do, they keep too busy snorkeling and fishing and zooming around in the "family car," the dinghy, to notice much.

We started a "homeschool newsletter" to keep our friends and relatives apprised of where we are and what we're doing; the kids have enjoyed writing articles and stories for that while getting in some practical writing experience. We talk about fractions and measures while cooking together, and learn about latitude and longitude while plotting our courses. Homeschooling on a boat is often very practical.

We do have a small TV, but out at sea and when cruising foreign countries, reception is often variable at best, so we got in the habit of reading aloud before bedtime. Brian read *The Hobbit* while we were cruising in Mexico, and we also got through the whole series of *Little House on the Prairie* and the *Chronicles of Narnia* together. History and science books are also often read aloud. Being just two years apart, the kids can study a lot of the same things, and we find books that are interesting to all of us.

Everywhere we go, we find wonderful museums to tour. Some of our favorites have been: the Air and Space Museum in Pensacola, Florida; Cape Canaveral; the marine museum on Soloman Island in the Chesapeake; the Nautilus submarine in Groton, and Mystic Seaport in Connecticut; Jamestown, Virginia; Plymouth, Massachusetts; and of course, Washington, D.C., where we spent

Debbie, up the mast.

almost three weeks and still didn't see it all.

Our children have added so much to our cruising experience. We're glad we didn't wait until they were grown and gone. Debbie has lived half her life on the boat, and Tim remembers only a bit more about what "living on land" was all about. We have found cruising and home-schooling to be a good experience for all of us, and the times we have stopped and stayed in one place for awhile (here now in the Clear Lake, Texas, area, and once before in Virginia), we have enrolled the kids in public school for the duration, and they both have made the honor roll, so we must be doing something right!

We've stopped our cruising at this time to sell our Lord Nelson 35 — a wonderful cruising boat, but becoming too small for us as the kids get bigger (they always seem to do that!). Our future plans include getting a Kady Krogen 42 and doing more inland water and coastal cruising, but wherever we go, we'll have "kids on board!" ✍

From a Teen's Point of View

Jamie Avery

My name is Jamie Avery and I am fourteen years old. Two years ago my parents and I moved aboard our 1968 Chris-Craft. We had been looking for the "perfect boat" on and off for about a year-and-a-half. One of the boats we saw was a 47' Chris-Craft. It needed work, but we took delivery of *Gypsy Magic* in New Orleans, Louisiana. That began a two-day rush back to our home town of Destin, Florida. Our boat hasn't seen full-speed since.

While we were still landlubbers, we remodeled the interior. She had her original sixties interior — complete with gold shag carpet, orange crushed velvet, and avocado Naugahyde. The first four months of boat ownership I spent my free time sanding the mahogany trim down to the bare wood. I smelled mahogany for weeks after that.

The teenage years can be stormy times for families. That's not the case for this teen (other than the odd hurricane). For him, a boat is an ideal place to come of age.

We finally moved aboard after countless garage sales, sending stuff to grandma's house and learning to live in the fiberglass confines of our home. Memories of living in a house are now distant. It seems that I've always lived on a boat. In the first six months of life on board, we experienced hurricanes Erin and Opal; luckily, with no damage to the boat. The only damage I recall is the bicycles that I had lashed to a piling circled around and were turned into pretzels by the boat next door.

On board, I have different chores than in a house. I don't have to mow the yard; but, on the other hand, I never had to wax our house. There is one thing for sure: boatwork is a lot more fun than housework. One day about a month ago, my Dad instructed me to polish our heavily corroded aluminum davit. When I first started, it took me four hours to get about six inches of a six-foot davit looking like a mirror. Then I thought "well what if I sanded it?'" So I sanded the davit with 220 grit sandpaper on a palm sander. After the metal was smooth I cut a piece off an old pair of flannel boxers to fit the sander. Then with the flannel on the sander, I applied Collinites no. 850 to the davit and sanded. That method took a bunch of time out of polishing. After machine polishing I recommend hand polishing to remove excess metal dust.

I love living aboard and hope to travel soon. Both my parents work and I'm in public school, so, unfortunately, we will have to wait. I think living aboard is the ideal place to raise a family. I don't watch television much. I usually read or draw concept boats on the computer. When I'm not reading or polishing metal, I'm sailing or helping out at the marina office. Well, I think I hear my Dad calling — another thing to polish and no complaints.

To Have or Have Not — A Dog Onboard, That Is

Marlene Parry

My husband and I had been cruising for three years, moving from anchorage to anchorage, when I suddenly asked a big question: "Can we get a dog?" During our working careers we didn't feel we had the time to spend training and caring for a puppy, but now it seemed like the right time. We had friends with dogs, cats, and birds aboard, so how hard could it be, right?

If you are a dog lover who is living aboard, the question of whether to have a dog live on the boat with you is sure to arise. Here's how one cruising couple answered that question and lived happily ever after.

We knew the breed we wanted was a Pomeranian. We had previous experience with this breed and they are a smart and (important to us) a small dog. We could not envision lifting a 60- or 70-pound dog on and off the boat and into our dinghy for shore leave. Another attractive characteristic of the Pomeranian is its energetic, affectionate, confident, albeit sometimes mischievous, behavior. A great companion, the Pom lives to around 14 to 17 years, so we realized that we were making a long-term commitment. We wanted a young puppy so we could train him from the start to relieve himself on our forward, starboard, or port decks. We had spoken with other cruisers who had to limit their travels because their dogs would not go aboard the boat no matter how much their owner encouraged the dog. We checked the newspapers for breeders and found 8-week-old Pomeranian puppies advertised. We chose a male dog and named our new first mate Kodi Bear.

Boat Training

When we initially brought Kodi Bear onboard we spent a great deal of time on potty training. It really was not that difficult because with puppies their meals go through their tiny systems within an hour. When we thought it was about time for Kodi to void we would take him to the bow of the boat and wait. After he peed and pooped, great praise was given to him, along with a liver treat. In less than a month Kodi was boat-trained. We also considered it important to visit friends with houses to train the dog not to have accidents in a home. Kodi now understands that carpets are not a place to urinate. This will be important if we leave the boating life and move ashore. We won't want our dog doing his "business" just anywhere. During the early weeks with Kodi we made it a policy never to take him on a walk unless he had already relieved himself. Now that he is older, he makes the transition from shore to boat without confusion.

One accommodation we made for Kodi was to put netting on our lifelines. We are one of those sailboats that when you spot us you say, "They either have kids or animals." We did buy Kodi a life jacket which he manages to squirm out of, so when we are sailing in rough seas he has his harness on and his leash is attached to our instrument post. We prefer a harness rather than a collar; the harness allows us to quickly retrieve him without injuring his throat. His first ocean voyage was in 9-foot seas and winds of 30 knots and it didn't take Kodi long to get very seasick. He now knows the meaning of the phrase "sicker than a dog." Under calm seas and winds, it doesn't take him long to get his sea legs. He studies the winds and carefully positions himself on the leeward side of the deck to avoid getting wet when he's doing his business. When we are under sail, Kodi's favorite spot is at the helm next to the captain.

Another thing we had to deal with is barking. Bear in mind that a dog's way of communicating is by barking, and a dog will bark at other boats and dinghies passing by. We have tried to discourage indiscriminate barking, but a dog becomes very territorial, and if he feels someone is entering his space, he will let you know. Kodi takes his responsibility of protecting us very seriously. The least sign of intrusion, the smallest sound or a hint of invasion from someone outside our boat, will bring on a burst of furious indignation. There have been occasions when this behavior has been very helpful. When we were below and another boat was about to drag down on us, it was Kodi who first alerted us to the danger. However, when we are at a dock, getting him to not bark at everyone passing by our slip was difficult; but, with patience and consistency, we managed to put a lid on the noise.

Pet Travel & Accommodations

All dogs seem to love the beach — running and digging in the sand comes naturally. However, there are few places on the eastern coastline that permit dogs to be on the beach There is beach area between Jupiter and Palm Beach Gardens, Florida, where dog owners can take their dogs for a walk, but this is rare. A potential dog owner should keep this in mind. We have found certain other areas that are extremely doggie friendly, such as South Beach in Miami and Key West. Kodi has dined with us at Kelly McGillis' restaurant in Key West; he has walked with us on Lincoln Road in South Beach, and has sat with us at outdoor cafés — us with our cafe latté, him with his bowl of water. At the News Café in South Beach, dogs are permitted at your table in the outdoor dining area. If you want your dog to accompany you to such places, you first need to work out the commands of "sit" or "lie."

Like any sailor, Kodi looks forward to a ride in the dinghy for shore leave.

With cruising, there may be occasions when you need to book a flight. What to do with your dog can be an issue. We generally do not stay in one area long enough to become familiar with boarding kennels, so we take Kodi with us. We have a carry-on bag, and Kodi fits under the seat. He stays calm with a little help from a doggie Valium. Most airlines charge $50 or $75 per trip leg for your dog to be under your seat or in the cargo area. I complain to the airlines about how it is not fair that Kodi doesn't qualify for any frequent flyer miles, but my complaints fall on deaf ears. When you book your seat on the plane, make certain you book a seat for your dog. Most airlines allow only two animals per flight in the cabin.

Kodi's realm is our sailboat.

Food & Bathing

We have cruising friends that travel with two large dogs. When the couple provision for the Bahamas, they usually begin their journey with 200 pounds of dry dog food. This they stretch by adding rice to the meal. A 5-pound bag of dry dog food usually lasts our small dog three months. If you plan to stray away from civilization, you should discuss with your pet's veterinarian a medicine kit for your dog. When taking your dog to foreign ports, be sure to research their requirements before your arrival. Many countries have processing periods, so plan ahead. You will need your pet's health certificate for customs clearance.

Since Kodi is a small dog, we can bathe him in our galley sink and he does not put up a fuss. His size assures us that all have a place to sit in the cabin or in the cockpit. I have seen a Great Dane on a 30-foot sailboat and I can't imagine dealing with that situation. Kodi's favorite movie is "As Good As It Gets;" his favorite star in the movie is, of course, the dog. His favorite treat is cherry tomatoes, and, unlike one of our former presidents, he also enjoys his broccoli.

We have introduced him to other dogs of varying sizes and as a result, he likes other dogs and gets along well enough. He wants to make friends with cats, but the feeling is not mutual. We have done the same with people, and Kodi loves to have human guests visit our boat. He is so good-natured that we do not have to be concerned about him snapping at or biting a visitor. In our current marina, the personnel run about in golf carts. When they see Kodi and me on a walk, they stop the cart. Kodi runs to them, jumps up onto the cart seat and lands a big kiss on their faces and gives a few licks to their ears.

Anyone who loves dogs, knows how wonderful they can be. They do take a lot of care and handling, but if you spend the time training a puppy, your efforts will be rewarded threefold — you will have a companion, loyalty, and a great dog for the rest of his life. So, would we get a dog if we had it to do over again? For us the answer is a resounding "yes." Our world is special because he is in it. Our sailboat is Kodi's realm and he feels an obligation to love, protect and entertain us.

The Company of Dogs

Michael Beattie

There are times when I wish I could just stick these dogs on a plane and get them far, far out of my life. Like the time Emma found a deliciously cool, muddy creek and decided a black mudpack was just the thing to counteract this humid Panamanian climate. Or when Debs, crashing through the bushes on a Costa Rican beach, came back with a grossly swollen, suppurating eyeball. Fortunately the damage wasn't permanent, but we had a scary (and expensive) few days, organizing a car rental, finding a good vet and making the inland trek to Costa Rica's capital, San Jose, to give the wretched dog a checkup. Meanwhile, our pet-less cruising friends lounge around in the shade of

When Michael Beattie and his wife, Layne Goldman, planned their cruise, they never considered leaving behind two members of the family. So what's it like to cruise with two large dogs?

their awnings, watching us haul our dogs to the beach twice every day, rain or shine, constantly sweeping hair balls out of our cabin and lugging bags of grossly expensive dog food back to the boat. Having active dogs onboard means we are always walking inland from every anchorage. It's not always picturesque, trudging through slums or industrial zones, but we've learned lots about the less touristy parts of countries we've visited.

Our dogs get to run free because a dog on a leash is viewed as *bravo*, or fierce, a lesson we learned early on when our two leashed dogs cleared the sidewalks in Cabo San Lucas, Mexico. Sometimes we fear for them with all the hectic traffic and crowded sidewalks, but we've trained them to stay close, and so far they've shown more respect for the aggressive style of driving down here than I would have given them credit for. The other cool thing, aside from no leash laws, is that the dogs are welcome almost everywhere. We used to tie them up on the sidewalk outside a store, but pretty soon we found the storekeepers wanted to meet these fabulous creatures from another world. Like the clerks in a Puntarenas, Costa Rica, pharmacy who persuaded me to lift my 85-pound Labrador on the counter so they could pet her, with their boss smiling his approval! We routinely take them shopping, which for them is much more exhausting than waiting for us in the car as they used to have to do in California. Debs got so overwhelmed one hot day in Playa de Cocos, Costa Rica, he lay down in an aisle of the supermarket, near the freezer, and fell fast asleep. There I found him stretched out, snoring, with the customers politely stepping over him to get their ice cream! Another time in La Union, El Salvador, Emma decided she had had enough, and without our noticing she simply stopped walking and got on a bus. Fortunately my wife, Layne, noticed the missing Labrador and we doubled back through the stream of pedestrians crowding the sidewalk, calling for our dog. A man, giggling wildly, pointed into the bus, and there was

Emma keeps watch with Michael aboard Miki G.

Emma panting away next to the driver, who was pretty much ignoring his non-paying passenger. I have no idea if he would have simply driven off with her, but we got the message and found a cab willing to haul us and our dogs back to the dinghy landing.

Officials have thus far been very casual about our hairy crewmembers. The port captain in Barra de Navidad, Mexico, brought his office staff out to meet Emma, a dog that shared a name with his wife. He thought it was a huge joke, though I can't say if his wife agreed. In San Blas, Mexico, the port captain invited our panting crew into his air-conditioned office while we did our paperwork.

However, it hasn't all been fun. The port captain in Playa de Cocos looked stern and told us we shouldn't have brought them ashore until he'd checked their vaccination certificates. When we offered to rush back to the boat to get them, he broke into an enormous smile and said, "No, no, I just need to make sure you have their papers." I guess we passed the honesty test. Here in Panama, we have come up against every dog-cruiser's worst nightmare — the dreaded quarantine! According to the information we had, Panama's 40-day quarantine was applied only to animals arriving by air, but unfortunately there has been an election, and apparently the bureaucrats have been reshuffled and now they have decided that the quarantine applies to all animals. So Emma and Debs are confined to the boat for 40 days: the first dogs to face this requirement here in Puerto Pedregal, Panama. That's according to the marina manager, who was so annoyed that she went and asked the customs agent what he was doing to her customers. His inflexible ruling on the new quarantine restrictions is the bad news, but this is Latin America, so an accommodation is possible with a little flexibility on our part and a little blind-eye-turning on theirs. The manager told us the hours the customs agent works and guess what? When he's in the office, Emma and Debs are languidly draped on deck watching the world go by, up and down the Pedregal River. I'm figuring they can easily do a 40-day quarantine in the uninhabited islands that line Panama's Pacific Coast and be all fresh and ready to go ashore when we finally reach the metropolis of Panama City!

Quarantines will indeed restrict your travels if you boat with a pet. Bird owners returning to the United States can enter only at one of six selected ports that have quarantine facilities for the birds. Most South Pacific islands have quarantines, including Hawaii and American Samoa, so dog owners don't usually travel there. Several Caribbean islands have restrictions, as do Ireland and Great Britain. The best resource I've found is Jimmy Cornell's massive tome *World*

Cruising Handbook. The *Commodores' Bulletin* of the Seven Seas Cruising Association often carries updates from members traveling the world. Be sure to ask fellow cruisers for their experiences if you are traveling the same route. We did, and had we arrived in Pedregal a week earlier, the old customs agent would have allowed Emma and Debs ashore no problem! In this lifestyle, it pays to be flexible, and if you have a problem in one port, smile politely, agree to whatever, and move on!

The issue of going ashore raises another thorny question. Where do the dogs relieve themselves? It's a very good question, too, because if your animal is properly housetrained, as ours are, they will be extremely reluctant to go on your boat/home. We are lucky enough to sail a Gemini catamaran which not only remains level underway but also has no steep companionway or high freeboard to make it hard to get in and out of the dinghy. On most boats, dogs can get to the foredeck, the least lived in space. In desperation, our dogs go there. After ten months of travel, they are starting to realize its okay to go there. I must admit, even in print, that when underway, I have tried to set an example by going there too. (Layne declines to assist me in this heroic effort on the grounds it's a man's job.) Relieving yourself, deliberately, on your own sparkling deck will give you some idea of how difficult it is for the dogs. We praise them massively every time they do.

Even this practice has its risks. One morning in Bahia Calabria, Costa Rica, we woke up and went to put the kettle on in the usual way. Layne said to me, "I can't find Debs!" In my usual half-witted masculine way I replied, "Of course you

---

Before deciding to travel with a dog, ask yourself if you are willing to live with certain restrictions:

- Will your route take you through countries where you can't landyour animal?

- Do you enjoy inland travel, and if so, can you afford to rent cars? Most long-distance buses, even in Central America, won't carry pets.

- Does your cabin need to be immaculate at all times? Dog hair gets everywhere on a boat. Your dinghy will be a vile carbuncle filled with hair, sand and water all the time.

- We carry a garden sprayer and lots of towels, and after every trip ashore, the dogs get cleaned of all sand and salt-water residue before entering the cabin.

- Once a week we thoroughly shampoo the pooches, and each month they get flea and heartworm treatments.

- How do you feel about going ashore twice a day, every day? Starting a long passage at dawn becomes a lot harder when you have to start with a trip ashore, plus the clean-up in the cockpit — all before the sun is up!

- Some cruisers really miss their pets and will love the opportunity to be around yours. However, not everyone loves dogs, and if your dog is a barker or a jumper or otherwise undisciplined, the entire cruising fleet will feel less than friendly to you in short order.

- Every country we have visited has had some sort of pet supply center. Even the poorest nations in this hemisphere have enough rich people with pets to require the sale of food and supplies. You may have to travel to find food, and it will be expensive, but you don't need to carry a year's supply of food. Treats are much harder to find, especially in bulk.

- Leave home with a vaccination certificate and an international certificate of good health. In a crisis, a piece of paper, any paper, no matter how old, may save face for the official and enable your dog to go ashore.

- Before returning to the States, get a good health certificate from your last foreign port.

can, you just aren't looking properly." Well, there aren't many places a 70-pound dog can hide on a 34-foot catamaran. All we had left of Debs was his last "deposit" on the foredeck and no sign of the brat. Probably he went forward as nature called in the middle of the night, heard a fish splash and being the hunter he is, checked it out and fell overboard. Happy ending, though. He was sitting cold and disconsolate on the beach waiting for us to wake up and collect him. He at least was smart enough to swim ashore. Marta on *Altair* admitted to us that's her worst nightmare, waking up and finding her spaniel, Skipper, gone. She says she gets up two or three times each night to make sure he's asleep on his beanbag on deck. Incidentally, Skipper holds the "no-pee" record of the Pacific cruising fleet this year. It seems he won't go if land is in sight, and when *Altair* was south of Acapulco, Mexico, the transmission broke and Skipper had to hold it for five days as they drifted around trying to sail back to port.

Anecdotes we've heard from other cruisers include the story of the strict vegetarians who hunted and killed fish in Mexico's Sea of Cortez to keep their pooch happy. Then there was the single-hander on a motor cruiser who was traveling with five huge Newfoundlands. Those who met him in Mexico described him as surprisingly relaxed except while docking in marinas. The dockhands were too scared to get close and take his lines! We met a guy traveling with a Saint Bernard who had rigged a Rube Goldberg-type ramp on the stern of his sailboat to enable his dog to get in and out of the dinghy. And the whole Mexico cruising fleet was in awe of *Ilie*, a small sailboat carrying a very happy couple and a pair of huge, active German shepherds. *Camelot* travels with Sam, a little schipperke, supposedly a dog bred for boats, but Sam is scared of the water! When the boat's owners Eric and Faye had to go home for a family reunion, the airline declined to take the dog unless it was in a "proper" cage. Guess what? They couldn't find a proper cage in all of San Jose, Costa Rica, and the last we heard they were waiting for one to be sent down before they could leave. That crisis came after months of struggling to solve an overpowering flea infestation plaguing their dog.

Sabrina, a husky mix, lives aboard s/v *Sea Yawl*. She takes up most of the floor, I mean cabin sole, space when she is napping or trying to keep cool under the air-conditioner. A lot of her hair flies off to lodge in corners, filters, the bilge etc. Potty-time while underway is a con as we must stop but the pro list is a whole lot longer than the con list! No one has ever stolen as thing from our boat even in high crime areas where other boaters have lost bikes and other deck items as Sabrina likes to sleep on deck watching for wildlife. Walking her is good excuse for daily exercise as well as exploration and we make friends along the way as well as feel very safe in any neighborhood.

– Pat Poupore

My favorite was the story of Lope on *Cuckoo's Nest*, a huge Canadian monohull with enormous freeboard. Diane and Randy found Lope starving on a Mexican beach and took her onboard. I guess life aboard was better than anything Lope had known before because she instantly learned not to cause problems. If she needed to go ashore, or cool off, Lope would fling herself in the water and swim ashore. When it was time to go home, she'd swim back to *Cuckoo's Nest* and — I swear this is true, I personally watched her — climb the boarding ladder unassisted! If only Emma and Debs could do the same!

There was another dog story that had a less happy ending. Detroit-based Irwin on another Gemini cat, *Speck*, was single-handing in Mexico this past year and decided he wanted a dog. He bought a cute little Mexican lapdog and took

Peewee everywhere with him. In Puerto Madder, Mexico, Peewee wandered off and was returned to Irwin only on payment of an $80 "ransom." The last we heard, Peewee wandered off again in Costa Rica and has not been seen since.

So, would I recommend traveling on a boat with a pet? After ten months on this Central American odyssey, I can safely say no way! But if, like us, your family includes a non-human member, what else are you going to do? We simply couldn't leave Emma and Debs behind. So here they are, up a stinking humid river in Northern Panama, 3,500 miles from home and another 1,500

Emma, Debs and Layne arrive in the dinghy.

to go before they get back to the States, but they are where they want to be — with us. And at the end of another day of tropical stress, dealing with a harbor official, lugging water or hunting down lost mail, we come home to a boat filled with doggy love. There is nothing quite like a quiet anchorage, a good book and a big, hairy, snoring dog lying at your feet to make you feel properly at home aboard.

It really is a dog's life!

We recently returned from a two-month trip on our 34' trawler with our two cats. One cat did beautifully; the other got seasick every time we went off-shore. They're wonderful company and have been part of our family for nine years. This was our first trip of any length and we plan to do more. The litter box was a pain! We'll do some off-shore fishing during this summer and take off again in the fall for two to three months. Next spring, we plan to do a nine-month to two-year trip.

— *Joan Self, Bayou Vista, Texas*

Four-Legged Crew

Darlene Goodman

It's been three days, and the kitten is still hanging around. The adoring eyes look up at you with so much hope. As you pick her up, she rubs her face on your cheek, and purrs with contentment while you stroke her fur.

How could you take this little kitten home with you when you live on a boat? There is barely room for all your things, where would you stow a litter box? In the shower stall, a voice in your head answers. Yes, it would fit there and could be lifted out for the time each day you need the shower for yourself. And what other space did a cat really need?

What cat lover could resist a fluffy, big-eyed stray kitty roaming the docks? Not Darlene Goodman who gained a new member of her crew and became an expert on kitty care.

Food and water bowls — that was easy. A place to sleep — no problem.

You hugged the kitten tighter, this might work. How wonderful it would be to have someone to come home to.

Ashley — oh my, now you have given her a name. But quite a perfect name for the gray kitten.

As you ponder whether or not you should give in to this kitten, you realize there is more to owning a pet than a litter box, food and water, or even love. A commitment to daily care, veterinary needs and teaching this young pet how to live in the boating world. A living thing is a long-term commitment, not just something you will try, and if it doesn't work, dispose of like a sack of garbage.

What if you were away from port and she became sick? Certainly these problems have been solved by others who boat with pets on board.

Many liveaboards share their boating homes with a pet. Most often a dog or a cat. For those who moor permanently at a marina, pet care is similar to living ashore.

Boaters who travel regularly with their pet aboard, need special plans to insure its well being. The best solution is preventative medicine. Cats need to maintain their shots. A pet who spends little time in an outdoor environment cannot build up any natural immunity to disease. Therefore shots, especially rabies and FeLV (feline leukemia virus), are important.

Fleas can be a problem even to a pet that never leaves the boat. Their human housemates can easily bring them aboard on their shoes, especially in the sandy beach environment where boats spend their time. The new once-a-month medications are easy to use. Ask a local veterinarian. Except for an unusual cat, sea sickness is seldom a concern; nor are heart worms, unless you spend a great deal of time in a highly infected area.

It is a good idea to have a self-help veterinary book in your ship's library. *The Well Cat Book*, by Terri McGinnis, D.V.M. and the *Cat Owner's Home Veterinary Handbook* by Delbert Carlson, D.V.M. and James Giffin, M.D. are two good reference books. These will offer you an emergency plan, or assistance in evaluating a medical problem. When in doubt check the yellow pages for a local veterinarian. You may wish to keep the following phone numbers available for help, if no local help is nearby. The National Animal Poison Control Center can be reached at 1-800-548-2423 for a one-time $30.00 charge placed on your credit card. Follow-up calls are free.

Dr. James Trash, who cares for many boating pets in his Fulton, Mississippi Veterinary Clinic, indicates the greatest problems for liveaboard cats are petroleum products and fish hooks. Cats that come in contact with petroleum products such as antifreeze, gas and oil need emergency care. For skin contact with these products, simply wash the area with a degreaser soap. If the petroleum was ingested, feed the cat an infants dose of ipecac syrup (one teaspoon) and follow up with water. Use a syringe to force the liquid into the mouth, but in very small amounts or the cat will choke.

To remove fish hooks, Dr. Trash recommends first wrapping the cat in a towel to calm it and restrict its movements. Next, push the hook through the skin, so the barb is visible. Then cut the barb with a pair of wire cutters and pull the hook back out. Be sure to disinfect the area when finished. If a hook is in the mouth area the cat will need to be seen by a veterinarian. Again wrap the cat in a towel to immobilize it for transport.

Keep fishing gear stashed and in a case designed for its storage. It is easier to put things away than to watch a pet suffer because of carelessness.

One final area to consider is food and water. If you travel a great deal, keep a container of water especially for your cat. As you use the water replace it in the container with boiled and cooled fresh water. Cats are as apt to get diarrhea from an ever-changing water supply as are humans. Store the water in a cool place and be sure to clean the container regularly to reduce bacteria.

The type of food you choose to feed your cat is important. While it is tempting to buy the brand on sale at the local grocery store, remember that a high-quality premium cat food may cost more, but your cat will eat a good deal less. The inexpensive brands have byproducts and fillers added, so your cat will need to eat more to get all the nutrients necessary for a healthy diet. Premium foods will maintain your pet in better condition, with less food to purchase, less to store in your limited space, less stool to smell and remove and a reduced amount of kitty litter to purchase. It's not difficult to figure the savings. Premium cat foods can be purchased at pet stores and any local veterinary clinic. Brands such as Hills Science, Hills Prescription Diet for cats with special conditions,

Eukanuaba, or Iams, are readily available throughout the country. Some companies maintain toll-free numbers to assist you in locating local dealers for their brand.

If these aspects of kitty care are things you can easily commit to, by all means adopt a cat for your boating home. Cats are the easiest pet to maintain on a boat. They have been boating since ancient times and will fit into the lifestyle you love.

I'm not on board (temporary situation) now but when I was I had a great six-year-old Dobie. I was able to leave the boat unlocked when I left to shop or do other chores ashore. And when I returned he and the boat were safe and sound.

He was a great sailor too. When I'm ready to go aboard for good, "Dutch" is going too. He's a great companion, protector, can warn of any strange odors aboard. Wouldn't have any other pet!

— Daniel Bendit

Information about beaches which welcome dogs, pet-friendly accommodations and other tips for traveling with pets can be found on the World Wide Web. Here are a few sites to get you started:

- **dogfriendly.com**
- **petswelcome.com**
- **petvacations.com**
  These three sites have lists of accommodations that allow pets, searchable by city, state, zip code, and some by name of hotel.
- **takeyourpet.com**
  Free newsletter and travel guides
- **dogpark.com**
  Dog parks nationwide that accept dogs on and off leash.
- **travellady.com**
  Top ten tips for traveling with your dog — some good general advice.

We have two adorable, loving miniature Shihtzus. They weigh under ten pounds each which makes them very portable. If we fly somewhere they go with us on board in the luggage compartment. The one disadvantage is having to get them ashore if we're anchored out, but we feel they're well worth the trouble.

— Barbara Chodos Newberg,
Jersey City's Newport Marina

- 6 -

WHAT WORKS
Ideas for the Liveaboard Boat

Life on a boat creates different connections and fresh points of view; it also requires figuring out new ways of doing familiar tasks as well as finding solutions to unfamiliar problems. Throughout the pages of Living Aboard, *veteran boaters describe what they have done to make life aboard more pleasurable. It's the next best thing to actually visiting each other's boats. And who doesn't enjoy visiting other boats to see what their owners have done to make them comfortable homes as well as seaworthy vessels?*

This "how-to" of boat living is at the heart of Living Aboard *magazine and one popular column is devoted to unique ideas for making your boat more livable and easier to maintain. The "What Works" column is filled with innovative tips and novel solutions to everyday problems:*

- *Keep hair and soap scum out of the shower sump: find a bottle cap that fits snugly inside the shower drain, punch holes in the cap's sides, drill a small hole in the top.*
- *No rolling pin aboard? Peel off the label and use a wine bottle.*
- *Store "pourables" such as rice in plastic, two-liter drink bottles.*
- *Squirt a 50/50 mixture of white vinegar and cooking oil in the head at night. The vinegar will help keep the lines clean, and the oil lubricates the head's valves.*
- *If a hose or through-hull fails and you don't have soft wood tapered plugs aboard, use a raw potato to plug the leak. If the potato is too big, take a bite out of it and drive it home.*
- *Mesh bags costing about $10 in boating stores cost about $2 in discount stores. Look in the laundry supplies section.*
- *To clean dirty fenders, try using water-soluble brush cleaner, the kind for use on rock-hard brushes.*
- *Good egg? Bad egg? Put them in a bowl of sea water; if the egg sinks, it's good; if it floats – fish food.*

Well, you get the idea. From its beginning Living Aboard *has been dedicated to offering information and ideas not easily found in books and boating magazines. In this section you'll find innovative but workable solutions to common liveaboard problems as well as some creative ideas just for fun. Maybe one of these suggestions will turn out to be "what works" for you.*

Creative Storage Solutions

Eileen Schott

Our six months aboard *Proton*, a 41-foot Gulfstar Ketch, have taught us some good lessons about cutting down on unnecessary gear. Those of you who live on smaller vessels might think that forty-one feet is plenty of space for two people and two small dogs. So did I, until I began to try to transfer the "must have" articles from our ten-room home, especially those from my 120-square-foot country kitchen. We could have sunk the boat if I hadn't put the brakes on!

Less gear and a new way of thinking will give you more space and comfort aboard.

Fortunately, one of our desires in taking up the cruising life was to cut back to basics. In our half-century of living we finally caught on to the fact that you don't really own things – rather, they own you. Translating that theory into our new lifestyle, however, was sometimes easier said than done. I'd like to share a bit about how we did it for those of you just starting out. We adhere to four basic principles. They are: Think small, multiple purpose, recycle, different.

Think "Small"

A clear plastic 9" x 12" envelope was my first step in size reduction. Instead of storing old magazines that contained a couple of reference articles I wanted, I clipped them and took up a fraction of the space. That one change started me looking at other space gluttons. My "jewel box" (and I use the term very loosely) has been replaced by a little suede bag. On the rare occasions when I dig it out, it offers just enough baubles to make me feel dressed up.

I loved my huge stainless steel colander back home, and used it for everything from draining pasta to washing vegetables. Unfortunately, I'd have had to sleep with it in the bunk if I'd taken it along. Instead, I drain my spaghetti with a pasta spoon right over the pot. One spoonful fills the dish, and I've eliminated a step in serving. Smaller noodles can be drained in a six-inch strainer. As for those vegetables, a flat plastic drain tray that fits over the top of the galley sink and has a removable cutting service works perfectly. This item taught me the next principle in gear reduction . . .

Think "Multiple Purpose"

In addition to veggies, I can use the half-inch grid drain for dishes and small articles of clothing, and the corrugated cutting surface makes an effective washboard for hand laundry. I do that laundry in my most versatile piece of gear – a plastic picnic cooler shaped like an upright cylinder 14" deep and 11" wide. On a choppy day, I fill it with hot soapy water and clothes, secure the lid tight, and pop it on the floor of the V-berth. An hour later I have well-agitated, clean garments ready for rinsing. The same cooler serves as a foot stool, an extra chair, a spare bucket, a storage compartment and even, when the tides are low, a step up to the dock. Of course it goes on picnics with us. Best of all, it serves as a great tote for ice!

Visitors chuckle when they see that I have a high wooden stool in my galley, since it takes up over a quarter of the floor space. What they don't see is Don using it as a work bench for sawing and hammering projects, me using it as a desk for my computer in the aft stateroom or as a seat between the "V" that puts me at just the right height to use that surface as a cutting and sewing table, or the dogs using it as a hiding place when the cabin is crowded and they don't want to get stepped on. They also don't see the tired muscles I'd have if I spent all my galley time standing up.

Other multiple purpose items have earned their place on board *Proton*. A large, inexpensive plastic bowl is not only used for mixing batters, it serves salads and chips, holds rinse water for dishes and is a rising bowl for bread dough. The broiling pan that came with the stove makes a cookie sheet or jelly roll cake pan and its perforated drip rack can be used to cool those goodies on. A large lockable plastic trunk provides storage room on the boat, rests in the trunk of a visiting guest's car to make room for him and because it is lockable and designed for shipment by air, can become generous luggage for an emergency trip home. A small flashlight converts to a lantern and makes a good stern light for the dinghy as well as for the handlebars of our folding bike. A sun awning with a center opening becomes a water collection sheet when draped in a different way. It might even make an emergency collision mat in a pinch. Beginning to get the idea? Then let's move on to . . .

> A little hint for our boating friends. I had no place convenient to store the V-berth blankets, mattress cover, sheets and pillows, so I bought heavy upholstery fabric 60" wide and made two 30" square pillow cases with Velcro openings that hold a complete bed set. Then I prop them up at the ends and they are very neat looking.
>
> – Jane Hogan,
> Union City Tennessee

Think "Recycle"

This principle is good for the environment as well as the boat. Plastic shopping bags are wonderfully versatile items that every boater should make the most of. Small produce bags kept under a cushion or in a drawer can be used for icebox storage and as catch-alls. (If used for food, don't turn them inside out. The printing often contains lead that could contaminate food.) Larger bags are handy for wet swimwear, laundry, and dry storage of everything from clothing to paper. I use one particularly sturdy bag to hold my produce in the fridge. It contains odors, prevents the loss of small pieces of vegetable in the depths, and I am able to pull everything out at once when running the cold plates. In this way I don't inadvertently frost the more cold-sensitive among them. I loop other sturdy-handled bags over hanger necks to keep scarves and knit tops with their matching outfits.

After they have been used for everything else under the sun, tired bags go into the lazarette to become catch-alls for things the captain wishes to dispose of.

While talking about the recycling of plastics, let me mention that it can pay to try fitting those plastic lids that come on some canned products onto your other

Safe Solutions for Clean Living

Many of the products which we use every day in our homes are perfectly safe in that environment. On our boats, however, where cleaners are discharged directly into the water without any treatment, the same cleaners can be lethal to marine life. Here are safer alternatives:

- Detergent & Soap – elbow grease
- Scouring Powders – baking soda
- Floor Cleaner – one cup white vinegar in two gallons water
- Window Cleaner – one cup vinegar in one quart warm water, rinse and squeegee
- Head Cleaner – pour in baking soda and use a brush
- Shower Cleaner – wet surface, sprinkle on baking soda, rub surface with scouring cloth
- Aluminum Cleaner – two tablespoons cream of tartar in one quart hot water
- Copper Cleaner– lemon juice and salt
- Brass Cleaner – Worcestershire sauce or paste made of equal parts salt, vinegar and water, rinse thoroughly
- Chrome Cleaner/Polish – apple cider vinegar to clean, baby oil to polish
- Fiberglass Stain Remover – baking soda paste
- Drain Opener – disassemble or use a plunger and/or a plumber's snake; toxic substances should not be used in a thru-hull drain
- Mildew Remover – paste using equal parts of either lemon juice and salt, or vinegar and salt
- Wood Polish – three parts olive or almond oil and one part white vinegar (interior, unvarnished wood only)
- Hand Cleaner – baby oil or margarine

– Information courtesy of the Puget Soundkeeper Alliance, Seattle, Washington

containers. The ones from stackable potato chip cans fit snugly onto the tops of my plastic glasses, making each one an air-tight food container as well as a drinking vessel. That's different, isn't it? What a sneaky lead-in to my final principle, which is . . .

Think "Different"

Be as creative as you can possibly be, especially with items you make yourself. For example, bright yellow striped terry cloth covers with draw-string closures for your comfortable cockpit throw cushions are not only decorative and washable, they become our shower kit bags when we make one of our rare marina stops. They have even served as emergency toweling when a runaway shower nozzle attacked and soaked the intended bath towel.

One of our most creative inventions took the place of our Christmas tree. We had a Christmas pineapple instead! Propped up in a shallow, holly-filled basket, trimmed with miniature ornaments and fluffs of tinsel and topped with a slender candle set deep into the fronds, it was splendid. And when's the last time you enjoyed taking down a tree . . . and got to eat it, too?

Meeting the challenge of living a comfortable and convenient life aboard without resorting to lots of "landlubber" paraphernalia can be an interesting part of the adventure, and picking up ideas from other sailors is a great way to begin. I hope mine will be helpful ones for you. See you on the water!

The Litter-Free Cat Box

Lyn Foley

Selling the possessions was easy compared to deciding what to do about our cat, Muffin. Muffin was 14 years old in 1990 when we moved aboard our sailboat Sanctuary. She was used to a house and big yard, and, after all, she was already an elderly cat. Should we bring her aboard? How would she adjust to life on a boat? There was also the question of the litter box — where would it go? How would we change the litter? And could we find litter (or sand) everywhere we went?

We loved her and just couldn't go without her, so Muffin (and her litter box) moved aboard. We were happy, Muffin was happy — but the litter box was a mess. Luckily, a liveaboard neighbor with two cats

Cats are enjoyable companions aboard – especially if you can rid your boat of the litter nuisance.

introduced us to the litter-less cat box. We made one, trained Muffin, and she used it through years of cruising — no more worrying about where to buy or stow the litter, and no more mess. Leaving the litter behind made living aboard with a cat much easier.

We were sad when Muffin died at age 19, and decided not to get another cat. But while we were in Spain, a blue-eyed, stubby-tailed kitten adopted us. So Chiquita moved aboard, and we immediately began training her to use a box without cat litter.

The litter-less box consists of a screen platform raised approximately one inch off the bottom of a plastic pan. When the cat uses the box, the liquid goes to the bottom of the pan and does not touch the cat's paws. The solid matter sits on the screen. The cat, instead of clawing in litter or dirt, will claw the screen to "bury" the matter (even though it stays visible on the screen and is not "buried"). The box is cleaned according to instructions below. Here is how to make the box, and train your cat to use it.

Building the Cat Box

You will need:

- A dishpan-type plastic box of size and shape appropriate to your cat and boat. Ours measures 12" x 18" x 4" deep.
- Square piece of galvanized wire mesh-type screen, also known as hardware cloth, 6" longer and 4" wider than your box size. The mesh should have square openings no larger than 1/2".
- Lightweight small-link chain, galvanized or stainless, 12" long.
- Two 1/2" stainless-steel split rings.
- Two plastic wire ties.
- Wire cutters, pliers, ice pick or drill.
- Newspaper pages for shredding.

Measure your box and cut the wire screen to 4" longer and 4" wider than the dimensions of the bottom of the your box. For example: For a box 12 x 18 inches, cut the mesh to 16 x 22 inches. Cut a 2-inch square out of each corner of the flat screen. You now have a rectangle the size of your box, with 2-inch strips on each side. Bend down the extra 2-inch strips to form a 90-degree angle. Fold 1 inch all the way under and back up on the inside. You will have made what looks like a mesh box lid. Cut and or fold away any bits of protruding mesh, so there are no snags of wire.

From the remainder of the screen make a center support. Make a small support similar to the top, only 2" x 2" x 1". Again fold or cut away any snags of wire. Attach this support in the center of the underside of the main screen using the two wire tires. Cut off the extra tails of the wire ties.

Check the screen now for a snug fit in the bottom of the plastic box; adjust as necessary.

Drill or punch a hole in one corner of the box, near the lip. Attach a split ring to each end of the light chain. Attach one split ring to a corner of the screen. Later you will attach the other end to the corner of the box. Put the screen aside for later use. Get ready to train your cat and leave the litter ashore!

Chiquita looking into her litter-less cat box.

Training Your Cat

Before you begin training your cat, remember these two points: First, you can never go too slowly, but you can go too fast. Alter the speed of the steps to suit your cat.

Second, follow these directions, and it will work. The only cat owner we know who did not succeed with this method did not follow the steps exactly. (We trained our 14-year-old cat in one week, our new kitten took two weeks).

1. Put the screen you have made aside and move your cat and litter into the new box. Let the cat use the box "normally" with litter until a bit of smell has transferred to the box. Change the litter, but do not wash the box perfectly clean. The cat should recognize this as its place to go.

2. Add a small amount of shredded newspaper to the litter. Each day gradually increase the amount of shredded newspaper and decrease the amount of litter. The end result of this process is to move to using 100 percent shredded newspaper and no litter. The rate at which you increase the shredded paper and decrease the litter depends on your cat. Change the paper as you would litter.

3. Once the cat is satisfactorily using only shredded newspaper, attach and insert the screen under the shredded paper.

4. Gradually, again according to your cat's temperament, reduce the amount of shredded paper each time you change the box until very little shredded paper remains. You will end up with no paper, just the screen.

5. The cat will scratch the bare screen to attempt to "bury" its stuff. The liquid will go below the mesh, and the cat's paws will not get wet. The hard stuff remains on top of the screen. The box can be cleaned by either putting hard stuff in your toilet via scoop or toilet paper — or dumped and rinsed in saltwater overboard, which is why the screen has the chain. For saltwater rinsing, attach a tether to the chain, and toss the screened box overboard. Let soak if necessary. Be careful if underway — five knots might rip the screen or box from the tether. We learned this the hard way — and had a terrible time getting Muffin to use litter again until we could replace and remake her beloved dirtless box. She hated that messy litter on her paws!

6. We add a bit of water and cleanser to the bottom of the box to help with odors. If underway and heeled, reduce the amount of liquid cleanser to prevent sloshing. The lightweight plastic box is not as stable as one filled with heavy litter. We secure the box into place using a bungee cord.

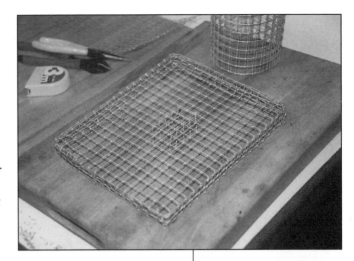

The finished product resembles a mesh box lid, top photos. Bottom photo shows how little shredded paper is used toward the end of the training period.

Editor's Note: Since Lyn Foley first sent us plans for a litter-free cat box she has refined the idea somewhat, and no longer uses galvanized chicken wire for the "grid." Lyn has found a plastic, snap-together, multi-purpose floor-type tile that works better. They can be easily cut to fit the box, and two layers are self-supporting; and, of course, plastic is non-rusting. Lyn writes that they bought the plastic tiles, cut them to fit and, although they snap together, she added wire ties to make sure they don't unsnap and float away when tossing the box overboard. Two layers of stacked tiles supports the cat better and no wet paws. She also switched to a line lanyard instead of light chain. Everything is now completely rustproof and also easier to clean.

A Valuable Piece
of Sailing Equipment:
The Sewing Machine

Linda Knoll

In preparing for our trip aboard *Simple Gifts*, we evaluated many different types of equipment. One of the most valuable things we brought with us is a small portable sewing machine.

I had taken a few sewing courses when I was younger but had not used my 1970-vintage Singer portable much for years — I've been too busy and all that. We had read about cruisers who take special hand-cranked sewing machines aboard with them and my conclusion was that making sails was not something I would be likely to do, so there was no need for a sewing machine on our cruise.

Singer still makes a version of the Featherweight; however, the original is more highly-prized. If you can find an original Featherweight – and they are available – expect to pay up to double the price of a new one. Contact any sewing machine dealer for a new or used Singer.

But one night a few weeks before our departure, we stopped in to visit a Singer dealer who had done some repairs on my machine. I was interested in those new, small machines called sergers and wondered whether one might make sense for the boat, though I was skeptical. The dealer talked us out of that idea fast, because apparently sergers don't do basic sewing, which is what I was interested in (and all I know how to do). What he did show us, and what we ended up buying, was a 40-year-old Singer Featherweight, a tiny little portable, which is no longer made (it has long since been replaced by bigger, electronic models with lots of plastic parts, I guess).

This machine is a godsend, especially because it is so small and dependable. It fits in a case that is only 11" x 14" x 8", with space inside to spare for thread, manuals and other sewing things. It's really cute — just a miniature version of a traditional Singer machine. The parts are all metal, and it has a zipper foot and even a zig-zagger (which I haven't tried yet). It was made in 1951 and has a centennial medallion on it indicating that the same machine had been made for 100 years. According to the dealer, and to other, more objective people we have met while cruising, it will last another lifetime with proper care. We paid $250 for it.

This machine has proved itself up to the challenges of boating every time we have called on it. My newer Singer portable, which is bigger and less capable, was left behind in storage. It had often failed me; it is unable to handle thick fabric, for example, or Velcro tape with adhesive backing. But not the Featherweight — it takes just about everything I put in it and just keeps on stitching. Its only disadvantage is its diminutive size; the space under the arm is small, so sewing in the middle of big pieces of fabric is harder than with a bigger machine. But compared with the high cost ($600 and up) and low reliability of other machines designed and marketed — especially for boaters — I'd vote for the Featherweight anytime. Featherweights are only available used, from dealers who generally buy them from estates. If you have one in your attic or your mother's attic, you are blessed — any Singer store can make it work beautifully again.

Since we have been on the boat, I have used the Featherweight to make weathercloths for the cockpit, fitted sheets, vinyl bags for our folding bikes, a colorful blanket cover from two sheets sewn together, a huge mosquito net for the cockpit, a zippered screen for the companionway, a bag to store the main-hatch drop boards, and a storage bag for the charcoal grill.

We still have a long list of sewing projects I haven't got to yet: a dinghy dodger, a dinghy carrying bag, slip covers for the settees, a curtain to conceal the junk in the quarterberth, and a cover for the GPS. Some boats have very pretty table linens and other decorating touches as well as all sorts of customized storage bags, all made possible by having a sewing machine aboard. The small space this machine occupies is well worth the possibilities it provides.

One aspect of sewing on the boat has really required an adjustment, and that is space. At home, I could lay fabric out all over the living room floor if I needed to cut or match large pieces. But on *Simple Gifts*, our main floor space is about 4' x 4'. I have had to sew on docks, in marina lounges, and practically in mid-air to deal with large pieces of fabric. And there is no way that I can be sewing in the cabin with Jay doing anything at all in the boat — sewing takes up all the available space. We have developed a rule: only one project is allowed in the cabin at one time — there just isn't room for two. But we have found ways to work around that, even if the other person has to disappear for a while or take some enforced leisure.

The end results, both in the successful completion of the sewing project itself and in the feelings of accomplishment and creative fulfillment that go with it, are definitely worth the effort. It really feels good to be back to sewing after so many years away from it.

Fellow liveaboards: Don't get rid of that sewing machine. If you do not have one, you may want to run out and get one. Make it a heavy duty one.

Twelve years ago, when we began to live aboard, my husband insisted I keep my sewing machine. Five years ago he had it overhauled. "Why?" I thought. "I don't mend, what made him think I would sew!" Well, a couple of years ago, he got me to do a few projects for him. I soon discovered sewing on canvas was a cinch and vinyl equally as easy. The obvious projects were drapes, matching pillows, place mats, and bed spread. I soon learned that I could stuff the pillows with towels, bedding and scraps of material – an attractive and useful way to stow these items.

Bags – you can't have enough tote bags aboard. Canvas makes nice waterproof and nautical tote bags. They are great for carrying food and drinks from one boat to another by dinghy. I enjoy making and designing these, so if you are a friend of mine you are bound to have a tote bag personalized for you on your boat. Vinyl is great for small bags I designed for cellular phones and VHF radios.

Our dog, Jennie, has her own soft and cuddly pillow bed made of colorful fleece and stuffing. She took to it right away, not like her "El Niño" rain gear which is made of bright red vinyl and clear plastic visor. She may feel silly in it, but it keeps her warm and dry.

If you have ever bought the fender covers made out of thin terry cloth, you know they are expensive and not too durable. I use a heavy vinyl – just wrap the fender and add drawstrings at each end. They will last as long as the boat and still give good protection. Vinyl, because it is waterproof and has a soft lining, is great for covering the fish finder, GPS and compass.

After putting so many different items in bags, I soon discovered it is wise to label the bags. Even the propane can and barbecue have their own vinyl bag. Let's get sewing. This is a great liveaboard hobby.

– Janet Jones, aboard Lady Janet,
Huntington Beach, California

*Jennie may feel a little silly in her "El Niño" rain gear,
but it keeps her warm and dry.*

Back-Burner Baking

Darlene Goodman

Is an oven but a memory of days gone by? Do you long for the aroma and taste of homemade bread and chocolate cake? Don't despair. They're all yours again with a single burner and a large pan with a cover.

My onboard oven died a slow and painful death — rust and old age. Replacement parts were no longer available. In cooler autumn weather, home-made bread is a family staple, comparable to summer hamburgers on the grill.

Once I resigned myself to the fact my onboard oven would never be more than a storage unit for pots and pans, I remembered my son earning his Boy Scout cooking badge. As the family's cook, it was my job to help him. One badge requirement was baking in a Dutch oven over a campfire. Why wouldn't this work on the galley stove?

Say you are hungry for meatloaf, but don't have an oven aboard. Or maybe you do have an oven – and a chocolate cake would also taste really good, but you just can't bear the thought of heating up the boat yet another several degrees. What to do? Darlene Goodman has a solution.

The first consideration was the oven. All I had was the large pan that came with my inexpensive seven-piece cookset. It had a cover but no rack. I needed something to get the baking pans off the bottom of the oven, but only about half an inch. Warm air needs to circulate around the baking without scorching the bottom. I used the rack from my pressure cooker, a perfect fit. Select a rack with holes to allow warm air to rise evenly over your baking. A throwaway aluminum pie pan would work well, add a few holes around the edge for air circulation. Be careful not to add too many holes, or the rack will not be strong enough to hold your filled baking pans

If you feel uncertain about regulating the temperature, preheat the pot using an oven thermometer. Just remember every time you open the lid, the small interior area will cool down quickly. My stove did perfect baking on a setting of medium heat. Temperatures do not have to be perfect. I found things took less time to bake than a conventional oven. The smaller oven required smaller pans, all this reduced baking time.

Potential baking pans can be located in a variety of places. You might even have some stashed in your cupboards. I found mine at Wal-Mart. Small-loaf aluminum pans for bread, an old layer cake pan for biscuits, and a scaled-down bundt pan for chocolate cake. When recipes make a full-sized cake, I cut the recipe in half. Smaller quantities of goodies are eaten quickly, reducing the need for storage.

For homemade bread I followed my favorite recipe, to the final rise. At that point I shaped the dough into small loves and placed them in well greased little 3-inch x 6-inch loaf pans for their last rise. I could bake two pans at a time in about 15 minutes to a golden brown.

Be sure to allow a bit of space between the pans for air to circulate in the oven.

The bundt cake pan was best for cakes. It allowed the warm air to rise through the center for more even baking of the dense batter. Drop biscuits are always a big success and probably the easiest way to hone your stovetop baking skills. They are more forgiving of uncertain baking temperatures and the time factor. Leave out the biscuit in the center in the pan; it will help your biscuits bake evenly.

It is important to allow warm air to rise around all sides of the goodies as they bake. Avoid thick dough in the pan or leave the center open. Place a small ring in the middle of the baking pan if necessary to retain the dough, This will help warm air reach all sections of your baking.

Fruit pies do well, but keep them small and not too high in the center. I line the inside of the oven with aluminum foil to catch the juice overflow. Rolled or drop cookies require more space than a Dutch oven allows. Bar cookies do well.

Meatloaf and casseroles are possible, but be careful of the center thickness of your meat. It needs to cook thoroughly without causing the outer edges or the bottom to burn.

A stovetop oven is a lot like Grandma's old wood stove. You learn to regulate the heat and time based upon experience. This is but a starting point. Once you learn what your cookware and stove require, your homemade goodies will be the envy of other boaters.

Chocolate Chiffon Cake

1 egg, separated
3/4 cup sugar
1 cup sifted flour, less 2 Tbsp.
1/3 tsp. soda
1/3 tsp. salt
5 Tbsp. plus 1 tsp. cooking oil
1/2 cup buttermilk (sweet milk can be substituted in this recipe)
1 square (1 oz.) unsweetened chocolate, melted

Beat egg white until frothy, gradually beat in half the sugar. Continue beating until very stiff and glossy. Set aside.

Sift remaining sugar, flour, soda, salt into another bowl. Add oil, and half of the buttermilk. Beat one minute at medium speed on the mixer. Scrape sides and bottom of bowl constantly. Add remaining buttermilk, egg yolk and melted chocolate. Beat one more minute, scraping bowl constantly. Fold in meringue. Pour into greased and floured bundt pan. For this recipe I use my 8" bundt pan.

Gently place onto the rack in the "oven." Bake on a medium stove setting. Check with a toothpick after 15 to 20 minutes. When toothpick comes out clean, carefully lift the pan from the oven and allow to cool on a rack a few minutes before inverting to a plate for final cooling.

I'm just about to go and burn dinner, which is a triumph, and one I want to share in case there are other frustrated liveaboards with propane ovens that take hours to bring food to room temperature. We've lived aboard almost 13 years, and that's how long we struggled with our Hillerange propane oven, which much prefered to cure food, rather than cook it

We had in repair people, we worked on it ourselves, we wrote the manufacturer and chatted at long-distance length with the dealer. The best anyone could do, after replacing pressure regulators, checking propane lines for kinks, enlarging the orifice, messing with the air flow, was to speed the thing up slightly, and only temporarily at that.

Then I talked to a liveaboard friend. She, too, had been battling with her propane oven (a Force 10) but she'd actually found the solution! It's a tool called an orifice reamer, available at welding supply shops for $3.50 or thereabouts. It consists of nerled wires of various thicknesses. And five minutes of cleaning out the oven's orifice has made the thing heat like a flash, attaining temperatures close to 500 in 10 to 15 minutes, rather than hitting a max 375 after three-quarters of an hour. My friend says she has to use the reamer once every couple of months — just one of those regular galley cleaning chores.

Here's how to use the orifice reamer according to my husband, Nick, who actually did the work:

Take the burner off the jet (take out the screws that hang the burner, and slide it off the jet). Then unscrew the jet, which is a thick brass cylinder with one end closed and a pinhole in it. Find the right size nerled wire on your new reamer tool. This is a trial and error process; Nick ended up using the third smallest in the set. The wire shouldn't enlarge the actual orifice hole; it's designed to remove encrusted gunk, not metal. Slide the wire in and out. Nick did this for about 30 seconds (the whole job from start to finish took 5 minutes), but our orifice was nearly plugged: yours might not be so bad. He also says there's a feeling of the wire moving in and out more easily when you've done enough, but the only way he knew for sure was to reinstall the orifice and the burner and turn on the oven. Voila! A healthy sized flame, and a 400-degree oven in less than 15 minutes.

As I say, I'm going to burn dinner now. What a treat!

— Deborah Pearce,
Aboard Chrysalis, C&C Landfall 38

Living Aboard
with Whiskey & Wine

J.J. Stives

> *Whiskey 'n wine, / Whiskey 'n wine, / I'm lookin' for a bottle, / 'cause the captain's got mine.*
> *The bottle will help me, / And I'll feel most sublime, / But sooner or later / I'll have whiskey and wine.*

> — Old sailor's chantey

I'd like to have a dollar for every sailor who has at some time in his or her life aboard yearned for a safe and accessible place to keep his spirits. A few boat designers have created the little liquor cabinets for a few bottles, and others have even put in two or three little circular holes intended to hold a bottle or two near the galley. But the boats with real and proper storage space for whiskey and wine are far too few.

If you enjoy the occasional sundowner, here's some advice about storing spirits. But if you bring aboard that Grand Cru Bordeaux you first cellared in 1994, plan to drink it sooner rather than later. Not a problem, we're sure.

The best wine storage I've ever seen was aboard the Forbes' *Highlander.* And a proper wine cellar it is, with climate control for a few hundred bottles, a lovely etched crystal door to display the bottles, and a cooler for champagnes and white wines. In my three trips aboard the *Highlander,* I don't ever recall anyone ever going to the cellar though. The wines that were served seem to have come from a less conspicuous place, but they tasted fine.

For those of us unable to match such elegance, there remains the problem of what to do with alcohol in bottles and how to keep it. The obvious answer is simply to drink it and buy more in the next port. But there may just be another solution. For wine storage, you have four requirements: darkness, reasonable ventilation, temperature stability and safety from breakage.

For us, aboard *Laphroaig,* the toughest issue was temperature. Like other skippers I know, we found that the bilges offer the best storage areas for wine. But we also have three or four other acceptable areas for liquor and wine storage. Some of these may match your needs and facilities.

Reds we use often are stored on their side in a handy open cabinet in the saloon. The opening is secured with a panel of dark plexiglas and a bungee cord. They seem to do well there. Those reds needing long-term storage reside in a neat little area I discovered between the outer hull and the storage locker inside the stall shower. The upper area of this locker is pantry space for canned goods, but beneath the pantry is a cool (water temperature), dark place for a few precious reds. They get a 360-degree shield of plastic bubble wrap. (More on bubble wrap uses later.)

In a top opening space originally created for glassware, another dozen or so reds and whites survive very well. The area is dark and the temperature matches that of the cabin, sharing air conditioning as needed.

For some years, while I still drank, I pondered where to keep the real drinking alcohol — the malts and sipping whiskey. After some experimentation and loss of a few bottles, we took to using a locker behind the portside settee in the saloon. This had a lift-out door that was easily modified with hinges and a Velcro closure. Stuffed neatly in there are some 15 fifth- and liter-size bottles. They have survived for more that 10 years and undergone some rough weather. Every now and then, a too harsh pounding at sea will result in a broken bottle, but that has never been a serious problem. If we anticipate a long or rough crossing, the bottles get an extra bubble wrap. This locker is next to a wet locker for plumbing equipment, hose, pumps, etc., and it's held an even temperature in a variety of locations, from Houston's Clear Lake to Little Harbor Marina in Portsmouth, Rhode Island, to the Florida coast.

Once a storage area for glasses, this little bin (above) holds more than a dozen wine bottles in the preferred horizontal position, and it gets the benefit of cabin air conditioning.

The wet locker behind the settee (right) makes an excellent storage bin for liquor bottles. Note the center bottle with bubble wrap.

Two things that will damage your wines, especially the reds, are harsh temperatures and excessive agitation. There will be times when you cannot avoid either, but we have generally had good luck while living aboard.

Being a single-malt fan brought me some added benefits. Many malt whiskeys are sold in cylinders or tins. These make excellent storage containers for the bottles at sea, and the locker accepts them equally well. The "good stuff" thus resides in individual containers. The cheaper items get a wrapping of bubble wrap, like the wine bottles. We have never had a wine bottle break aboard using these methods.

But nothing is perfect. Recently, we opened a couple of very old bottles of red wine and found that some had not done as well as expected. Some old California reds from the mid-'80s had gone bad, and a prized 1976 Chateau d'Yquem was losing its cork and seeping a bit. The d'Yquem was opened and shared with a few valuable friends around the marina one night. The constant question was "where did you get this?"

"Oh," my shipmate Christine and I alternately responded, "it's just something we found rolling about in the bilges." In a wine shop, if you could ever find such a bottle, it would have fetched more than $200. But we drank it freely and had a great time. So much for perfect storage aboard!

In Praise of Bubble Wrap

We protect our precious bottles of wine and liquor by wrapping them in bubble wrap finished with a circle of clear tape and an ID label. (Some of the best labels are the plastic strips from a Brother label maker. Water or dampness does not effect them.) But we've found many other uses for this remarkable material.

As space-age materials go, there are probably a lot of things that are more interesting than the clear, plastic, flexible bubble wrap you find packed around china or crystal for breakage protection. This is the stuff that you can "pop" by squeezing the individual bubbles. But if you pop it, you lose its benefits, not only for breakage protection, but for its insulating qualities as well. The best thing about the material is that it is not affected by water. Also, it's cheap, reusable and really never wears out. It weighs nothing and can be cut with scissors or knife or razor blade. Pretty cool stuff. You can buy rolls of bubble wrap in office supply stores, or places that pack goods for shipment. We carry one small roll on board all the time. Here are a few uses we have found:

Three types of bubble wrap: large bubble wrap (right) is the most effective, regular bubble wrap (bottom) and non-skid shelving sheets (top left). All three are sold in most supermarkets.

• While we are in a slip or rafted with other boats, we use one or two thicknesses as a privacy shield in our deck hatches. We place the sheets under the clear hatch, using a little tape or, as we have screens, between the hatch and the screen. The bubble wrap blurs images like a shower door and gives curious dock wanderers less to look at, especially at night.

• Used the same way, as above, the wrap is helpful as additional insulation in winter and summer. We found that our many large hatches were a source of heat loss in winter and heat penetration in summer. The bubble wrap makes a nice heat shield and is very easy to remove quickly.

• If you carry firearms on board, the bubble wrap is useful for water-resistant, shockproof, safe storage of the arms and ammunition.

• Electronics gear, such as portable GPS units, night vision glasses, and hand-held radios survive better if wrapped in a couple thicknesses of bubble wrap.

• Line the bottom and sides of your binocular holder with the wrap.

• Occasionally, we will bring aboard something in glass. Last summer it was several glass jars of homemade jam from a tiny little store we found in the Black Hills of South Dakota. The bubble wrap protected the glass and insulated the jelly from our hot summer temperatures.

Next to Velcro, I think bubble wrap is my favorite multi-use material. See what you think. Try it. I've a bunch of stock in the company that makes it! (Right, I wish.)

— Jeff Stives, aboard Laphroaig

Alarming Developments

Rick Kennerly

We sighed "Great day" as we sank into our bunks and drifted gently on the tides of sleep. Phoebus Apollo, blazing his chariot from horizon to cloudless horizon, had gifted us another perfect day. Now fair Artemis, wielding her silver bow, chased celestial prey across a star-splattered heaven and watched over our small boat. Even after we'd retired for the evening, the gods did not abandon us.

Playful Zephyrus blew through the open hatch, toying with a wisp of Gayle's hair and tickling my nose with the free end, as mighty Poseidon rocked us gently in his massive arms. The breast of the Tidemaker sighed as it rose and fell in a deep and abiding peace. It's easy to wax poetic in the land of Homer and Sappho, and who is to say that a dolphin isn't a visiting god in disguise, or that the enchanting fisherman who'd stopped by to chat isn't Odysseus returning to his Penelope, or even Hermes sent by Zeus to test your hospitality to strangers?

> Whenever he anchored in remote areas, Joshua Slocum, the first solo circumnavigator, placed tacks on the deck to protect the boat from barefoot intruders. But in the 100 years or so since, burglar alarms have become more sophisticated. Some work well; some are more trouble than they are worth; others are expensive. Rick Kennerly devised a simple, inexpensive and portable system.

As I lay in my bunk I surrendered myself to the care of the gods. Hypnos drew his cloak over my eyes, and I loosed my grip on this idyllic ancient world to spiral deeper and deeper into the dream world of Morpheus. We were young then and on our first charter — the Ionian Sea. Dinghy sailors with Homeric dreams of cruising.

Like all Greek harbors, small fishing boats plied the waters around us day and night. Most putt-putt-ed far away from the little nook where we anchored, yet some passed nearby. Our chartered boat would rock gently in their wake when they came close aboard, sometimes so near that low murmurs of muffled conversations, punctuated by the aroma of Turkish tobacco, wafted through our open ports. Their fishing lanterns cast yellow phantasms on our cabin sides, creating animated shadows that passed before us by like the shades of heroes past approaching Odysseus in Hades.

Only half awake, I was nevertheless conscious of one boat that passed unusually close by, turned, and throttled back. The voices of two men, conspiratorial and hushed, flooded through the hatch as the light from their yellow lantern was snuffed out and their engine choked to a halt. By then I was fully awake and alert to every sound, every motion. I felt more than heard the rough wooden rubrail of their old fishing boat touch our port side. I awaken Gayle and whispered, "prowlers," which sounded a good deal less alarming than screaming "Pirates!," I thought. I reached up to close and dog the hatch above the berth as I looked around for a weapon — underwear, a duffel bag of clothing, boat shoes, a copy of the Iliad. In the area of self-defense, my Achilles heel was obvious — as was everything else. I was fumbling with my shorts when we heard a thump and clank on deck.

No time to hesitate! I sprang from the bunk naked as a jay bird and screaming like a madman. Gayle rushed to turn on every light she could find. I grabbed the airhorn as I passed through the cabin and sprang into the cockpit, me shouting curses and the horn squealing like the wrath of a hundred Harpies. Cabin lights came on all over the harbor, flashlights stabbed the darkness from nearby boats and beams searched the water. Cruisers called out from the darkness to discover what was the matter. Emboldened, I rushed forward to face and repel the boarders, but found no one.

As I reached the bow, however, I did glimpse the dark outline of a boat and for just a flicker I saw the stricken faces of the fisherman who had befriended us the day before and his son. Carried away on the broad shoulders of the tide, they drifted in stunned silence out of the pool of light surrounding our boat and faded forever from our lives into blackness.

When faced with the task of securely locking up the boat, hatches tend to be a real problem. Install two stainless steel tubes (1.5" diameter or so) across the inside of your large hatches. Space them so that they are close enough that a person cannot enter the boat via the hatch. But you say, "they can easily be hacksawed!" Not so. The secret is a piece of commercial 3/4" rebar inside of each tube. If anyone tries to hacksaw through the tubes they will encounter the rebar. Because the rebar is not attached, it will rotate with the hacksaw teeth, thus preventing its being sawed in two.

– Sue Meckley,
aboard Menage-A-Trois

At my feet was the only evidence that they had come — a half sack of nuts, a tiny flagon of olive oil, and a jar of octopus soaking in seawater, killed with a bite through the eyes. An offering of peace and friendship for his American visitors delivered after a long night of fishing. Although we took the dinghy and searched for them the next day, we never saw them again. And then it occurred to me that if the fisherman was indeed Hermes sent by Zeus to test our hospitality to strangers, we had failed the gods miserably. To this day we regret those Greeks bearing gifts.

How to Construct Your Own Onboard Alarm

We were young and inexperienced cruisers back then. And my career as a police officer and Gayle's as an emergency room nurse had pretty much conditioned us to expect the worst from people, and from life. Thankfully, with the passing of time and the gaining of experience, we've mellowed considerably since those days. Even so, as we traded up to larger and more complex boats and as we chartered over the years, I began working on a portable alarm system that could be moved from boat to boat without ripping up the woodwork as well as be taken on charters. In addition, the alarm had to be not only loud and give a visual indication of where the sound was coming from, but also, considering how badly I still feel about my Greek visitors, it had to be dependable.

The biggest problem to overcome was finding a reliable triggering device. At first I experimented with a portable traveler's ultrasonic alarm designed to be used in hotels. We mounted it near our cabin and aimed the detector at the companionway hatch. At least we wouldn't be surprised in our sleep, I thought. That didn't work, however, because the movement of the boat was enough to set off the alarm.

Then I tried infrared detectors. They didn't work either, but it took me a long time to figure out why. Night after night the alarm would trigger for no reason that I could see. Finally, slipping out the hatch and sitting on the foredeck one evening, I discovered that big south Texas bats and night hawks (attracted to the insects, which were in turn attracted to the anchor light) were the culprits. As they flew past the open companionway hatch, the infrared detector would sense their body heat and set off the alarm.

Step pads (a staple of the shoreside alarm business) were also an expensive error as they were not constructed for the marine environment and quickly deteriorated. They were also heavy and awkward to transport. The final solution to the tripping mechanism didn't occur to me until I was reading Alex Haley's novel, Airport — which should give you some idea of how long I've been working on this project.

In that novel a character took a standard wooden clothes pin (with spring closure) and placed a metal tack on the inside surface of each jaw so that the force of the spring held the two tacks in contact. Each tack was wired to different sides of a battery which, in turn, was wired to the device (Figure 1). By inserting a small piece of non-conductive plastic inbetween the two tacks and then attaching a string to the plastic, the story's character had created a tripwire circuit that closed when the plastic was slipped from between the tacks by a jerk on the string.

Working backward from this epiphany, the rest was easy. The beauty of this alarm is that it doesn't use any power unless tripped, is cheap to construct (less than $25 in parts and supplies), is almost impervious to the marine environment, and is nearly foolproof.

I already had a small wooden box, although any sturdy box will do. On the side of the box I mounted a wonderful old dual-tone horn from a wrecked Chevrolet Caprice. On top of the box I mounted a tri-color and anchor strobelight salvaged from a broken mast at our yard (all the bulbs were wired to come on when the circuit was energized). Wiring needs

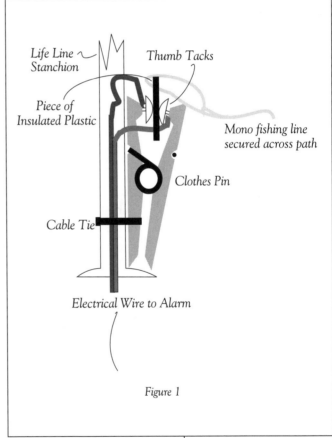

Life Line Stanchion

Thumb Tacks

Piece of Insulated Plastic

Mono fishing line secured across path

Clothes Pin

Cable Tie

Electrical Wire to Alarm

Figure 1

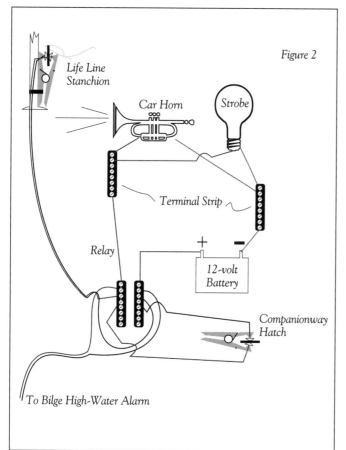

Life Line
Stanchion

Car Horn

Strobe

Figure 2

Terminal Strip

Relay

12-volt
Battery

Companionway
Hatch

To Bilge High-Water Alarm

to be heavy as the current load is pretty high (although those with a bit of experience can wire in a relay or solenoid to make the electrical current load on the trip wire circuits less severe). I used ripcord, designed for household lamps, for most of the wiring. There was enough storage inside the box for the power cord, which had two battery clips on one end. The whole thing went together like this (Figure 2). If you can't scrounge a strobe, both Radio Shack and J.C. Whitney catalogs have several 12-volt automotive distress strobes for sale for a reasonable price. Add a few cable ties, some lengths of wire, a few terminal strips, and a roll of monofilament fishing line and you're all set.

Once you've assembled the box, how do you set up the alarm? One of the most appealing aspects of this system is that it can be set up to protect anything you need protecting and is adaptable to almost any situation aboard a boat. Construct as many trip devices (clothes pins) as you need, attach them to a stanchion or other solid support with a cable tie and run the wire from the clothes pin to the box. Rig the monofilament as a tripwire across side decks-or face high like a spiderweb, across the companionway, to the dinghy (make a big loop of monofilament and secure the loop with a cable tie to allow for some movement of the dinghy), or to secure the fore hatch or companionway slide (Figure 3). Insert the plastic insulator (we used an old Tupperware lid cut in pieces) between each pair of clothespin jaws on the system. Once all of the insulators are in place, hook the battery clips to the house battery. Your alarm is set!

If you carry a spare bilge pump float switch, you can also have this alarm double as a simple high-water alarm, too — just remember that when tripped the horn and strobe are going to be competing for electricity from the battery with your bilge pump. If help is not quickly at hand, weigh the risks before setting up a high-water alarm that will drain your battery dry and cause your boat to sink faster than it would have otherwise. With a bit of creativity and experimentation, you can rig this alarm to protect you boat from burglars while you're ashore. I do have one extreme prejudice, however — a holdover from my police days. If you set up this alarm as a burglar alarm while you are ashore, particularly on an extended trip, make sure that a neighbor has a way to get into your boat and knows how to silence the alarm. One of my greatest aggravations as a cop were irresponsible residents with alarmed homes who left town for vacation and left no way to silence the outside horn. After a night or two of continuous racket and increasingly strident complaints from the neighbors, I often returned to the area on a call for gunshots at the house with the ringing alarm only to discover the offending horn shotgunned off of the wall! No arrests were ever made, yet justice seemed to be satisfied.

While under sail, spool it all together and store it in a locker (unless you're using it as a high-water alarm). You can spend a lot more on an alarm system and get a lot less.

As a final note, for those who decide to have an alarm on board, it's a good idea to instruct the dockmaster nad nearby friends on how to disable it. Also, be sure they know how to contact you in case of a real or false alarm. ✍

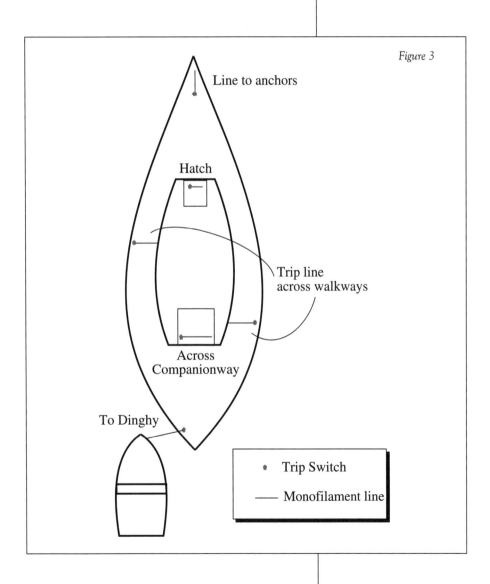

Figure 3

Line to anchors

Hatch

Trip line across walkways

Across Companionway

To Dinghy

• Trip Switch

— Monofilament line

La Cucaracha

Mary Heckrotte

Most folks think Caribbean cruisers sit around discussing spectacular sunsets while they sip rum punch at happy hour. Well, just the other day, a few of us were sitting at the Trinidad and Tobago Yacht Club having piña coladas instead. First thing you know, a bunch of us women got into a conversation about unwanted critters crawling through our provisions. It seems that by the time they reach the West Indies, an awful lot of cruising boats are giving rides to the most unwelcome of all critters: roaches. Those aggravating things fly through the air, hop out of bunches of bananas picked up at the outdoor market, and perch on packs of gourmet jellybeans to glare at us from the upscale supermarket shelf. As far as I know, though, we don't have any on *Camryka*.

Webster's Second defines cockroach as "a troublesome pest in houses and ships." They got that right! Here are some pest management strategies for keeping your boat critter-free.

It took just one close call to make a preventionist of me! One day I set a cardboard flat of Cokes in our cockpit and was lifting the cans out when a giant roach scuttled from under a six-pack. Operating on automatic pilot, I threw cardboard, cans, roach, and all overboard! (Sorry, Mother Nature!)

Since then, I take everything possible out and discard its cardboard before bringing it aboard. One solution is to carry along zipper-style or other plastic bags when shopping. People may give me a funny look when I stand by the grocery's trash bin emptying boxes and tossing them, but hey, better funny looks than creepy-crawlies on board! Besides, most groceries are easier to manage in my backpack and in the dinghy without square-cornered boxes. Once on board, everything that doesn't go in the fridge goes in a plastic bag, glass jar, or a Tupperware-type plastic container.

Diatomaceous earth can be an effective deterrent for bugs on board and in marina areas. As the insects crawl through the diatomaceous earth, the powder sticks to their bodies. When they clean their bodies, they ingest the powder, and it kills them. Try a bit in the boat's bilge area, or in the bottom of out-of-the-way lockers. To keep bugs off the docks, liberally apply the powder around the area where the dock abuts land.

– Paul Johnson

Whether it's from the outdoor market or the regular grocery store, all produce needs a bath. We even wash the items we'll peel or cook. In the dinghy or on the dock at a marina, it's easy to dump everything in a bucket of water with a few drops of bleach in it. Let it all soak 15 minutes. Not only will that chase out the roaches, you'll also kill the nasty critters that cause dysentery.

The precautions needed on a boat aren't limited to buying economy items or shopping in economy locations — or even to cruising in the Third World. Living aboard for a year in the United States, we were as exposed to roaches, weevils, rats, and mosquitoes, as we were during our year on the Rio Dulce in Guatemala. Grocery stores and marinas in particular seem to attract all such critters.

The only item that we've had go bad with critters in the past year was a Rubbermaid plastic container, closed tightly and completely sealed with duct tape. It was filled with the contents of four boxes of expensive U.S.-purchased treats for our dog. The bugs were obviously already in there when I sealed the container — but at least they didn't get out to contaminate anything else.

Lest you think I'm an obsessed exterminator disguised as a cruiser, I'll tell you that I've never gone as far as some books recommend: I don't remove labels from cans. I do, however, maintain up-to-date store-bought roach and ant motels and offer any visiting roach a "cookie." Roach cookies are made by mixing boric acid (from the pharmacy) and a few drops of sweetened condensed milk together and shaping it into little patties that look like candy mints. Roaches of any nationality just love them. I make big batches, wrap the extras in bits of waxed paper and store them in a covered glass jar with "Poison" marked clearly on the outside. About every five feet of *Camryka*'s remote hidden space gets a "cookie." I just have to make sure they are inaccessible to our miniature schnauzer or any child that might come aboard.

We count our blessings that we've lived aboard five years, including nearly two years in Central America, without getting infested. I hope we can report the same news after an equal time in the Caribbean! Of course, it never hurts to bow east, say three Hail Marys, and throw salt over your left shoulder! And have another piña colada while the veggies are soaking. ✍

Here's another idea for keeping your boat from becoming a roach-motel. Fill a bowl with cheap wine and set it in the locker under the galley sink (no laughing, you skeptics). The roaches will drink the wine, get immediately drunk, fall into the wine and drown. Thus two problems solved: 1. How to get rid of the roaches, and 2. What to do with that rot-gut wine you got at the last port.

– *Bonnie & Phil Ojeda*
of the s/v Hey . . . it Floats! *of Alameda, California*

Roach Cookies

- Powdered boric acid (available at most pharmacies in 12 oz containers)
- Sweetened, condensed, evaporated milk

Mix together 8 teaspons of powdered boric acid and 3 teaspoons of the sweetened condensed milk. Drop by small amounts onto a dish or cookie sheet covered with wax paper. Place in a sunny spot to harden slightly.

After the cookies harden, leave the wax paper under them and cut around each one. Place individual cookies around the boat in areas where roaches might be found, especially the galley.

Makes 6 to 8 cookies.

– Lyn Foley
aboard Sanctuary

Phalarope's Dockside Garden

Richard Manning

Mary stepped down the companionway and handed me some freshly picked tomatoes and a handful of fresh basil and chives for the pasta sauce I was busy making in the galley. Meanwhile she arranged the impatiens, marigolds and assorted herbs she carried in her other hand in three miniature vases. She placed one on the cabin table, one in the head and one on the galley counter.

With the pasta sauce simmering on the stove we stepped out into the cockpit and sat drinking a glass of wine beneath the beautiful bougainvillea hanging in a pot from the boom of our sailboat. On the floating dock beside us, the last rays of the setting sun shone on the luxuriant and colorful plants of *Phalarope's* dockside garden.

Does it sound far-fetched? Living aboard a boat does not mean you cannot have a garden. A cruising or anchored boat is limited in what can be grown aboard, but a boat at dock can have fresh herbs, vegetable and flowers throughout the growing season.

> Don't throw out those seed catalogs when you move aboard. You can combine the love of cruising with the love of gardening. Corn and sunflowers might be a bit difficult to grow aboard a boat, and pumpkins are probably out, but you can have a variety of herbs, flowers and vegetables on board and even more along the dock.

In *Phalarope's* container-grown floating dockside garden in Charleston, South Carolina (Zone 7), spring is heralded by bright bursts of color from miniature azaleas, daffodils and other bulbs. Fresh chervil, parsley, thyme, chives, cilantro, mint, tarragon, basil and rosemary grow profusely between the flowers. Geraniums, impatiens and bougainvillea follow the azaleas; then come the nasturtiums and marigolds. We like to hang one prize blooming specimen from the boom under the sailcloth awning over the cockpit.

Outside the galley porthole a window box contains pots of herbs, handy and waiting to be picked.

Our favorite plants include a bushy chili pepper that has profuse white flowers, followed by tiny green and red peppers that provide color through the fall months; they are unlimited spicy additions to sauces, soups and chili dishes. Tomato plants are our prized possessions since nothing is more satisfying than biting into a freshly picked tomato — unless it is an ear of corn, but that we have not yet tried!

In fall, the cold weather herbs return, and pansies, Johnny Jump-Ups, deep purple and crimson petunias, and asters take over. Many continue blooming until spring returns.

Winter is the time to peruse the gardening catalogs that still find you, and it's also the time to plan next year's garden. By following the demands of the climate and the season you can plan and grow a garden to suit your taste in size and plants wherever you may live. If it is properly maintained with consideration for safety and your dockside neighbors, it will be a source of joy and admiration and an asset to your marina. Some practical considerations:

Climate

Being close to the water moderates the temperature and extends the growing season. We cover our plants with a tarp on nights with frost warnings. Plants must also be protected from salt spray if that becomes a problem. There are many micro climates around a boat at dockside, and plants can be moved around to take advantage of them. Shade or frost protection can be found under the cockpit, for there is morning sun on one side of the boat and northern light or afternoon sun on the other.

Garden Pests

Isolation makes a floating dockside garden remarkably free from pests. Our neighborhood river otter did sample a basil plant but did not return for more. Other garden residents, too, are more pets than pests. A small frog lives under the rosemary bush, and a green anole sometimes leaves its leafy hideout and boards *Phalarope* by the mooring lines to see more sun. Migrating butterflies add moving color as they linger by the fall flowers.

Containers

Heavy clay or concrete pots are best on the dockside since they will not blow over in the wind. Light plastic hanging pots and window boxes are best aboard since they are easier to lift ashore or to stow when you take off sailing.

Gardening Tips

Sprouts are another fun and easy item to grow on a boat. You can buy sprout seeds at a health food store. You'll need a jar with a screen top for drainage. Soak a couple of tablespoons of seeds in the jar overnight with warm water. In the morning drain the water and place the jar at an angle with screen lid facing down. This will ensure prop[er drainage and ventilation during sprouting. Rinse sprouts every morning and evening. Sprouts will be ready to eat in three to five days. They are loaded with vitamins, enzymes, amino acids and minerals. Use the soaking water to water herbs or use as a base in soup or sauces as it is rich in nutrients.

– *Sharon Reed*
aboard Poet's Place

More Gardening Tips

After dumping several plants while sailing, which we do regularly, I tried a gallon-size, clear, plastic jar with a top. Small orchids and octoi greens grow fantastically and travel in the sink or shower beautifully. I have to water only about once a month. I do herbs in another jar. keeping the top off except when sailing. I simply clip the herbs as they pop out the top. No fuss, no muss! We are writers who live and work aboard our 48' Irwin, *Barefoot.*

– *Doe & Bill Saderup*

Maintenance

We replace plants frequently as the season progresses; our limited space has no room for tired specimens and invalids. Due to limited root space in the pots, plants need to be watered often and fertilized frequently with liquid fertilizer or fertilizer sticks. Our dockside neighbors enjoy watching our garden grow and are more than willing to take over watering when we are away. In return they have fresh herbs and flowers for the cabin table.

Tools

A hand trowel and a good pair of scissors are all you need.

Safety

Take care to keep plants clear of dock edges and cleats so as not to impede access and interfere with docking operations.

Planter Boxes

Plastic planter boxes are ideal for use on many boats or the dock. They can be purchased at Garden Centers and Home Building Supply Stores. Most do not have adequate drainage. That can be remedied with a bit of ingenuity.

1. Using a $^3/_8$" diameter sharp drill bit at low speed, carefully drill a hole on the side of the planter box, about $^1/_2$" from the bottom. Plastic can crack and split, so do proceed carefully.

2. Insert a 6" length of $^3/_8$" diameter clear plastic tubing in the hole, allowing $^1/_4$" to remain inside the planter box. The outside section of hose will drain water out of the box and away from the planter.

3. If the hole is misshapen or larger than desired, secure the hose in place with silicone for a tight fit.

4. Fill the bottom $^1/_4$" of the planter with small sized gravel, being careful not to block off the drainage hole. Add a good quality planting soil, but do not overfill.

5. Position selected plants as desired. Allow room for plants to grow.

These boxes can be placed anywhere near the edge of a dock to drain into the water below, attached to the boat's hand rail so they can drain directly overboard, or placed near a scupper hole on the deck. Position the drain hose to direct drainage overboard, inserting a longer hose length to the planter if necessary to reach a suitable drainage location.

– Darlene Goodman,
aboard Wild Goose

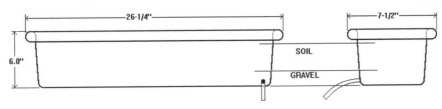

What Works in the Galley

It's not your mother's kitchen, but there is no reason why your galley should not be just as convenient once you learn to "think different." Here are some ideas to get you started.

Doing Double Duty

Galley equipment is one of the most difficult to sort out when you move aboard. On land, items that are used occasionally can be stored in the back of the cupboard or pantry. On board, the back of the cupboard is precious storage space! On *Simple Gifts*, a Crealock 37, Linda Knoll saves a bit of storage space by leaving the rolling pin behind. When she needs one, she pulls a bottle of wine out of the locker, peels off the label, and uses it just like the "real thing."

"Cool" Idea

Jeannette Deale took the wine bottle idea one step further: "Being in a warm climate I discovered it was hard to roll out pie or biscuit dough because the dough became sticky very quickly. I discovered using a cold beer or soda can as a rolling pin worked wonderfully. No sticking, no dusting the rolling pin with flour and when you are finished just rinse and return to the cooler.

Galley Storage

For most "pourable" items such as rice, the plastic two-liter drink bottles provide good storage. Transfer the rice to a clean dry bottle, screw on the top and you've got great storage. Another good "free" storage container is the wide-mouthed plastic jug with a handle on it that some dry dog food, pretzels, and other goodies come in. They are rectangular rather than round and thus store better on a shelf. Ask your friends to save them for you. Be sure to put a bit of plastic wrap under the lid to insure a good seal.

Mary Heckrotte aboard *Camryka* has some thoughts on galley storage. "You have to be careful using Ziploc-style bags" Mary comments. "We find that most plastic bags are not really airtight or moisture-proof. Buy only excellent quality bags and think twice about what you store in them and where you store them. For example, rice stored, even in a Ziploc brand bag will, with the boat's motion, eventually poke tiny holes in the plastic. Once the hole is created, in come the little weevils, and you'll play host to a great colony of critters.

"We bought one of those vacuum/heat sealers and found most of the plastic bags designed for them to be inadequate. After some experimenting, I found we could take almost any heavy-mil plastic, cut it to the size we wanted, seal each of the edges with the machine, and make our own bags as needed. Try industrial supply catalogs to order plastic if you can't find it at a local hardware or paint store."

Mary says, the sealers sold at discount stores for about $30 will not do what you need for storage on your boat — they just don't have the power to create a real vacuum. The really good industrial machines are very expensive at about $300. After much shopping, Mary found one sold by J.C. Penney for about $90 that created enough vacuum inside to suffice. Their first year cruising, she used the machine to "seal a zillion bags" storing leather shoes, special books, and to double-wrap already well-sealed packets (like packages of English walnuts or chocolate chips). It's a close call but Mary thinks the machine pretty much justifies the space it occupies.

Keeping Things Crisp and Fresh

Louise-Ann Nunas aboard *Akama* also has experience with vacuum heat sealers. She uses one to re-seal anything that comes in a plastic wrapper and, these days, most things do: cheese, vegetables, fruit, breakfast cereal, pretzels, potato chips, cookies, nuts, raisins, candy, the list is endless. And once these packages are open, the remaining contents begin to go stale overnight, no matter how carefully you roll or fold the bag. This is especially true in the humid environment on a boat. Louise-Ann and her husband, Maurice, lived for several years in Singapore, which is nearly right on the equator. "So when you talk humidity," comments Louise-Ann, "we know what it is all about. Stand still long enough and you'll start growing moss! Of course, you can put things in Tupperware containers, but those things take up way too much space."

So Louise bought a Decosonic heat-sealer at Costco. It is made of plastic and is about a foot wide, two inches high and four inches front to back. It comes with special material for making up plastic bags, and has a little vacuum pump to evacuate the air from the bag, as it is supposed to be used for food you want to freeze. The owner's manual carries dire warnings about only using the special bags that the company sells (for a hefty price). That turned out to be nonsense. Louise uses it to seal virtually any plastic bag — even those silvery ones that chips come in. She opens a bag, takes out what she needs, then reseals the bag right away. Louise said, "Everything will keep so fresh, you'll think you are living back on shore! It is probably the single most-used appliance in our galley. It only draws 170 Watts at 120 Volts. Since it is on for only a few seconds at a time, you can even use it off the inverter. We figure it takes only 0.06 Ah to seal a bag. The more you use it, the more uses you will find for it."

Another Way of Sealing Plastic Bags

If you can't justify the money or space required to own a commercial sealer, Darby Goode of the good ship *Some Best* in Nova Scotia, has an idea for you. She says that you can seal any plastic bag by placing a piece of aluminum foil over the end to be sealed and running a hot iron over the foil. Make sure you have foil on both sides of the plastic to be sealed so it does not stick to the ironing surface. Remove the aluminum foil and the bag is sealed — with no expensive sealing gadget required.

Save the Wine Glasses

Julie Bertch, and her husband cruised the Great Circle Loop aboard *Insight,* a Monk 36 trawler. She came up with a way to keep the wine glasses from banging together and breaking while underway. At the end of a day's cruising one definitely wants to find the wine glasses intact!

Julie uses those soft ponytail hair bands. She says they slip on the hanging glass easily and keep the glasses from actually touching each other, no matter how the boat moves. She also uses them for her plastic glasses; plastic won't break, but it will scratch if the glasses collide.

Conserve Cold Air

Carol on s/v *Suka* out of Alameda, California, says she hangs 3" vertical strips of flexible plastic completely across the front of her refrigerator, on the inside of the door opening, like they do at the grocery store to limit excessive cold air loss.

Crock Pot as a Solar Cooker

Nanci Whitley aboard her Catalina 30, *The Journey,* says a crock pot will cook anything unplugged, in the full sun, that it cooks plugged in. She even bakes bread and cakes in it. And, yes, with a clear lid and a dark interior, it'll work on cold, sunny days. Fill it with water, you'll be surprised how fast it gets hot enough for coffee.

Nanci, who cruises the Florida Keys and the Bahamas says, "I've also cooked on my engine while underway. But I got the idea for the solar cooking from a news article about a woman who cooks this way, only with a very complicated foil-lined box. As I thought about it, I figured a crockpot would work, so I tried it and it does! Since I have a 2-burner Origo and no oven, this "little oven" is perfect for me. It has added benefits: you don't have to stay on board while you're baking and you don't heat up your cabin if you're in the tropics. Plus, it's impossible to burn anything."

How to Cook in a Thermos

Here's a recipe for cooking in a thermos. Doug Cooley's mom (a non-sailor) suggested he use this method aboard his Westsail 32. He says it's great for open sea when the galley may not be the most comfortable place to hang out and prepare a meal.

- Choose a glass lined pint thermos with a narrow mouth (garage sales and used stores are good places to look).
- Fill the thermos full of boiling water.
- Pour the hot water out of the thermos.
- Put in $1/4$ cup of organically grown whole brown rice, oat groats, hulled barley, wheat berries, or lentils into the thermos.
- Refill with boiling water.
- Screw on cap (helps keep it hot enough to cook).
- Lay the thermos on its side. If you leave it standing up only the bottom will cook.

By putting on to cook at night, you are assured of a hot breakfast the next morning (or next watch). It does not take eight hours to cook but will be kept ready to eat the next morning and even longer. Makes a good take along lunch or supper and will cook in about three hours if you fix it in the morning, you can have it for lunch, or you could fix it at noon and have nutritional food for supper.

- Pour into bowl.
- Add salt only when done. (Food salted first will not cook).
- Enjoy with fruit, etc. Also you can cook two things together like wheat and barley, or lentils and rice.
- Wash out the thermos bottle immediately, as it will be harder to wash when it dries.
- An old-fashioned lunch pail will hold two pint thermoses in the flat position for cooking and carrying.
- Don't put in more than $1/4$ cup of grain to cook or you'll find it hard to get out.

Enjoy!

That's Using Your Head!

*N*othing inspires more fear and loathing aboard a boat than problems with the head. Here are some solutions that will make life aboard a bit more comfortable and pleasant. But if you want to install a Jacuzzi with unlimited hot water, you're on your own.

The Dreaded Head Odor Problem

Have you ever lusted after that bigger boat? Well, even if you can't afford the bigger vessel, take consolation in that all boaters face the same problems! Captain W. R. Lee is a marine surveyor and the owner of a 65' Romsdal North Sea trawler. Even that impressive vessel isn't immune to the dreaded head odor problem.

Here's what Captain Lee advises: Purchase a small, raw-water strainer approximately the size of a small concentrated orange juice can (made by Sherwood, etc. and selling for around $20.00). Remove the screen and insert a K-Mart blue block toilet tank treatment (other alternatives would be 2000 Flushes, etc.) sometimes with a little force, into the bowl. Install the modified filter in line as close as you can to the sea cock (your incoming salt water). You will instantly have deep dark blue water which will last considerably longer than any of the other chemical treatments for a fraction of the cost of replacement chemicals available in the marine stores. It should last an average of 3-4 months. You can use either just the blue block or blue block/scent.

An additional benefit for those with smaller holding tanks — the "blue water" is so highly concentrated that odors are eliminated even when urinating two or three times between flushes. This system also helps to keep the lines clean and breaks down the effluence and other respective chemicals and odors. Be careful when it comes time to change the block. Wear latex gloves and keep a wad of paper towels handy because the blue dye in these tablets is very concentrated and could quickly make you look like a real blue blood.

Bob Young aboard *Polaris* agrees that blue blocks are a big help with odor problems. He traced his problem to odors emanating from the hose connecting his vacuum flush system head to the various tanks, pumps and valves. This hose is very expensive to replace, so he first tried spraying it frequently with Lysol, which helped some.

Then he found a small chemical dispenser kit in a marine store. It consists of a Tee adapter for the flush-water line, and a plastic bottle of solid chemical. Installed, it helped some, but the chemical doesn't last long and replacements are quite expensive. Bob bought "one of those blue hockey-puck things" for domestic toilet tanks, for slightly over $1 at the supermarket, cut it into small pieces and stuffed them all in the plastic bottle. He gives the bottle a squeeze each time he uses the head before flushing. It turns the water dark blue but odors are almost completely eliminated, and it keeps the bowl stain-free. One tablet lasts months. Cheap and effective, but there is a *caveat*: Be careful that the hockey puck doesn't contain chlorine. Chlorine will eat the rubber parts of your head.

Many veteran liveaboards say they squirt a 50/50 mixture of white vinegar and cooking oil (the cheaper the better) into the head on a regular basis. Mix up a batch in a small squeeze bottle, store it next to the head, and it's easy to give the head a few squirts when it needs it. The vinegar will help keep the lines clean, and the oil lubricates the head's valves.

Jay Knoll aboard *Simple Gifts* said one source of the smell may be a buildup in the lines from inadequate flushing. If you're using the boat in salt water, you'll find a buildup of calcium on the inside of the hoses. This scale can quickly reduce the interior diameter of the hoses with a totally undesired result. You might try a preventative treatment of muriatic acid. Read the directions of the bottle and prepare a 10% solution of the acid. But be careful. Wear protective clothing, gloves and eye protection, this is serious stuff! Pump the solution into the head, wait a bit, and then pump it a bit more. The amount of pumping will depend on the length of your hose run. You want to leave the acid mixture in the hoses for the scale to be broken up, but not so long that it will attack the head's metal components. Flush with fresh or sea water once you've completed the process, and then re-lube the head using the 50/50 vinegar/oil mixture.

TP or Not TP?

Tammy Phillips and her husband Bruce did the Great Circle Loop aboard their 38' Vista motor yacht, starting in Geneva, New York. Tammy and Bruce sold their home before setting off and therefore have a lot of "stuff" on board — things they didn't want to pack away for a great length of time. Tammy says, "Because of this most of the lockers and closets are filled to capacity. And, while it is definitely a necessary item, I just hated to take up a whole locker with toilet paper so I improvised. I purchased several spring loaded curtain rods and put three in our forward day head. (We do not use this head for showers so it stays dry.) I put the curtain rods up over the side window in the sink alcove and then some up over the head. By leaving the wrapping on the four rolls of paper and punching a hole through the ends you can hang 2 packages (8 rolls) in a rather small space. If you need to store more, just add more rods.

Maurice & Louise-Ann Nunas aboard *Akama* lived for awhile in Southeast Asia, and learned some tricks that transfer to the boating environment.

Maurice writes with a "solution" to the "toilet paper problem": Nope, not special TP. As many know, special TP for marine use has two problems. First, it is expensive, second it just does not work right. (We'll spare you the details but you know what we mean if you have tried it.) Of course, quality household TP has its problems too. Putting too much of it in the head makes you wish you could call a plumber at sea. We've seen other solutions such as "use just a little" (not acceptable to us) or dispose of the used TP in the waste bin (ugh).

Maruice offers a solution: Go down to the hardware store and buy some plumbing fittings, copper pipe, a shut-off valve, an adapter and one of those little sprayers intended to be installed on the kitchen sink. Mount the shut off valve on the bulkhead beside the commode. Make up a little bracket and hang the spray nozzle in a handy spot nearby. Plumb the fresh water over to the valve with the copper pipe (plastic would work fine, too). Using an appropriate adapter (depends on the valve you have) hook on the spray hose. *Voila*, instant bidet!

To use, open the valve, position the spray nozzle at the appropriate angle and press the little lever on the top of the nozzle. Use a couple of squares of TP to pat dry and clean up any over spray. (Maurice advises that once you get the hang of it, there won't be any.) That paper will be relatively clean and it can go in the trash bin. Maurice said, "We learned this while living in Southeast Asia. Once you start using this, you will see that millions of Asian people are onto something that we somehow missed."

Shower Fix

Keeping clean while living aboard is one of the more interesting aspects of the boating life. Most vessels don't have the tankage capacity to support long hot showers. Nevertheless, for those lucky enough to be able to shower aboard, Chris Nero aboard *Chris' Craft* in New Bern, North Carolina, suggests an easy fix for recalcitrant shower sump pumps. He points out that the automatic float switch in the shower sump is a high failure item. A combination of soap scum and hair often causes the switch to stick in the on position, requiring you to get down to the sump and push the float switch down by hand. Chris found that by epoxying a one-ounce fishing weight to the switch he never had this problem again. You still have to clean the sump out, but not when you're showering!

Al Flesher on *Sentimental Journey* suggested a way to keep hair and soap scum out of the shower sump. He found a bottle cap that fits snugly inside the shower drain. He then punched holes in the cap's sides and drilled a small hole in the top (to keep the cap from floating out of the drain). After showering, it's an easy job to pull out the cap and clean off any collected residue.

Welcome Aboard

Tom & Bobbie Vandiver

Previous visitors have requested a written list of suggestions that would familiarize them with our boat and our "seafaring" way of life. Since many of our family and friends are not experienced at living on a boat, we agree that your safety and enjoyment would be enhanced by some simple explanations.

Friends and family who come to visit are often not "boat people," so it's a good idea to let your guests know the "house rules" before they come aboard. If that deters some people, well, so be it. For the rest, it will ensure that a good – and safe – time will be had by all. Tom and Bobbie Van Diver aboard s/v *Satori* in Pensacola, Florida, have put together a comprehensive list of tips, advice and rules for guests.

Satori is our home, our transportation, and our essential "life support system" at sea. We know you will treat our boat with the same care and consideration that you would like us to display toward your home.

We dreamed of this lifestyle for many years, worked hard to achieve it and sincerely enjoy sharing our world with family and friends. It is our concept of paradise and we love it! Those of you accustomed to the hustle-bustle of the work-day world may find our lifestyle a little boring. Please think of it as "enforced relaxation"; enjoy the beauty of the ocean, sea life, islands, and the lack of many of the pressures of society. Come prepared to swim, fish, explore new places, read a book, or just sit on the afterdeck and relax.

Safety

We want your visit to be happy and safe. Since there are many differences between a home on the land and one at sea, the following suggestions are offered as assistance.

1. Controlled Substances (non-prescription or illicit drugs). We know that none of our friends or relatives use any illegal substances. However, the current emphasis on this issue; *i.e.,* the U.S. government's "zero tolerance" policy demands that we assure that everyone aboard *Satori* understands that illicit drugs are not permitted. In the event we were boarded and searched by authorities of the U.S.A. or any country we are visiting, and any minuscule amount of drugs were found, we would all be arrested, jailed and our home/boat would be confiscated. Due to the seriousness of the possible sanctions, you will be asked to sign a statement indicating you are aware of our rules and do not possess any controlled substances. Coast Guard regulations require that we ask you to display the contents of all baggage brought aboard.

2. Weather. Time is the prime consideration when at sea. We have the most recent high-tech weather and navigation instruments, plus many years of experience on the sea. We do not wish to lose our lives, the lives of our friends, nor to lose *Satori*, therefore, decisions to travel or stay in port will depend on weather. Your input or feedback is welcome and will be considered, however the decision of the Captain is final. It is better that you miss your airline reservations than that we lose our lives or boat. In the event we are surprised by rough seas or high winds, do not be alarmed. We will provide additional instructions and anti-seasick remedies. *Satori* has sailed completely around the world once without problems, and we have faced many adverse conditions at sea. Don't worry, storms do not last forever.

3. Life Preservers. USCG-approved life jackets are located in the aft deck box. We will demonstrate how they are worn and under what conditions we may ask you to don them.

4. Overboard Drill and Gear. Located on the starboard (right) side of the radar arch is a long, white pole with orange floats, a horseshoe life preserver and a battery powered strobe light. In case you fall overboard, keep calm, swim to the float and wait for rescue. In case anyone else falls overboard:

A. Immediately begin shouting, "Overboard, overboard" and extend one hand pointing toward the person in the water.

B. Throw any of the deck cushions toward the person. They will provide positive flotation for an adult.

C. We will immediately turn the boat to retrieve the person.

5. Fire Protection. We have an automatic fire extinguisher system in the engine room, two smoke detectors in living spaces, a combustible gas detector in the bilge and eight hand fire extinguishers located throughout the boat. We will familiarize you with their location on arrival. In the event of fire, sound the alarm and move aside.

6. Cook Stove. Guests are requested not to use the LPG cook stove without our immediate supervision. The fuel is heavier than air and extremely explosive.

7. Smoking. Smoking, *i.e.,* cigarettes, pipes, cigars, etc. is not permitted anywhere aboard *Satori*.

8. Blocking Access. The main companionway (door from the deck to the pilothouse) must remain unobstructed. You are welcome to go above or below as you wish, however, please do not stop or tarry in this "doorway." Our instruments and controls are not all duplicated at both pilot stations, therefore, it may become necessary to move quickly from one steering station to the other.

9. Dinghy. After a few minutes of instruction, you are invited to use a dinghy for exploring, short trips, or fishing. Please let one of us know when you are leaving and when you expect to return. Be cautious of your wake near other boats and swimmers. Tilt the motor up before beach landings or in shallow water. Assure the dinghy is securely tied up or beached before leaving it.

Comfort & Convenience

1. Clothing and Luggage. Please bring only soft luggage, preferably one bag per person. Shoes should be soft soled and non-marking. Our lifestyle does not require fancy clothing. Only bring what is necessary and comfortable for the climate.

2. Gear Storage. Please do not leave personal items all over the boat. Clothing, cassettes, sunglasses, etc. that are not in use should be stowed in your bag.

3. Freshwater. With our "watermaker" we have a theoretically limitless supply of pure water. Reality is, these type of machines are relatively new and subject to frequent failure. Therefore, we must concern ourselves with water usage. Drink all the water you want, it is absolutely safe and pure. Do not leave the water running while brushing your teeth, shaving, etc.

4. Head (bathroom). The ventilator fan switch is the chrome button on the front, port (left) side of the lavatory cabinet. The commode (potty) is flushed by depressing the foot lever (left side when seated, right side when standing). This allows water to enter the bowl when the hand lever is pumped fore and aft. Use slow strokes until all waste has been flushed. Then, position foot lever all the way up (it does not automatically go all the way up) and flush the bowl dry. Be sure the foot lever is left in the up position and the hand lever in the forward position. Do not, under any circumstances, deposit anything other than human waste in the bowl. This includes toilet paper. Use the waste basket. Paper or other articles will plug the valves and to unplug them is not a pleasant task.

5. Showers. We usually have adequate fresh water for each person to have one shower each day. Wet down, turn the water off, soap up and rinse off. Dry off in the shower, clean hair from the lint trap and leave the shower clean. Hang your damp towel, swimsuit, etc., outside on the life lines. Remove and stow as soon as they are dry.

6. Electrical Power. When the generators are not running, or we are not in a slip on dock power, we are on 12-volt battery power and therefore, the supply is limited. Turn off lights when not in use. If you are unsure about using some item, just ask.

7. Swimming, Snorkeling or Diving. We have enough gear on board for four people and will provide safety instruction. No scuba please, unless you are certified. No wet swimsuits, etc., below deck. Go into the shower via the deckhatch. Be careful diving from the boat so your splash doesn't wet someone or something.

8. Brightwork (painted or varnished surfaces). Please be careful with all varnished or painted surfaces. Do not place items with metal or hard bottoms on these items, (deck boxes, galley table, pilot house sole, etc.).

9. Hatches and Port Lights (windows to non-sailors). Our hatches and ports are very special, heavy duty plastic. They are strong enough to handle any weather (we hope), however, they scratch easily. Do not sit, stand or place anything on the hatches. Do not open any hatch or port light without asking. Do not attempt to clean or wipe any or these surfaces, we prefer to do them ourselves.

10. Refrigerator and Freezer. Refrigeration aboard a small boat is a major maintenance item, not at all dependable like your home unit. Determine what you want from the fridge or freezer before opening the door, then get it as quickly as possible and close the door. We normally have adequate ice for cold drinks and happy hour.

11. Cleanup. We prefer that our guests enjoy themselves. We will take care of cleanup, dishwashing, etc.

12. Entertainment, Eating Out, Etc. We are retired and thus on a fixed income, budgeting our expenses. Normally, we will eat out once or twice a week, sometimes at "pricey-tourist" places, but usually at the good places where the locals eat. We may or may not join you for visits to other local attractions. Remember, we have forever to visit.

13. Expenses. We will not allow any of our guests to share in any operational costs, (*i.e.*, chipping in for diesel fuel, food, etc.). You are a friend or relative and are invited guests. In addition, any contribution on your part could be construed as "paid" chartering by the U.S. Coast Guard and we could be fined because we are not licensed to charter.

We hope we have covered all pertinent items. If not, ask us. We love to explain our boat and lifestyle.

We have not intended to offend anyone with a list of "rules and regulations," so please take our suggestions as a means of enhancing the pleasure of your visit.

LIVEABOARD LINGO

When you take up a new pursuit you need to learn the language. A proper yachtie has to remember nautical names for everyday things. Forget walls, floors, ceilings, living room, and kitchen. Instead say, bulkheads, cabin sole, overhead, saloon and galley. Don't say pointy-end when you mean bow (even though it is the pointy-end), or back porch when you mean aft deck.

Remember that on a boat the bathroom is the "head." The bathroom up the ramp on the dock is still a bathroom because it isn't on a boat so it isn't a head. Windows are portlights, if they open. Stairs on a boat are ladders and beds become bunks or berths at which time they also become impossible to make up in the morning.

Here are some more terms to help you feel like an old salt (a sailor seasoned by experience) and sound like an old hand (a knowing and expert person).

Aground: Touching or fast to the bottom. You may run aground and you'll hate when this happens but most of us do it sooner or later.

Beam: The width of the hull at its widest point. And you needn't be embarrassed about your "broad beam."

Brightwork: The Brits say it's the varnished wood trim above decks, but we Yanks include any polished brass, bronze or stainless steel trim aboard a vessel. Whatever it is, you'll get to know brightwork on a deeply personal level while maintaining it.

Burgee: A swallow-tailed or triangular pennant either displaying the name of the boat or, more often, the insignia of the owner's yacht club. Remember, it's not a "little flag."

Ceiling: The inside linings, usually decorative, of the cabin sides. The ceilings on the boat correspond to the walls in your house ashore, and the ceilings in your house are the "deckheads" on your boat.

Chandlery: Items of nautical gear or the shop in which they are sold — *a.k.a.* the place where you can easily spend your kids' inheritance.

Clew: The back lower corner of a sail. Most powerboaters don't have a clew.

Dolphin: A fixed pile of concrete, metal or timber used to moor a boat and sometimes for navigational purposes.

Draft: The depth of water required to float a boat.

EPIRB: Emergency Position Indicating Radio Beacon. In an emergency, sends out a signal on frequencies monitored by aircraft or satellites or both.

Fender: A cushion, placed between boats, or between a boat and a pier, to prevent damage. While first learning to dock, you'll need several of these.

Forecastle: The cabin furthermost forward. It is pronounced "focsle" as in "*folks'll* never believe you can sleep in that tiny space."

Founder: From the Latin *fundus* (bottom), it means to sink, especially in deep water. This is best avoided.

Ground tackle: A collective term for the anchor and its associated gear.

Hanging locker: A storage space for full-length garments. With any luck you will convert it to better uses such as a place to stack your shorts and T-shirts, because that's all you ever wear.

Headstay: Wire running from the top of the mast to the boat and to which the jib is attached. The headstay supports the mast and prevents it from falling backward. That's a good thing.

Heel: The sideways tilt of a boat under the influence of wind. If a boat lies over to one side because she is heavy, she "lists" — a good sign that it is time to throw out all those old boating magazines (except, of course, for *Living Aboard*).

Helm: The apparatus for steering a ship. When you are at the helm and doing your job, you're the "helmsman" — even if you are a woman.

Inflatable: An inflatable boat commonly used by liveaboards to travel between ship and shore. We don't know why it's not called a "deflatable."

Jetsam: Goods thrown overboard to lighten a vessel in danger. Also refers to rubbish wantonly abandoned. That's illegal. Goods accidentally lost overboard are "flotsam." Material floating on the surface of the water after a vessel has broken up and sunk is also flotsam.

Knot: A measure of speed equal to one nautical mile (6,076 feet) per hour.

Lazarette: A storage space in a boat's stern area. (That's the back of the boat.)

Lines: The smaller-sized ropes carried aboard. They are usually about the size of a clothesline (remember those?) or smaller. Just to confuse things, the "lines" of a boat are those lines drawn on paper plans to show her hull shape.

Lunch hook: A light anchor used for temporary stops.

Mooring: An arrangement for securing a boat to a mooring buoy or a pier.

Nun buoy: A floating mark anchored to the bottom which is diamond-shaped when viewed from any side. Large in the middle, it tapers to the top and bottom and doesn't look anything like Sally Fields.

Overboard: Over the side or out of the boat. This is not a good thing.

Port: The left side of the boat as you face forward. The right side is "starboard." It is widely believed that the word "posh" started as an acronym for "port outward, starboard home." That is probably incorrect, but no one knows for sure.

Quarter: The sides of a boat aft of amidships (*a.k.a.* back from the middle).

Raft: Mooring several boats side by side all lying to a single anchor or moor. This usually happens on weekends and there is often alcohol involved. Great fun unless you are an early riser.

Ropes: If you can't find the ropes on your boat, look for hawsers, cables, sheets, halyards, painters and lines. They are all ropes of one sort or another.

Sheets: While it conjures an image of something large and white, these are not the sails on a boat. Sheets are the ropes attached to the sail.

Skeg: An extension of the keel at the after end of a boat, designed to support the rudder and improve steering. Northern liveaboards complain that in the winter it gets cold enough to shrivel their skeg.

Sole: The deck of a cockpit or interior cabin.

Sounding: A measurement of the depth of water, which is a good thing to know (see "aground").

Sternway: When a boat moves (or drifts) backwards. Sometimes the movement is intentional, sometimes not. In either case remember that the rudder will work in the opposite direction from when you are making "headway."

Stow: To pack or put things in their proper place. Ashore, you store things; on your boat, even though it makes you sound like Elmer Fudd, you will put them in "stowage."

Tender: A smaller vessel tending a larger one. When you move aboard you'll probably call your tender a "dinghy." Note that the spelling is not "dingy."

Topsides: The sides of a vessel between the waterline and the deck. It can also refer to going up onto the deck.

Underway: Vessel in motion — that is, when not moored, at anchor, or aground. Don't confuse it with "under weigh" which has to do with pulling up the anchor.

Very light (or signal): A flare projected to a goodly height from a special pistol. Part of a system of signaling named after Lieutenant Samuel W. Very who invented it in 1877.

Waterline: A line painted on a hull which shows the point to which a boat sinks when it is properly trimmed. Liveaboards try to stay out of the shopping malls lest they lose sight of their waterline.

Xugia: The second bank of rowers in an ancient trireme. You probably won't hear this term often. Well, you didn't expect us to leave out 'X' did you?

Yacht: A pleasure boat of a certain size and luxury. You may or may not have a yacht but know that a true yachtsman always refers to "my boat" not "my yacht."

Zephyr: The west wind, but generally considered to apply to any light, pleasant breeze.

Well, dear reader, that's enough to get you started on the unique and uncertain language of boating. We hope you find the boating world as much fun as we do. Fair winds!

CONTRIBUTORS

Jim Akers has cruised our nation's rivers for over 50 years, starting as a teenaged crewman aboard a towboat. He has lived aboard full-time since 1994, traveling the Cumberland, Tenn-Tom Waterway, Ohio and Mississippi Rivers. He lives aboard his Chris Craft Flybridge Express, the *Missa Lynda,* with his little dog, Kristi.

Jamie Avery lived aboard a 1968 47' Chris Craft Commander, "almost fully restored," in Destin, Florida, with his dad, Jim, step-mom, Lois, and Tasha the Maltese. Jamie says he "loves that boat more than anything." Now 18 and about to graduate, he plans on moving to Ft. Lauderdale to pursue a career as a steward on the mega-yachts. Long-range plans include buying the Chris Craft when his parents sell it, and hopefully starting his own family aboard.

Barbara Baur is a liveaboard mom, a self-taught sailor, boat-based professional and pressure-cooker aficionado. She is the author of *The Complete Pressure Cooker Book* and also runs Quintessence Designs, a Mac-based nautical software company. She has been living aboard since 1992. Barb lives on *Quintessence,* a Whitby 42 ketch, with her husband, Lary, daughter, Wendy, and dog, Sounder. They are currently living and working in east central Florida and preparing to go cruising again.

Michael Beattie lived aboard for 10 years in monohulls on Florida's West Coast and in Santa Cruz, California. Michael and his wife, Layne Goldman, purchased their Gemini 105, the *Miki G.* for a cruise down the coast of California, through Mexico and the Caribbean to Florida, where they have temporarily swallowed the hook to earn more "freedom chips." Their dog, Debs, died in 2001, but Emma the yellow Lab, Michael and Layne still live aboard the *Miki G.,* where they all look forward to the next cruise. Their e-mail address is <goldbeat @hotmail.com>.

John Callahan is a technology writer. He and *Amy,* his 31' Cruise-A-Home, ply the waters of Puget Sound.

Louise Coulson, her husband, Don, and Foggy, the kitty, have lived aboard *Caper,* a 48' Harpswell Trawler since 1991. *Caper* was a workboat that they converted into a comfortable liveaboard. Both of their children live aboard, one in the Caribbean and another in Texas. Don and Louise plan to start cruising in the fall of 2002. To build their cruising kitty, they are doing canvas work under the name of Caper CanvasWorks. Once they start cruising, they intend to maintain their CanvasWorks business. You can reach them at <caper@pocketmail .com>.

Robyn Coulter left the Canadian cold and now lives in a warmer place. In 1996 Robyn and her partner, Manny, sold *Free Spirit* and settled on land in Eilat, Israel, on the shores of the Red Sea. For the next four years they worked and saved for their next boat-home. In June 2000, they bought a 32' sailboat, named her *Manana,* and began renovations with the goal of moving aboard. Between boat repairs they sail the Gulf of Aqaba and celebrate the return to life afloat.

Susan Davison is a freelance writer for the *Post Tribune* in Northwest Indiana. She and her husband, Rich, live aboard their 37' Irwin, *Caribbean Knight.* When they're not in the Bahamas they can be found cruising the East Coast. Susan can be reached at <Eyesea222@aol.com>.

Paula Day lives aboard in Ft. Myers, Florida. After purchasing their 43' Gulfstar trawler, *Clementine,* Bob and Paula Day sold their home, left their jobs, moved aboard and went on an extended cruise along the East Coast of the United States. Bob died in 1998, and Paula treasures memories of their cruise and is grateful for their "time out" aboard *Clementine.* As she says, "Bob lived his dream." Paula continues to live aboard *Clementine* in Ft. Myers where she is a nurse at the VA hospital.

Karen Dodd was a certified financial planner until 1997, when she and her husband, Denton, moved aboard their 32' Bayfield. Health problems caused them to rethink their goals, allowing them to give up "line dancing" when they bought their 27' aft-cabin Albin trawler, *Miss Karen.* Karen has published a book, *Carolina Comfort,* which you may order by sending $9.95 plus $2 shipping to Karen Dodd, 10072 Windward Drive, New Bern, North Carolina 28560. Please feel free to e-mail Karen at <kkdd@pocketmail.com>.

Karen Fisher is a retired teacher and freelance writer. Her husband, Andrew, is a realtor in central Pennsylvania. His business website is <www.andrewfisher.net>. Since purchasing *Whistling Gopher,* their 32' Nordic tug, Andy and Karen have crossed Lake Okeechobee in Florida from Jacksonville to Ft. Myers; traveled the ICW from Jacksonville, Florida, to Middle River, Chesapeake Bay, Maryland; and have made numerous shorter trips around the Bay. They have a five-year plan with the goal of spending months at a time traveling the coasts, lakes, and canals of the U.S. and Canada. Andy and Karen would love to be contacted by e-mail at <afisher@eppix.net> or <onmynordictug@yahoo.com>.

Lyn Foley and her husband, Jim, last wrote from Yakutat, Alaska. They have nearly completed a ciricumnavigation. In 2000 they sailed from Lemut, Malaysia, to Singapore and then Borneo — with stops in Brunei and Sabah, Malaysia — then to the Philippines and Japan. From Shingu, Japan, they crossed the Pacific Ocean and after 32 long days arrived at Dutch Harbor, Unalaska, Alaska.

Darlene Goodman is a retired home economist and a freelance writer. She lives aboard *Infinity* on the Tenn-Tom Waterway with her husband, Larry, and their cat, Tommy.

Gary Graham, often described as an "incorrigible wanderer," lives on his Hunter 34, *Mariah,* currently at anchor in Key West while he works as the ship's engineer on the historic schooner *Western Union.* He also writes personal histories and is co-owner of Herbs on Board, a natural-health mail-order company for boaters. He has a home port of Astoria, Oregon, and can be reached (eventually) at P.O. Box 2221, Gearhart, Oregon 97138.

Mary Heckrotte, her husband, Carl, and their chief security officer, Tashi, a miniature schnauzer, are in their 10th year of cruising, first on a Westerly 36' called *Mariah,* and now on a Pan Oceanic 46', *Camryka.* Their home port is Jordan Creek, North Carolina.

Rick Kennerly and his wife, Gayle, and Cairn Terrier, Scruffy, sail their Westsail 32, *Xapic,* wherever the Navy sends them. A life-long sailor, and a once-and-future live-aboard, Rick has served as Net Control for the Pacific InterIsland Net and as a regional relay station for several other cruising-oriented Ham nets in the Pacific. He also operated the Seven Seas Cruising Association's Cruising Station-Guam

and is active in the Westsail Owners Association. When not on the air or on the water, Rick runs Mouseherder Communications <www.mouseherder.com> and an online vinyl boat lettering and graphic design business.

Jay and Linda Knoll have been sailing since 1971. Starting on Lake Ontario with a Tartan 27, he and his wife, Linda, moved to the Chesapeake when their careers took them to Philadelphia. Linda was a founding partner in a marketing research firm, and Jay was a vice president in a large, international human resources consulting firm. They have crewed on several passages, including Bermuda to the Virgin Islands, Brindisi, Italy, up the Yugoslavian Coast to Venice, the Turkish Coast, and down the Mosel and the Rhine. On their own they have made several passages from the Chesapeake to Maine. In 1992 they quit their jobs and moved aboard *Simple Gifts,* their Crealock 37 and have cruised the East Coast of the U.S. and the Bahamas. They presently live in Vero Beach, Florida.

Art Kreiger is a retired chiropractor. He and his wife, Liz, cruise the New England waters on *Anneliese,* their Bristol 35.5, from their home on Sterling Harbor in Greenport, New York.

Kevin LaGraff and Susan Atkins have been living aboard their 36' Krogen, *Mana,* for the past 12 years in Sausalito, California, and loving every minute of their unique lifestyle. Thanks to lower overhead since moving aboard, they both retired at 50 and lead active lives, most of which are centered on water activities, including acting as cruise hosts with Golden Bear Travel in northern California. You can reach Kevin and Susan at <skal1956@compuserve.com>.

Philip Lange has been living aboard for 23 of the last 30 years. Currently he and his mate, Marilyn, cruise aboard *Kuan Yin*, a Searunner 37 Tri. They have spent most of the last 10 years in the eastern and western Caribbean. Philip says, "I think the best cruising is right here in the U.S." They are currently looking for a suitable vessel to cruise the inland waters.

Steve Madden and his wife, Barbara, live in Woodstock, Georgia. They are not yet retired, not yet living aboard but feel they are moving closer to their goal now that they have found the *Final Answer*, their new boat.

Richard Manning and his wife, Mary, sailed *Phalarope*, their Pacific Seacraft Dana 24 along the East Coast from Maine to Venezuela.

Shirley and Fran McGoldrick spent a year cruising aboard s/v *Ariel*, celebrating the new millennium with palm trees and boat drinks. While they re-stock the cruising kitty, they are living aboard in eastern Pennsylvania. Fran will retire in October 2003, at which time they intend to cruise "'til whenever." Shirley has published a book, *Men Go to Port, Women Go to Starboard*, which can be purchased online at <www.buybooksontheweb.com> at <Amazon.com> and <Barnesand Noble.com>.

Nancy Mills and her husband, David Perkins, live aboard and cruise on their 34' trawler, *Summer School*. It is an apt name for the boat, since they are both former university professors of engineering. Prior to her academic career, Nancy also enjoyed success as an industrial engineer and engineering manager, primarily in service industries. She has published articles in *PassageMaker, Living Aboard, Boating for Women* and *Coastal Cruising* as well as contributing numerous "helpful hints" to *Motor Boating, Sailing and Sea Magazine*.

Marilyn R. P. Morgan is a freelance writer and editor who is currently working toward a Ph.D. in communication and rhetoric from Rensselaer Polytechnic Institute. Her liveaboard dreams are temporarily on hold while she completes her degree.

Tom Murphy has been living and cruising aboard *Monday Morning*, his 30' Bristol sloop since 1993, enjoying Monday and every other morning.

Tim Murray is a sailor and former publisher of *Living Aboard* magazine. Believing there is a relationship between sailboat racing and successful stock-market trading, Tim established the *Briar Patch Stock Market Letter*. For a trial subscription, logon to <www.briarstock.com>.

Lisa Odaffer is a stay-at-home mom and a part-time writer. She and her husband, Jay, and four boys, Alex, 14, Jamie, 5, and John, 4, and baby Sam live on their 45' Hardin ketch, *Blue Heaven*. Their home port is Alameda, California. They are currently docked in Bradenton, Florida

Marlene Parry and her husband, Bob, have been cruising aboard their 42' Tartan sailboat, *Tik Hai*, for the past three years. They have logged over 10,000 miles and are currently in Palm Beach Gardens, Florida.

Robert Perkins is former president of the Houseboat Association of America and founding editor of *Houseboat News*.

Nina Pratt lives and writes on the shores of Narragansett Bay in Rhode Island. Her non-fiction books about the art business are available online through Amazon.com. She has published articles in *Living Aboard*, *Art Business News* and *Décor Magazine*. Her short fiction has appeared in *Snowy Egret* and *Lines in the Sand*. She is working on her third (as yet unpublished) novel.

Robert Reib, *a.k.a.* "Skipper Bob," is the author of *Cruising the New York Canal System*, *Cruising the Trent Severn Canal, Georgian Bay and North Channel*, *Cruising Comfortably on a Budget*, *Anchorages Along the Intracoastal Waterway*, *Marinas Along The Intracoastal Waterway*, *The Great Circle Route*, and *Cruising the Rideau and Richelieu Canals*. To order copies, contact Skipper Bob at 802 7th Street, East Rochester, Pennsylvania 15074, phone (724) 775-5892, e-mail at <skipperbob@ worldnet.att.net>, website <skipper bob.home.att.net>.

Jeff Stives, his partner, Christine Ascherman, and their Golden Retriever, Opus, live in Vero Beach, Florida. Jeff is a freelance writer, and Christine is a professional photographer. Jeff wrote his first nationally syndicated story for UPI in 1963 and has spent the years since then handling public relations for international firms. Christine has photographed three U.S. Presidents: Carter, Reagan and Bush Sr., as well as Bob Dole. More recently, she has contributed cover shots for *Living Aboard* and other magazines. Both are divers and sailors, having spent more than 10 years living aboard. Their email address is <jjstives@ aol.com>.

Nellie Symm-Gruender and Zachary Symm, along with Nellie's husband, Gene Gruender, and Ninja, the ship's mouser, have cruised aboard their 1981 Hunter 37 Cutter, *Rainbow Chaser*, along the ICW and Gulf Coast and to George Town, Exuma, Cuba, Jamaica, Grand Cayman, and Isla Mujeres. They are currently in Austin, Texas, refilling the cruising kitty. You can contact them via e-mail at <rain bow_chaser@compuserve.com>.

Peg Travis and **Dave Hirchert** live aboard *Gypsy*, an 80' steel-hulled three-masted schooner which they built between 1979 and 1992 and launched out of the Port of

Anchorage, Alaska. When not cruising, engaged in oceanographic research projects, remodeling fishing vessels in remote villages or doing private charters, Dave works in the Alaska North Slope oilfield. Peg, recently retired from the oilfield, keeps busy on *Gypsy*.

Leslie Woodcock is a stay-at-home dad who uses his degree in education to homeschool daughter, Samantha, and son, Teague. His wife, Dana, is a nurse at New Hanover Regional Medical Center in Wilmington, North Carolina. They all live aboard *Tabasco* with NautiCat the cat and Mickey the Chihuahua. You can reach Leslie via e-mail at <sailordad38@hotmail.com>.

Marge Ziegler's home port is Sodus Point, New York, where she lives aboard a 38' 1968 ChrisCraft Roamer, *Ki-Ki*, with her partner, Tim Williams. Tim has a business selling shrinkwrap and supplies. He can be reached at W.W. Products, (716) 265-4945. Marge and Tim intend to travel the ICW to warmer climes after they retire.

INDEX

Discover *Living Aboard* magazine!

Other boating magazines tell you to spend, spend, spend.

Living Aboard helps you *enjoy* the time you spend on your boat . . . whether a weekend, a month, or a lifetime. Learn from people who have actually made the move and how you can reinvent your life to live in a style most people only dream of.

Subscribe today and start working toward the dream.

A reader-written magazine covering power and sail.

"I drop everything when I get your magazine and read it cover to cover." — B.W., Brooklyn Park, Minn.

L·I·V·I·N·G
A·B·O·A·R·D

For more information
or to subscribe, visit us online at
www.livingaboard.com
or call toll-free in the U.S. and Canada
800-927-6905
outside U.S. & Canada call (512) 892-4446
24-hour fax (512)892-4448
info@livingaboard.com